Art From Many Hands

Multicultural Art Projects

by Jo Miles Schuman

Field Work by Pat Jackunas
Burns Park School, Ann Arbor, Michigan

Davis Publications, Inc.
Worcester, Massachusetts

Front cover:

Stenciling a masi kesa, 1995, Suva Fiji.
This Fijian woman uses an old X-ray plate to stencil a design.
© Federico Busonero.

Indonesian tjap batik. Detail of a sarong in cream, soya brown, and indigo blue, c. 1925.
Collection of the author.

Cave painting of horse, c. 15,000 to 10,000 BC, Lascaux, Aquitaine, France.
Photo courtesy of robertharding.com.

Carved emu egg by Bluey Roberts, 2000. 5" high x 12" circumference. Lower Murray River
region, South Australia. Photo by permission of the artist. Collection of the author.

Back cover:

Zoe cleans stained glass.

Dillon works on his felt mini rug.

Publisher: Wyatt Wade
Editor-in-Chief: Helen Ronan
Senior Editor: Nancy Burnett
Production Editor: Carol Harley
Manufacturing Coordinator: Georgiana Rock
Copyeditor: Sharon AvRutick
Editorial Assistance: Jillian Johnstone
Design and Electronic Page Make-up: Cyndy Patrick

Printed in China
Library of Congress Catalog Card Number: 2002112360
ISBN-10: 0-87192–593–1
ISBN-13: 978-0-87192–593–0
10 9 8 7 6 5 4 3

To all children, everywhere, and the creative spirit they inherit as human beings, and to the committed teachers and parents throughout the world who nourish this spirit and its expression in art.

Jo Miles Schuman taught art for many years at Burns Park School, Ann Arbor, Michigan. She is now a woodcut printmaker and writer living on the coast of Maine. She received her B.A. degree in creative arts from Antioch College and her M.A. in art from the University of Michigan.

CONTENTS

Bison Licking Its Flank. Engraving on reindeer antler. Abri de la Madeleine, Tursac, Dordogne. Paleolithic. © Réunion des Musees Nationaux / Art Resource, NY.

PREFACE TO THE REVISED EDITION

One of the most moving experiences of my life was when I was able to fulfill a long time dream and see some of the cave paintings in southwest France. It was overwhelming to realize that people 15,000 years ago could make art with as much skill as any of us today. What compelled them to create the delicate, sensitive lines and forms and colors? To speculate that the paintings and carvings may have been created for rites of passage or other religious ceremonies cannot explain it all. These early people must also have realized that what they made was beautiful in itself. There is much the same mystery and awe about a great work of art today: it is hard to explain, but it is a wonderful and precious part of human life.

I would like to erase the stereotype of the club-toting cave man. There may indeed have been brutality in the fight for food and life, but brutality is still part of the world today. It is shown on television almost every night. However, it is our privilege and joy as art teachers to be able to nurture and bring forth in children the creative, positive aspects of human nature.

Twenty years have passed since publication of the first edition of this book. I feel that the issues addressed in the original preface are even more important today than they were two decades ago. An understanding of the universality of art, across all cultures and throughout the span of human time on earth, can help children identify with and respect people in all parts of the world. The understanding can perhaps reduce, at least in our own communities, some of the intolerance and distance between people. Teachers have an important role in bringing to children a positive awareness of other cultures (even those with whose governments we are at odds), and to help them, at the same time, to find pleasure and growth in their own artistic expression. Creativity, wherever it is found, must be fostered and encouraged.

I have added twenty-three entirely new projects to this edition and retained all but three of the earlier projects. In the latter, a few changes have been made due to the availability of new products, and also because of an increased awareness of safety concerns.

The earlier acknowledgments remain true today, but in writing the second edition I have received important help and support from many additional people.

I retired from teaching art in 1984 to devote full time to my own woodcut print making. When approached by Davis Publications to prepare a revised edition, I thought it impossible without returning to the classroom. However, Pat Jackunas came to my aid, and this book would not have been possible without her. I developed the new projects in my studio in Maine, sent them to Pat (who now teaches art at Burns Park School, in Ann Arbor, Michigan, where I once taught) with instructions and visual aids, and she introduced them to students in her classroom. She also took photographs of the children working on these projects. (All photos of children working on new projects, with the exception of Fig. 6-8 and the children working in felt, are by Pat Jackunas.) She then sent me their finished work, from which I selected pieces and photographed them for the book before returning them. Her feedback on the projects was invaluable and resulted in a number of contributions to both media and processes. Pat is a talented teacher, and I am indebted to her for her hard work, patience, support, and good cheer throughout. I am indebted also to the many students at Burns Park School whose art graces these pages—they trusted me with their work and waited patiently for its return.

The felting projects were carried out in Vermont, at the Dotham Brook School in Wilder, and at the Chelsea school in Chelsea. These projects were taught by Janet Cathey, a felt artist, and now an art teacher. It was a privilege to watch her teach, and to see the enthusiastic participation of the students. She wrote the sections on making felt balls and mini rugs. I thank the teachers, Kate Townsend and Joan Feierabend, who allowed us introduce this art in their classrooms. Beth and Larry Bede helped with the felt project, reading the manuscript, and offering valuable suggestions.

They graciously provided the photograph (Fig. 5-84) of a rug in their collection. Mari and Istvan Nagy and Anna Vidak also made important contributions to the manuscript and illustrations (Figs. 5-83 and 5-85). (The traditional way of making felt balls was taught to Mari by her grandfather.) I received help from Peter Hagerty, of Peace Fleece, in obtaining slides of Kyrgyzstan rug makers. These are the photographs generously contributed by Mary Badcock, Figs. 5-81 and 5-82.

Nancy and Jim O'Neil got me started on the stained glass project by donating an abundance of colorful glass. I received information from Mrs. N. E. Mees, Parish Secretary, concerning the Gilbert White Memorial Window in Selborne, Hampshire, England; and also information concerning the windows in the little church in Brockenhurst, Hampshire, England, from the Revd. Francis Cumberlege.

I am especially indebted to Delly Hackell and Bluey Roberts for their contributions to the chapter on Australian Aboriginal Art. Delly read the manuscript and offered many helpful suggestions. I am grateful to Werner and Elena Obermeier of Boomerang Arts and Crafts who made possible the acquisition of Bluey Roberts' exquisitely carved egg and put me in touch with Delly. Linda Zillman also made valuable contributions to this manuscript. I would like to thank Hawk Henries for letting me photograph didgeridoos in his collection, and for the enjoyment of hearing his skillful playing of these remarkable instruments. Frank Deutsch sent me emu eggs from Australia, and answered many questions.

Marilyn Hudson, of Mandan and Hidatsa tribal heritage, read the manuscript on Plains Indians and encouraged me to use the new project on Plains Indian shirts and vests.

Ralph Bolton read the manuscript on the embroidery made by the children of Chijnaya, Peru, and offered very helpful suggestions based on his experiences in that community.

Brother Michael Grace, S.J., Loyola University, found, after much searching, the beautiful illustration for the Greek sculpture project, Fig. 4-15, a photograph taken by Rev. Raymond V. Schoder, S.J., many years ago.

I am grateful to Jan Lorys, Director of the Polish Museum of America, Chicago, who responded to my request for an example of the colorful circular Lowicz wycinanki designs by lending me several to choose from and photograph.

I received much help from Krystina Helmick and Alyssa Dodge at the Peabody Essex Museum in Salem, MA, and from Nynke D. Jolly at the Peabody Museum in Cambridge, MA.

Kathy Bray brought me up to date on new materials available to use in making the ink drawings, and offered helpful suggestions. Janice Wright, artist and teacher, helped me resolve some important design problems. Her warm and creative spirit renewed my enthusiasm. Julie Steedman contributed the photos for Figs. 11-7 and 11-11, in addition to those listed in the original preface. All other photos, unless otherwise credited, are by the author.

Others who have helped along the way are Deb Andrews, Jacqueline Angot-Westin, Ferdinand Anton, Betty Boim, DeSoto Brown, Dave Burgevin, Federico Busonero, Ingrid Cole, Fraser Hall, John Houston, Sylvia Inwood, David McNeece, Anastasia Mikliaeva, Bernard Murdoch, Roger Neich, Matthew Pavlick, Julia Pogodina, Marilyn Rader, Carl Shaneff, Barbara Spiers, Lou Stancari, Krishna Swamy, Danuta Swamy von Zastrow, Richard Waite, and Irwin Weil.

I am indebted to Wyatt Wade, President of Davis Publications, for his belief in me and his gentle but persistent nudges which got me started on this revision. Nancy Burnett and Carol Harley, my editors, were always there for me with answers, valuable suggestions, reassurance, and unflagging good will. A grant from Davis Publications greatly assisted me in obtaining many of the illustrations.

Above all, my family has given me support and encouragement. My husband, Howard, has read the entire manuscript. He is a constructive critic with an emphasis on clear writing. He rescued me from many computer snags. Our daughter Beth, a writer and an artist in felt, suggested the felt project and contributed substantially to the writing; I could not have done it without her. She also initiated my computer education, answered myriad questions, and boosted my flagging spirits at critical points. Our son David, a painter and teacher, critiqued some of my drawings; and our son Marc, an electronic engineer, set me up with my own e-mail address and introduced me to the Web. He also helped by locating some of the artwork I needed.

In writing this edition, I have gained renewed admiration for the extraordinary skills of the many artists who created the original pieces that were my inspiration. My greatest debt is to them. My aim is to bring respect and appreciation for their work. If I have failed to do this at any point through lack of understanding, the fault is my own.

Jo Miles Schuman
Phippsburg, Maine
September 2002

PREFACE TO THE FIRST EDITION

From ancient to modern times, people have used almost every conceivable material from their environments to bring beauty into their lives and the lives of others. I hope that through this book more people will become aware of these arts and crafts, which are our inheritance as world citizens.

It is not expected that students will be able to create pieces of art as fine as the examples they are shown, which are usually the result of years of training and tradition. But when they work with materials with their own hands, students learn to appreciate the skills of those artisans even more. At the same time, they

A Celebration of the Chinese New Year by fifth-grade students. The girls in front carry Happy New Year signs. Behind them is a boy in a traditional lion mask; a girl carries a pearl that the lion chases; and a dragon, created by the students, follows.

Angela and Thea, third-grade students, work together on a Mexican art project.

enjoy the creative process themselves and gain some confidence in their own abilities. Exposing students to art from all over the world brings them the wonder of art in all its many forms, expands their knowledge of what art is, and shows them the variety of ways design problems can be solved. Inspired by these experiences, students often produce art of very fine quality that can stand on its own merits. This is true, however, only when students are helped to use the example as a springboard for their own personal expression, rather than as something to copy.

I also hope that in a world where differences in culture and ethnicity sometimes bring conflict, learning about cultural differences in arts and crafts can help students appreciate and respect one another. In America's communities and classrooms, where children of several ethnic backgrounds often live and work together, art can be a language of understanding.

If children are unaware of the artistic aspects of their heritage, learning about them can be an important growing experience. If they are already aware of this heritage, they might find pleasure and self-respect in sharing it. Children who are underprivileged in the sense that their community does not include minority groups will benefit from experiencing the richness of creative expression in cultures other than their own.

Children should be proud of their own cultural heritage, not in the sense that it is the *most* beautiful, but in the knowledge that it *is* beautiful. They should also have the opportunity to see the art of other cultures. We should help them realize that the creativity of all peoples is to be valued.

Sadly, in the late twentieth century most people have lost—and still more are losing—the ability and the confidence to create objects of beauty with their own hands. In few areas of the world is art still a part of daily living, a skill everyone engages in and hands down through the generations. It is a wonderful and valuable part of the human spirit that sees and enjoys beautiful things. People in the past, even in circumstances of privation, devoted hours to decorating tools and clothing and homes that would serve practical purposes just as well if they were left unadorned. But today this enrichment of our lives is left to specialists—trained artists—or to the few who design the products that are mass-produced. Most of us no longer have confidence in our own hands. Children do, however, until they become aware that adults do not sit and draw or engage in other arts or crafts, and then they lose their motivation and their confidence.

This is not to say that specialists in art are a new phenomenon. In many early societies, people who were exceptionally talented in the arts were set apart as specialists. The bas reliefs in the Parthenon were not the work of the common man, and Japanese sumi-e artists spend many years perfecting their techniques. Such arts are usually referred to as the fine arts, produced primarily for beauty rather than utility. Still, it is possible for students to engage in these arts, even though their own work is less skilled.

I have included in this volume projects based on both kinds of art—the fine arts, created by artists working as specialists in their societies, and the popular arts, handed down by tradition within groups and families. Tradition is really just another form of special training, and the quality of popular artwork is often on the same level as that of fine art.

Schooled and unschooled, young and old, ancient and contemporary—the examples of artwork chosen for this book come from many skilled hands.

In writing this book I have sought assistance from a great many people, all of whom have given generously of their time and knowledge. Some of the projects could not have been written at all without this substantial help.

Karin Douthit contributed many ideas and translated correspondence pertaining to the project on the flower-related arts of Germany. Yolanda Marino spent much time and was helpful in many ways with the projects on Puerto Rican arts and island maracas. The information concerning straw inlays was provided by Valentin Petrovich Kotov, Senior Artist of the factory that produces these inlays in Zhlobin, Byelorussia. Jody Hymes and Susan Walton of the Project on Asian Studies in Education at the University of Michigan, Ann Arbor, were very helpful with the Japanese projects and that on Wayang Kulit. Hitoshi Uchida contributed information to the project on making Japanese fish prints. I am much indebted to Vee-Ling and Richard Edwards for their helpful comments on the section on Chinese arts and to Vee for the calligraphy that illustrates that project. Without Ingrid Cole's advice on constructing and dressing a tapestry loom, and that of Lois Kane on the art of tapestry weaving, that project could not have come to fruition.

Others who have read chapters and made helpful comments or given ideas or advice on projects are: Elsa Adamson, Mrs. Surjit S. Bakhshi, Rabbi Martin Ballonoff, Lisa Berg, Joan Blos, Susan Buchan, Mrs. Vincent Chrypinski, Madelaine Conboy, Mrs. Andrew Ehrenkreutz, Cecelia Ference, Richard Ford, Zelda Gamson, Marian Gillett, Ruth Gomez, Elaine Headly, Mimi Khaing, Rickie Lauffer, Marianna Lis, Scott McGuilliard, Paul Melton, Cyril Miles, Margaret Miles, Christella Moody, Arvilla Muirhead, Mr. and Mrs. Rudi Ong, William H. Peck, Eugene Power, Judy Rothman, Sao Saimong, Seiichi Sasaki, Elisabeth Schuman, Aliza Shevrin, Meredith Shore, Joyce Tinkham, May Uttahl, Gretchen Whitman, William Wiercbowskie, and Bill Zolkowski.

Others shared special skills: Julia Moore taught me how to create the dashiki diagramed in the project on tie-dyeing, and Mr. and Mrs. Stephen Kuchta shared their knowledge of gourd-raising and drying with me. Thanks to Vee-Ling Edwards, Joyce Tinkham, Marianna Lis, and Saburo Ikeuchi, who, by demonstrating their arts in the classroom, gave a wonderful experience to many students.

I am indebted to Jill Bace, Registrar of the Kelsey Museum of the University of Michigan; Richard Pohrt, of the Chandler-Pohrt Collection; Cyril Miles, Museum of African Art, Highland Park Community College; Donald A. Sellers, of Plymouth House Galleries; Eugene Power; and Mr. and Mrs.

James P. Wong; all of whom went to some difficulty in order to let me photograph from their collections.

I am grateful to Amy Saldinger for translating the correspondence from Byelorussia, Janice Moore for her translation of an article relating to the Swedish cookie presses and for the pepparkaka recipe, and to Terry Johnson for translating correspondence from Germany.

Fred Crudder processed much of my film and without complaining got the best possible prints out of even the earliest negatives. I enjoyed working with Julie Steedman, who took a number of the photographs in this book. They are Figs. 1-4, 2-5, 2-6, 2-29, 2-30, 2-31, 3-17, 5-11, 5-56, 5-58, 5-59, 5-60, 10-6, 10-7, 10-42, 10-43, 10-46, 10-47, 10-64, 10-65, 10-66, 10-67, and 10-68. All other photos, unless otherwise credited, are by the author.

Ruth Beatty, Art Coordinator for the Ann Arbor Public Schools, has been supportive throughout this endeavor.

Thanks to *Arts and Activities* for permission to publish some of my photos and material that first appeared in their magazine in January 1975 under the title "Mexican Bark Cutouts" (Figs. 8-9, 8-10, 8-11), and to the Ramses Wissa Wassef Centre, Harrania, Egypt, for permission to publish photos of the tapestries woven at their Centre.

Parents of students at Burns Park School and friends traveling in other countries have enriched this book by obtaining photographs or pieces of art, often involving some hours of work or even discomfort. I must especially thank Nancy Rice for her contribution to the project on Swedish cookie presses; Elizabeth Arnold; Mary Clark; Edith Gesche; Tamiko and Yoshihiko Imamura; and Shirley Paul, who travelled by airplane from Mexico to the United States, cushioning a ten-pound, nineteen-inch clay sun on her lap.

Thanks to John Stafford, who designed the shadow screen for the Indonesian Arts project, and to John Lillie and Alan Klein, who constructed the marionette theatre.

I am indebted to several faculty members of the University of Michigan who were my teachers: David H. Reider, who introduced me to the art of photography; Douglas Hesseltine, who gave advice on the line drawings; and most of all to Irene Tejada, whose appreciation of arts from many cultures has inspired enthusiasm and creativity in her students for many years. She read and commented on several chapters and contributed substantially to the projects on marionettes, shadow puppets, and the seed necklaces of Puerto Rico, as well as bringing many of the arts represented in this book to my attention.

A warm thank you to everyone associated with Burns Park School in Ann Arbor, Michigan—parents, students, staff, and teachers—who have welcomed these ideas and helped make the artroom an exciting and rewarding place in which to work.

I am grateful to my husband, Howard; to my daughter, Beth; and to my sons, Marc and David; all of whom have contributed ideas, support, and help in countless ways over the past five years toward the completion of this book. (My husband, who is candid, urges me to note, however, that although he indeed edited parts of the manuscript and helped in many ways, he also provided a few roadblocks to climb, chasms to leap, and other obstacles to overcome. Our partnership is never dull.)

I am grateful also to my parents, Max and Margaret Miles, who instilled in me a respect for, and appreciation of, other cultures. Perhaps the earliest beginnings of this book can be traced to the influence of my grandfather, Henry Turner Bailey, whom I never knew, but whose silent studio I explored at an early age, coming across art pieces from many corners of the world that spoke of creativity in clay, paper, wood, and stone, in places far from our small New England town.

Finally, I am indebted to all the artists, ancient and contemporary, a few known but most unknown, whose work illustrates and is the inspiration for the projects in this book.

Jo Miles Schuman
Ann Arbor, Michigan

Fig. 1-1. Students draw inspiration from a paper Japanese fish banner while creating their own fish designs.

I A METHOD FOR TEACHING MULTICULTURAL ART PROJECTS

BEGINNING THE PROJECT

Where does one begin? There are many beginnings. The study may start spontaneously, through a news clipping that describes art from another culture; through something a child or parent or teacher sees or does or brings to class; or perhaps through research on a particular culture that is part of a social studies unit. No matter what sparked the study, if children are to engage in an art project, showing them an actual piece of art encourages the highest levels of motivation and involvement.

Children feel a certain magic about the real thing. You hear their breath draw in, watch their eyes widen, and sense their respect and wonder when they can see and maybe even touch an Inuit sculpture of smooth black stone, an intricate and vibrantly colored painting on amate paper from Mexico, or a hand-stamped and embroidered adinkra cloth from Ghana. Nothing can quite substitute for such immediacy.

Giving children this experience is not as difficult as it might seem. You can find surprising things in a local secondhand shop—a two-dollar clay animal from Mexico with lovely hand-painted designs (it does not matter if it is chipped); a backstrap loom from Guatemala, which can be used to show students how cloth is created; an old Polish wycinanki design for three dollars. These are chance finds, but as tourism grows, such small,

inexpensive items become easier to find even if one cannot travel oneself.

Most cities have an increasing number of art import shops. Although larger items can be prohibitively expensive, smaller handcrafted pieces are often within a teacher's budget. Many shops are willing to lend items to a school for one day if they are assured that the pieces will not be harmed. They may require a refundable deposit against loss or damage.

We often live in a community without ever tapping its human resources. Has someone in your community traveled abroad? Are there foreign visitors to your town—students or business representatives who may have art objects to show or skills to teach? Are there local residents with ethnic backgrounds in your area who have knowledge of a traditional craft? Invite to the classroom a Japanese student who can demonstrate ink painting, a Chinese visitor who can show the growth of a language through calligraphy, a Native American who can demonstrate beadwork, or a Polish-American who has learned to cut wycinanki designs. Many people are willing and happy to share such valuable experience with your students, but you will have to search for them—they do not advertise these special skills. In most cities there are international organizations that

Fig. 1-2. Items found in secondhand shops: a weaving on a Guatemalan backstrap loom, a plate and a papier-mâché bird from Mexico, a gold-leafed lacquerware owl from Burma, a Navajo silver and turquoise bracelet, and a Japanese toy papier-mâché beast of burden.

Fig. 1-3. Vee-Ling Edwards shares her knowledge of calligraphy with Dan, a fifth-grade student.

might help you. You can also inquire at universities, which often have students and faculty from many countries.

Perhaps the art you wish to see can be found only in a museum or art gallery. Then you have to take the class to the art. Make arrangements in advance with the people in charge and ask a guide to explain the artwork to the children. Take paper and pencils so that the students can sketch and bring home their impressions.

Failing an actual object, pictures are the next best thing. The public libraries are rich in resources. Most art books are beyond the budget of public schools, but public libraries often have a number of books with beautiful color illustrations for those with the curiosity to find them and the muscle to carry them home. If teachers request it, libraries will sometimes purchase or acquire through inter-library loan books that are not in their own collections. The bibliography at the end of this book lists resource books relevant to most of the projects described.

The illustrations in this book are necessarily small, but may be photocopied and enlarged—one copy per illustration—for students to use in your classroom. Creating a poster with these illustrations may help students understand the project.

Materials

Once you have chosen an art project, think about materials. Is the original material available, or can you create a substitute? If you are studying Pueblo clay pottery and the school is lucky enough to have a kiln, you can work directly in clay. Or you could create your own outdoor kiln in the Pueblo manner, as this book describes. For African masks and sculpture, wood is not a practical medium to use at the elementary level, so papier-mâché would be a good substitute. Children's enthusiasm is greatest when their materials are as close to the original as possible, but their imagination is boundless and can fill great gaps. Children are realistic and know that making sculpture of pure gold is impossible in the classroom, but they are delighted to see their cardboard sculptures (inspired by ancient pre-Columbian art) transformed by an application of gold paint.

The budgets of most public schools require that materials be as inexpensive as possible. Most indigenous art uses materials that are found naturally in the environment. The school usually has paper, glue, paints, and other basic art supplies. But look further into your community for other, sometimes free, and often more exciting materials. Look at the land where you live and at what grows there (naturally and by cultivation); look at the industries, the stores, and inside the homes.

In some areas, children can dig clay, an act that brings them to the source of their material. Slate for use in rock engravings can be found naturally. Sand can be colored and used for sand painting. Native grasses and weeds can be used for weaving and basketry. In many cultures, jewelry is made from natural objects such as seeds, bones, shells, and feathers.

Visit the industries in your area. Sheets of aluminum, which are excellent for making African repoussé panels, are waste material from offset printing. Iron foundries throw away large hunks of man-made sandstone, which is a perfect medium for young children to use for their own sculpture when they are studying Inuit carving. Look into the stores and services in your community. Refrigerator boxes can be used to make large structures, such as caves (page 57). Old rubber inner tubes can be cut into shapes and used for making prints.

Use waste products from the home. Cartons, boxes, and tubes can be bases for papier-mâché sculpture. Leftover balls of yarn become fine weavings.

Trying It Out

After finding the inspiration (in the form of art pieces or illustrations) and the materials, do the project yourself before presenting it to the class. There may be pitfalls in directions or construction that become apparent only after you go through the steps. The method may be too tedious or require a skill level too high for the age level you have in mind. (Sometimes, however, especially with older students, encountering difficulties and overcoming them together is a valuable part of the problem-solving aspect of the art process.)

In a few cases there may be dangers in the art materials that are not immediately apparent. By doing the project first, the teacher encounters these and can make the process safer before presenting it to the class. For instance, taping the overly sharp edges on cut aluminum or learning the safest possible way to set up hot wax for batiking can help prevent accidents.

Copy or Create?

Do you want replicas of ethnic art, or do you want to use an art form as a basis for inspiring the child's own creativity? This is an important question, and the answer will vary according to the purpose of the project. My feeling is that only *rarely* should an art form be literally copied. If the group is studying a particular culture and wants to get as close to it as possible so the children can participate vicariously

Fig. 1-4. Kate copies a photograph of an Indonesian shadow puppet as part of a class project to put on a wayang kulit performance of an episode from the *Ramayana*. It proved to be a valuable experience in learning about another culture.

in an aspect of that culture, then the answer may be yes, make replicas. For instance, if the group is studying Indonesia, they may choose to make shadow puppets (see page 121). Children enjoy doing research; choosing a story; learning its meaning in that culture; and using the particular shapes, symbols, and colors for each character. Children have some freedom to choose which characters to re-create. They can put on a performance, complete with instrumental accompaniment, for their schoolmates. The experience of attempting to make and use likenesses of the puppets and simulating the rhythm of the gamelon is valuable.

Even in this situation it is not a good idea to be rigid. Most children will find challenge enough in re-creating an intricate shadow puppet. However, especially creative children may use the inspiration to create their own characters, using their own symbols. This is how new forms are created within all societies, and sometimes they are then perpetuated by tradition. Such innovations should be acceptable within the classroom.

My own predilection, whenever possible, is to use the art form in question as a method of exploring new ways of seeing and of expressing *oneself*. Except for the previously mentioned re-enactment, which can be very rewarding, most children get little satisfaction from a copy—it falls short of reality and has too little of themselves in it. Children should learn the method and especially the *spirit* in which the art form was made and then use this knowledge to create their own artwork. For example, in making "bark" paper cutouts described in Chapter 8, authentic amate paper

Fig. 1-5. This two-headed bird-of-the-mountain design by a fifth-grade student was inspired by Otomí Indian cutouts. It is the student's own personal expression, not a copy.

cutouts are shown. The Otomí Indian method of making the paper is explained, as is the method we will use to simulate it. Then we talk about traditional Mexican designs. We look at examples in *Design Motifs of Ancient Mexico* by Jorge Encisco. We talk about how some of these designs spring from natural forms, even though they are not realistically drawn, and how others are based on geometric shapes. The children are encouraged to make imaginative designs based on a natural form or an abstract shape of their choice. The resulting designs, because of the materials and the original inspiration, have the spirit of the Otomí Indian work, but are as varied as the children themselves and are very much their own personal expressions.

Fig. 2-1. Adire eleko cloth from Oshogbo, Nigeria with a hand-drawn pattern made from cassava starch and indigo dye. Courtesy of Mrs. Cyril Miles.

2 ARTS OF WEST AFRICA

Although masks and sculpture are what first come to mind when one thinks of the art of Africa, this vast continent with its many different nations and ethnic groups is rich in other arts as well. Bronze, gold, ivory, textiles, and leather are used; pottery making, weaving, and many other skills have been carried on for centuries. The artist has traditionally held a place of respect and importance in the village. Art is an integral part of life, sometimes an expression of religious ideas through abstract symbols. Containers, tools, dwellings, and clothing are often designed to have special meaning to the society, and they are strong in color and design.

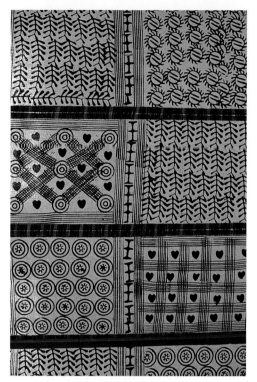

Fig. 2-2. Detail of adinkra cloth from Ghana. Photograph taken at the "In Praise of Hands" exhibition of crafts from around the world at the Ontario Science Centre, Toronto, Canada, 1974.

Fig. 2-3. Five adinkra stamps carved from calabashes. Courtesy of Mrs. Betty Okuboyejo. Photograph by Susan Buchan.

TEXTILES

Many villagers, especially in Nigeria, Ghana, and Senegal, still create textiles in the traditional manner. These are often richly colored and vibrantly patterned. Each village has its own particular style. The designs are created in several different ways: by painting, weaving, printing, tie-dyeing, resist-dyeing, and combinations of these processes. Projects for all age levels can be based on these arts.

Photographs of these textiles can be found in many books listed in the bibliography. There is an increasing interest in these fabrics; perhaps you can locate an import shop that will allow you to borrow and display cloth or clothing made in Africa.

ADINKRA CLOTH OF GHANA

Adinkra cloth, made in Ghana, is decorated with stamped designs. Each stamp is carved from a calabash, and has a handle made of strong sticks (see Fig. 2-3). The stamp is dipped in a black dye made from the bark of the badie tree and pressed on the cloth. Adinkra, the name of the dye, means "goodbye," and the cloth was originally worn when guests were departing or at funeral ceremonies. Traditionally, the glossy black designs were stamped on matte black or russet cloth because those colors were used for mourning. More recently, they are also stamped on white or brightly colored fabrics and used for decoration.

First, the artist usually divides the cloth into squares by drawing lines with a comb dipped in the dye. Then symbols are stamped within these squares. Sometimes the cloth is divided into small squares and the symbol is

Fig. 2-4. Adinkra symbols. Clockwise from top left: Adinkra 'hene, symbol of royalty, the most important adinkra design; Aya, the fern, symbol of defiance; Hye wo nhye, symbol of forgiveness; Fihankra, symbol of safety or security in the home; Akoma, the heart, symbol of patience and endurance; Dwanimen, ram's horns, symbol of strength.

Making Adinkra Designs on Paper and Cloth

For young children, a potato stamp can substitute for one made from a calabash. In fact, using this method, older children and adults can also produce beautiful results. First slice a potato into ¾" slabs. Then the children can cut the slab into simple shapes with table knives or plastic picnic knives (see Fig. 2-5). Brush tempera paint onto the cut surface and press it onto colored construction paper. Emphasize how a pattern is built up by repeating very simple shapes.

Fig. 2-5. Max, age eight, concentrates on cutting a stamp from a slice of potato.

stamped only once in each, but more often each symbol is stamped several times within a larger square.

There are many traditional designs used in stamping, and Ashanti names designate their meanings. Therefore, a finished cloth is not only a thing of beauty, but it carries a message as well. See Fig. 2-4 for some of the traditional symbols and their names and meanings.

In one type of adinkra cloth, one very large piece of fabric is stamped. However, in the usual, older method, long strips of cloth decorated in repeated designs are sewn together with brightly colored thread. The joining stitch uses a sequence of colors that is repeated at regular intervals (see Fig. 2-2).

Fig. 2-6. Melissa, age eight, has brushed her potato stamp with acrylic paint and is stamping it in one square of her piece of cloth. The edge of a piece of cardboard was used to print the squaring-off lines.

Fig. 2-7. Four finished pieces of decorated cloth by second-grade students. Clockwise from top left: by Erik, Mira, Thea, and Katie.

If there is concern in your community about using food for an art project, make the stamps from pieces of Styrofoam trays (the kind used for packing meat in the supermarket). The Styrofoam can be cut in shapes with scissors, and interior lines, circles, and dots can be made by pressing into the Styrofoam with a pencil.

Beginning at the second-grade level, children can work together on a group project to create a large piece of adinkra cloth in the traditional manner. It can be displayed in the school as a decorative hanging. But first, so that the children understand the process and will each have something to keep, it is a good idea to work on individual squares of cloth. Old cotton sheeting does nicely and can be dyed after printing, or the children can work directly on colored cloth. Acrylic paint, which is permanent after it has dried, should be used for printing. The square of cloth should be placed on a thick pad of newspaper, which will help the stamp give a stronger impression. The typical adinkra cloth design is created within squared-off areas. These lines may be made by painting the edge of a piece of cardboard and pressing this against the cloth. Then fill in each area with one of the symbols: paint the black acrylic on the stamp with a brush, and press it hard on the cloth. Repaint the stamp for each new impression (see Fig. 2-6). Wash the brushes immediately after use. When the cloth is thoroughly dry, it may be dyed. Commercial dyes available in the grocery store work well, and cut-down plastic gallon milk containers make fine dye pots.

To make a large hanging, tear a sheet into 12"-wide strips. Mark off squares the length of the strip (every 12") with a piece of cardboard. Each child fills in one square with his or her most successful stamp (see Fig. 2-8). When thoroughly dry, the strips may be dyed a bright color and then can be sewn together on a sewing machine or by hand. Although hand-sewing takes time, the traditional joining stitch (Fig. 2-9) in a bright, repeated sequence of colors adds a great deal to the beauty of the cloth. One second-grade class completed theirs in two weeks; parents directed four children at a time during part of each day. They are all very proud of the finished cloth (see Figs. 2-10, 2-11). The children used doubled embroidery floss, just as it comes in the bundle. The threads were kept short, for safety's sake, so the children would not raise their needles too high and endanger their neighbors. Students preferred to sew toward themselves. As the work progressed, the ends of the strips were checked to be sure they were even. Between sewing sessions, the cloth was taped to a pole and rolled up.

Fig. 2-8. Second-grade students print a strip of cloth for a large wall hanging. Rebecca is printing with a piece of Styrofoam, and Molly is making a design by printing with the edge of a piece of cardboard.

Older children, fifth grade and up, may want to duplicate some of the more complicated symbols used on adinkra cloth, learn their names and meanings, and create symbols that have special meanings for themselves. These symbols can be cut from potatoes, but since

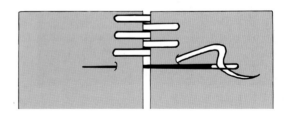

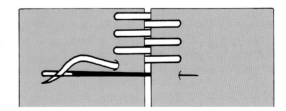

Fig. 2-9. The stitch used to join two strips of cloth.

Fig. 2-10. Second-grade students Jonathan, Rebecca, Susan, and Ori, under the supervision of a parent, take turns sewing the cloth strips together.

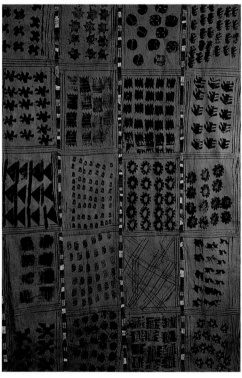

Fig. 2-11. A section of the finished wall hanging inspired by adinkra cloth from Ghana. Each of thirty second-grade students stamped one square. The cloth was dyed bright blue and was then sewn together with red, orange, green, yellow, and black embroidery thread.

such stamps will not keep more than a day or two it may be better to cut the shape from linoleum. Draw the design with a marker on a small piece of linoleum. Leave ample linoleum around the edge so that it can be held easily while cutting. Observing the safety rule of *always cutting away from the hand that holds the linoleum,* cut away from the design with linoleum cutting tools, leaving the design raised. With heavy shears, remove the excess linoleum that had been used for holding the piece, and glue the design to a block of wood for easy handling (see Fig. 2-12). A trial print with tempera paint on paper can show any changes that should be made in the stamps before the final printing. Put a thick pad of paper under the cloth, and make the squares by inking the edge of a piece of cardboard and stamping with it. Finally, stamp the cloth using slightly diluted black acrylic paint, or roll black oil-base printing ink on the stamp with a brayer (Fig. 2-13). Both methods produce a permanent washable design. Acrylic paint has the advantage of being water soluble before it dries, so that tools and hands can be easily cleaned. Oil-base ink requires turpentine for cleaning. When it's dry, the cloth may be dyed any color. Children may make individual squares, or a group of students may make a large hanging.

Fig. 2-12. A handle of scrap wood has been glued to a linoleum stamp for easier handling. This adinkra symbol is Aya, symbol of defiance.

Fig. 2-13. Brian, nine, rolls oil-base printing ink on his adinkra stamp. This design is Nsa, a motif from a cloth of that name.

ADIRE ELEKO CLOTH OF NIGERIA

The Yoruba people of southwest Nigeria make adire eleko cloth, a fabric with intricate white designs that stand out against the indigo dye. Adire eleko is created by placing a paste made of cassava starch and alum on white cotton. Sometimes the paste is painted on by hand with a feather or palm frond, and sometimes it is forced through a hand-cut zinc stencil. When the paste dries, the cloth is dyed with indigo. Although synthetic indigo dye is increasingly used, some villagers still make their own dye.

To make the dye, villagers chop and pound the indigo plant, dry it, and then combine it with potash in a complicated days-long process. The cloth is brown after being dipped in the dye and oxidizes to blue when hung in the sun. When the dye is dry, the cassava paste is removed; the paste resists the blue dye, creating the white design on a blue background. (Usually, since the paste is placed on only one side of the cloth, a little dye seeps in from the back, giving a bluish tint to the design.)

The Yoruba first draw lines that square off the material and then put designs within these boundaries. The designs are a combination of geometric lines and shapes (spirals, triangles, diagonals, dots) and shapes abstracted from natural forms (birds, flowers, snakes, fish). Fabrics made up of traditional combinations of these designs are given names such as olokun (see Fig. 2-14). It always includes the figures of birds around a stool seen here in a lower middle

Fig. 2-14. Detail of adire eleko cloth from Nigeria of the olokun design. Courtesy of Scott McGilliard and Susan Buchan.

square. Fig. 2-1 shows a pattern whose name means "cloth with two patterns." Squares of abstract tortoise designs alternate with squares of birds, letters, and other symbols.

Making Paste Resist Fabric Designs

Before beginning the project, the children should study a piece of adire eleko, if it can be obtained, or photographs of the fabric.

Students from about fourth grade on can make their own resist-dyed cloth by using a paste made of six tablespoons of flour, one teaspoon of alum, and two cups of cold water.[1] This should be cooked in the top of a double boiler, stirred until it becomes semitransparent and thickened. The somewhat glutinous paste may be painted on the fabric, but it is easier to manage if it is cooled slightly and put in a plastic squeeze bottle (mustard, hair dye, or soap bottles would do) and squeezed out. You can use the container as a drawing tool. After filling the bottle, test it first on newspaper to see if the consistency is right for drawing—not too thick to come out easily and not too wet. The paste should form a raised line. Beat in a little extra water if it is too thick; cool longer if it is too liquid.

Children should plan their design first, drawing it on paper equal in size to the cloth they will use. Remind them that the paste will be quite thick (1/8" or more) and that they should not make their figures too detailed. Place the cloth—use any white cotton, such as old cotton sheeting—on a pad of newspaper. As the students squeeze the paste onto the cloth they can refer to their drawing. The application of paste should be completed at one sitting; as it dries, it puckers the cloth so that there is no longer a flat drawing surface. The cloth should be placed on a flat surface to dry.

After the paste has dried *thoroughly*, for at least three days, place the material in a pot of

Fig. 2-15. A fifth grader uses a squeeze bottle filled with a specially prepared paste as a drawing tool. She first draws lines to square off the cloth and then will create designs in the squares.

[1] Taken from *Contemporary African Arts and Crafts* by Thelma R. Newman. © 1974 by Thelma R. Newman. Used by permission of Crown Publishers, Inc.

Fig. 2-16. A paste resist design by Wendy, eleven. Snake, flower, and leaf designs combine with geometric forms.

Fig. 2-17. Designs inspired by adire eleko, created by sixth-grade students David and Sue.

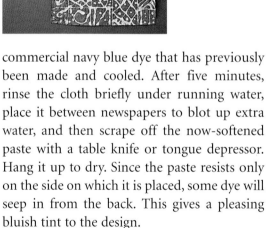

Fig. 2-18. Adrian has dyed his cloth dark blue and is now scraping off the paste to reveal the white designs.

commercial navy blue dye that has previously been made and cooled. After five minutes, rinse the cloth briefly under running water, place it between newspapers to blot up extra water, and then scrape off the now-softened paste with a table knife or tongue depressor. Hang it up to dry. Since the paste resists only on the side on which it is placed, some dye will seep in from the back. This gives a pleasing bluish tint to the design.

Very young children can make adire eleko designs on white or light blue paper instead of cloth. After being shown examples or photographs of the cloth, the children draw their own designs on the paper with a small candle or piece of paraffin. When the drawing is com-

Fig. 2-19. Samantha, five years old, brushes blue paint on a design drawn with a candle on light blue paper. You can tell that she has carefully observed the spiral and cross-hatched designs of an adire eleko design.

plete, the paper is "dyed" by brushing on dark blue watercolor or diluted tempera paint. The wax resists the paint, and the design appears in good contrast against the dark blue.

Fig. 2-20. Detail of indigo blue tie-dyed fabric from Togo. Courtesy of Mrs. Cyril Miles.

ADIRE ELESO, OR TIE-DYEING

In tie-dyeing a design is created by folding, bunching, or twisting material and then tying or sewing it very tightly so that the areas inside will resist penetration of the dye when the material is immersed in a dye bath. The art of tie-dyeing has been practiced for centuries in many parts of the world. Ancient examples of cloth decorated in this way have been found in South America, India, Japan, and China. Many West African countries also have a rich tie-dyeing tradition: Sierra Leone, Ivory Coast, Senegal, and Upper Volta, as well as those mentioned below.

In Nigeria, if the tied material is dipped in indigo, it is called *adire* (indigo) *eleso* (little stones) because often the pattern is created by tying in many rows of seeds or stones. In one traditional design, hundreds of tiny seeds are tied in concentric circles on a very large piece of cloth.

Often, more than one technique is used in creating a design. Fig. 2-20 shows a tie-dyed fabric from Togo. Rows of seeds were tied in, creating the small circles, and then the cloth was folded accordion style and either tied or sewn to create the larger diagonal pattern before being dyed in indigo.

The fabric in Fig. 2-21 is from Ghana. The large diamond, which is three feet long, was made by folding and tying the material in narrow pleats. The surrounding marbleized pat-

Fig. 2-21. Detail from a tie-dyed fabric made in Ghana. The diamond shape was created by tying small pleats in the cloth, and the marbleized background by tying the cloth in a tightly bunched ball. Collection of the author.

tern was made by bunching the material into a tight ball and wrapping it with string. The cloth was immersed in green and gold dyes.

The tie-dyed fabrics are worn in many traditional styles: wraparound skirts, robes, shirts, and head wraps. The fabrics are now also made into Western-style dresses and shirts.

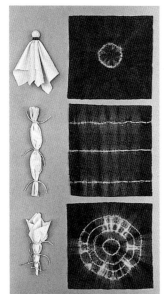

Fig. 2-22. Articles on the left are tied in the manner that produced the results shown on the right. From the top down: a marble, secured with a rubber band; accordion fold bound with string; a long point tied in four places with string.

Making Tie-Dyed Fabric Designs

Many items can be decorated with the tie-dye method. Students can design wall hangings or decorate T-shirts, pillow covers, or curtains. Some may want to make a dashiki, a traditional African men's shirt that is popular now for both men and women. An excellent film for younger elementary school children, *The Blue Dashiki*,[2] may be available through your library. It tells the story of a young boy in the city who earns the money to buy a dashiki he's seen in a store. But children enjoy making a piece of clothing themselves that they can wear with pride.

Instructions for making a dashiki are given in Fig. 2-24. The dashiki design is very simple and can be cut out and sewn in a few minutes. Plain white cotton cloth works best. Old sheeting is fine, but if it is *too* old, the fabric may be weak and tear easily. Avoid synthetic fibers, which often do not take the dye very well. On the junior high level, the students can sew the dashiki themselves; in elementary school, teachers or parents can do the machine

[2] *The Blue Dashiki, Jeffrey and His City Neighbors.* Encyclopedia Britannica Educational Corporation, Chicago.

sewing. Hand stitching is rarely strong enough to allow for wearing. When the dashiki has been made, it may be tie-dyed.

Students should experiment with tie-dyeing on scraps of cloth before they make their final wall hanging or decorate a dashiki. Essentially, the material is tied very tightly in certain areas with string, or rubber bands. (Pulling the string hard against a slab of wax will help it resist the dye.) Tying around marbles or beans makes small circles. Folding accordion style and tying makes different linear patterns. Try dipping a twisted and tied point of cloth in a light colored dye and then just the tip of the same area in a darker dye—this gives a sunburst with a deeper colored center (see Fig. 2-22). Experiment and see what happens.

Commercial dyes, which are available in most grocery stores, should be mixed ahead of time. Make strong colors by using less water

Fig. 2-23. This design by Myles, age twelve, in orange, red, and blue, was achieved by folding the cloth and dipping in the tips and edges. It was then unfolded, folded again differently, tied with rubber bands, and dipped again.

Fig. 2-24.

To make a dashiki:

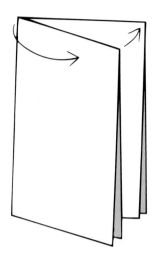

1. Double cloth lengthwise and hold against person for whom dashiki is to be made. For long sleeves, let it go from wrist to wrist; for shorter sleeves, cut at forearm. Cut at any desired length, leaving an extra inch for hemming.

2. Fold cloth over again, very precisely, matching all corners.

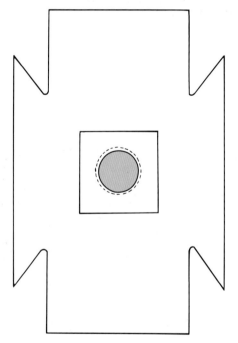

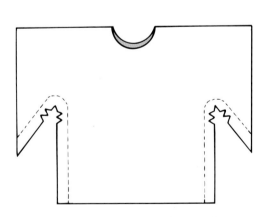

5. Open up dashiki and fit hole in square piece directly over hole in dashiki. Sew together to make facing.

6. Fold material down with *facing inside*. Sew on dotted line under arms and down the sides. Cut V-shaped notches out of edge under arm.

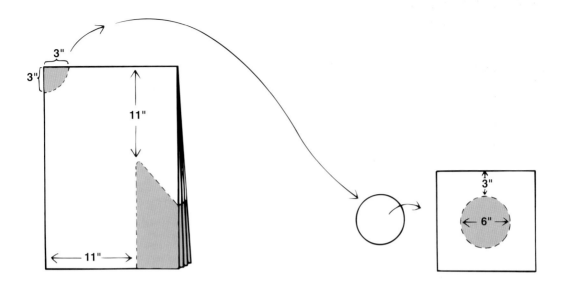

3. Mark the neck opening, 3" out and down from the corner, with a compass. Cut on dotted lines. Cut out piece to make sleeve: the folded dashiki should be 11" wide for an average student, 10" for a slight student, and 12" for a heavier student. Carry this cut up to 11" from the shoulder and then curve down to make sleeve, as in diagram.

4. Take the circular piece that was cut from neck hole in step 3 and place in the middle of another piece of cloth. Cut out a hole of the same size. The margin should be at least 3" beyond the hole all around. Discard both round pieces. This will be interfacing for the neck.

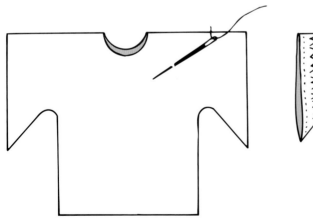

7. Turn right side out. Turn facing inside and tack-stitch at corners and front so that it will lie flat inside.

8. Hem sleeves and bottom to desired length. Decorate the dashiki by tie-dye method or by the batik process described in Chapter 5.

Fig. 2-25. Kristen's multicolored marbleized wall hanging was created by tying bunches of fabric in a few places and then crumpling up the entire cloth into a ball and tying it again.

than indicated on the package. Add salt to make them more colorfast. Plastic gallon milk containers are good for storing dye, and more of the same containers cut in half make good dye pots. Dip tied fabrics in the dye until the fabric is a shade darker than you want it to be. Rinse out excess dye. Let the pieces dry thoroughly before untying.

If the tie-dyed fabric is to be a wall hanging, it should be ironed and then glued or sewn to a dowel along the top edge. Leave just enough dowel extending at either side to tie on a length of yarn for hanging (see Fig. 2-25).

A dashiki should be ironed with a cloth dipped in diluted vinegar *before* it is washed the first time. This increases colorfastness. Wash separately from other clothing.

At first, tie-dyeing has many accidental qualities. If children are disappointed in the way their project turns out, they can retie the cloth and dip it in deeper colors for a different effect. If it is still not satisfying, they can use the color as a background and print over it using potato or linoleum cuts and textile paint. (See the directions for making adinkra cloth.) A border around the neck, sleeves, or bottom edge may be all it needs. African fabrics frequently combine several different methods of textile design in one piece.

Dashikis may also be decorated with batiked designs. Wax batiking is a similar process to the Nigerian adire eleko (cassava paste resist designs) described earlier. The country most associated with batiks is Java, and directions for making them are given in the section on Indonesian arts in Chapter 5.

Fig. 2-26. To decorate her dashiki, Jill picked up the front center in a long point and tied it in three places with string. It was gathered and tied around the neck, sleeve ends, and bottom to produce the parallel lines.

ANCIENT AND CONTEMPORARY METAL WORK OF NIGERIA

Items made of bronze were produced in Africa as early as 2500 BC, and work was done in iron as early as 400 BC. Copper, gold, and silver were used as well. Tools, weapons, containers, weights for weighing out gold, and jewelry of all kinds were made with these metals and varying techniques.

Beginning in the fifteenth century and continuing through the nineteenth, the Nigerian kingdom of Benin created many beautiful, realistic sculptures in bronze. Artists made portraits of royal figures that rank among the finest sculptures of the world. The palace walls and doors in Benin were covered with bronze plaques, cast in relief, with decorated backgrounds. These plaques provided records of historical events in the empire: scenes of hunting, battles, family life, and symbolic animal forms. Fig. 2-27 is a portion of one of these panels from Benin. The leopard

Fig. 2-28. Aluminum counter-repoussé panel by Asiru Olatunde, Oshogbo, Nigeria. Collection of the author.

spots are suggested by an overall decorative pattern of large circles, and tiny dots suggest fur. The background of dots and a floral pattern is typical of the Benin bronze panels.

Both the portraits and the panels were made with the lost-wax process. In this process, a sculpture is made of wax over a base of clay. The wax sculpture is modeled in very fine detail. The wax is then covered with a mixture of clay and charcoal. When this mold of clay and wax is heated, the wax melts and flows out of tubes set in the clay. Molten metal is then poured into the space left by the "lost wax." When it cools, the clay is broken away. This leaves a metal sculpture, which is then refined and polished. The lost-wax process of making bronze sculpture and jewelry is still used in Nigeria and in many other parts of Africa.

In Oshogbo, Nigeria, a Yoruba artist named Asiru Olatunde (1922–1995) became famous for his work in aluminum panels. He achieved a relief design in metal that resembled the Benin work of centuries ago, but did it by a very different method. Instead of

Fig. 2-27. Bronze plaque with leopard. Benin, Southern Nigeria, seventeenth century. Courtesy of Linden-Museum, Stuttgart.

modeling the sculpture in wax and casting it in bronze, he worked with aluminum. When he hammered on tools placed on the face of the panel, the metal expanded so that unhammered areas were raised into relief. This is called counter-repoussé. (In the more common form of repoussé, the raised areas are pushed out from the back.) Olatunde first sketched his designs on paper. He then used simple tools to create a richly textured aluminum panel. In the panel shown in Fig. 2-28, it looks as if he may have hammered on a nail set to form the background and used something like a screwdriver for the lines. Before he hammered the background, Olatunde made designs on the parts to be raised, such as patterns on clothing (typical Yoruba textile designs can be recognized) and fur and feather patterns on birds and animals. His designs, like the Benin bronzes, often showed village scenes or animals. The background was enriched with designs derived from nature: leaves, stars, and insects. Many of his ideas came from Yoruba folklore or illustrated aspects of Yoruba daily life, history, and traditions.

Making Aluminum Counter-Repoussé Panels

Sheet aluminum, 0.020 gauge, can be purchased at a reasonable price in hardware stores. (Do not use the tooling aluminum in art supply stores, as it is much too thin for this project.) However, a local offset printing company might donate one or two large used sheets, which would be ample for your project. Aluminum offset plates come in several thicknesses. For this project use the thickest plate, at least 0.008". Aluminum edges are *very* sharp. Before handling the sheets, always fold 1"

Fig. 2-29. Brian has taped the edges of his panel to preserve a border and transferred his design to the aluminum with carbon paper. Now he is making impressions on the design by hammering a dulled nail with a stick of hardwood.

masking tape over the edges. With steel wool and scouring powder, remove ink from the surface of the aluminum before beginning the project.

For fifth- or sixth-grade students, cut the aluminum sheets into rectangles about 3½ x 5". Older students, of junior high age, may want to work on a larger panel. Again, first make a ½" border around the aluminum pieces by folding 1" masking tape over the edges. This will preserve a border of unhammered aluminum and also prevent students from being cut by the sharp corners.

Next, work out a design on paper the size of the aluminum plate minus the border. The students should not try to get many figures on

Fig. 2-30. After impressing eye and flipper lines on his turtle design, Theodore uses a dulled nail to fill in the background. This raises the unhammered areas.

a small plaque. One central animal, person, or design is probably best. A large panel could show a group of people or a jungle, grassland, or river theme that includes a background of leaf, grass, or wave patterns. When the drawing is completed, it should be taped to the aluminum over a piece of carbon paper and transferred by pencil.

Remove the paper after transferring the design and place the aluminum over a thick pad of newspaper. Being careful not to penetrate the metal, first create designs *on* the figures. Feathers, fur, spots, or clothing and features are typical designs. Pressing hard with an old ballpoint pen (that no longer contains ink) can make lines; tapping with a hammer on various metal objects (nails, nail sets, bolts, and screwdrivers) can create eyes, fish scales, and feather designs. This is done with a somewhat lighter touch than the subsequent hammering out of the background. If there are not

enough hammers to go around, use 8–10" sticks of hardwood for hammers.

Once the designs on the figures have been completed, fill in the background with deeper, quite closely packed impressions. This will raise all the unhammered areas. A sharp nail will penetrate the aluminum (especially if you are using offset printing plates), so use a dulled nail (hammer the point flat), the head of a finishing nail, or a nail set or bolt. The nail sets and bolts give pleasing round impressions without the danger of making holes that pierce the panel. If the impressions are too close together, the effect is poor; if they are too far apart, the metal will not raise properly.

Fig. 2-31. Chandra has removed the tape that preserved a border and is nailing her panel to a block of wood.

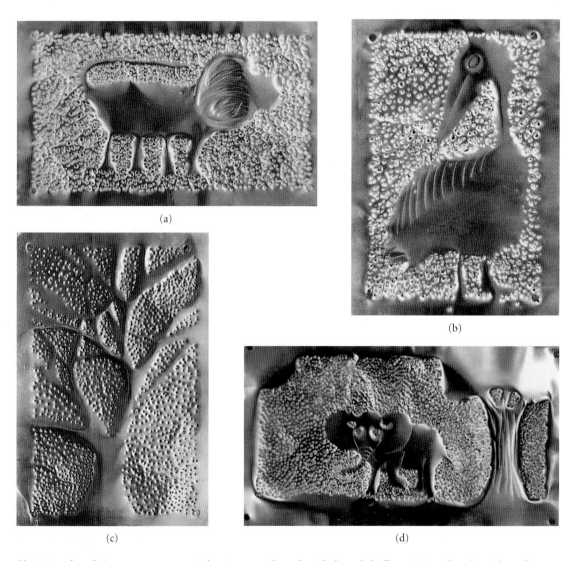

Fig. 2-32. a, b, c, d. Four counter-repoussé aluminum panels made with discarded offset printing plates by sixth-grade students. (a) *Lion*, by Chandra, (b) *Pelican*, by Meg, (c) *Tree* by Polly, and (d) *Elephant* by Paul.

When you have filled in the background, remove the tape and mount the panel by using small ⅝" no. 18 wire nails to attach it to a piece of wood. (Lumber companies will often allow schools to use their scraps; if you are using scraps, you may want to begin the project by cutting the aluminum to fit the different shapes of the wood pieces, rather than by sawing wood to fit the aluminum panel after it has been made.) Rub the completed panel with very fine steel wool to bring it to a high polish.

MASKS AND SCULPTURE

We see West African masks and sculpture in museums and consider them works of art. However, all these pieces were created for a particular purpose, most often for a religious or magical rite. Children in Western society think of a mask as a disguise. In Africa, masks are created and used for a number of very different reasons—usually as a link with the supernatural. They are only part of a more complete costume, and the accompanying music and dance are equally important in the ceremony.

Many West Africans believe that when dancers put on a mask, they become the spirit they are portraying. The masks are used for many different purposes. They are used in

Fig. 2-33. An antelope dance mask, worn by the Zamle Society, Guro, Ivory Coast; and a highly abstract Kplekple mask, commonly called "moon mask," Baule (bä-oo-lee), Ivory Coast. Courtesy of the Plymouth House Galleries, Plymouth, Michigan.

administering justice and in teaching young people the laws, history, and traditions of their society. Some of the ceremonies are an attempt to influence the forces of nature. In the mythology of the Bambara people of Mali, the Creator sent an antelope, Chi Wara, to earth to teach the people how to raise corn. Every year, in celebration of the birth of agriculture and to ensure a good harvest, the Bambara hold a dance. A male and a female dancer, each wearing a beautiful headdress depicting Chi Wara, gracefully imitate the motions of the antelope. (Fig. 2-34 shows a male Chi Wara headdress; a female Chi Wara headdress is in the form of a doe with a fawn on her back.)

Fig. 2-34. Chi Wara headdress depicting a mythical antelope, Bambara, Mali. Courtesy of Charles and Julie Steedman.

Some sculptures are made to ensure health. The Ashanti women of Ghana carry small sculptures resembling dolls to ensure the birth of healthy children. (Examples of these akua'ba statues can be seen flanking the antelope headdress in Fig. 2-36.)

Sometimes sculptures are made to embody spirits. In some cultural groups it is believed that when a person dies the spirit wanders until it finds a suitable home. An ancestor figure is created to make a home for the spirit.

Masks are traditionally carved by specially trained male artists, often after long apprenticeship in the art. The very tools the artist uses are considered sacred, and the artist uses all his skill to create a unique and powerful mask that is still within the traditions of his people. He works alone, in a special hut, with simple tools—an adze, a curved knife, and perhaps a chisel and hammer—carving in new, unseasoned wood.

African masks have been created in an astonishing variety of forms, sizes, and styles. Some masks cover the face only; some go over the head and rest on the shoulders. Others are worn as high headdresses. Such materials as

Fig. 2-36. John makes a sketch of a Bambara antelope headdress from Mali (on the shelf). It is flanked by two Ashanti statues from Ghana. Behind them on the wall is a Bobo butterfly mask from Upper Volta. Other masks from the Ivory Coast, Guinea, and Nigeria are on the floor. Courtesy of the Plymouth House Galleries, Plymouth, Michigan.

Fig. 2-35. A sixth-grade class sketching from a display of African art that shows a variety of masks, including two Dan masks from the Ivory Coast (upper left), a Bambara antelope mask from Mali (center), and a large round Baule Kplekple mask, commonly called "moon mask," from the Ivory Coast. Courtesy of the Plymouth House Galleries, Plymouth, Michigan.

shells, seeds, beads, and sheet metal are sometimes added to the wood to suggest hair and ornamentation. In some masks, the surface is incised or painted with geometric designs. The colors are derived from native materials—white kaolin, black charcoal, and other earth and vegetable colors (see Fig. 2-33). Artists rub oil or mud into some masks to darken the wood, which is polished to a satiny sheen; in other masks the wood is left untreated. Long straw or raffia fringes are frequently attached around the base of the mask to hide the identity of the person wearing it.

Although some masks are representational, most are not copies of nature but are highly

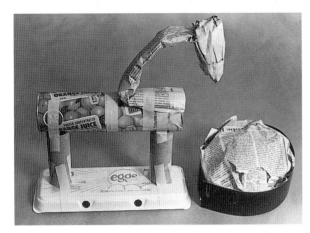

Fig. 2-37. The framework for a sculpture of an antelope is created from half an egg carton (base), toilet paper rolls (legs), two juice cans (body), and a roll and wad of newspaper (neck and head). Later, tubes from clothes hangers will be inserted in the head for horns. The base for a mask is made by clipping a strip of cardboard into a circle and filling it in with crumpled newspaper.

Making large wood sculpture would be an overwhelming project for most young students, but sculpture built of papier-mâché is a fine substitute. This technique can be used in many other art projects as well.

First, build a basic form or framework for the sculpture by taping or tying together boxes, tubes, other containers, or rolled newspaper. (See Fig. 2-37.) Then cover pieces of torn newspaper on both sides with wheat paste or other papier-mâché paste product and apply them to the basic form, as shown in Fig. 2-38. (See appendix for directions for making and using these pastes.) Apply at least four layers of paper for a strong sculpture. If one alternates between torn newspaper and torn

stylized and symbolic. This increases the psychological impact on the viewer. Aspects of the figure are exaggerated to emphasize strength and awesome qualities. The human and animal forms are often translated into abstract geometric shapes that stand for qualities of the animal or spirit being portrayed.

Papier-Mâché Masks and Sculptures

If it is possible to arrange a visit to a museum or art gallery that has a collection of African sculpture, such a trip would be a great inspiration to the students. Make arrangements ahead of time so that museum staff can be prepared to explain the items in the collection and answer questions. Students should take paper, pencils, and drawing boards (squares of corrugated cardboard work well) to sketch the pieces that most interest them. If a museum experience is not practical, offer students time to study the excellent books on African art found in most libraries.

Fig. 2-38. John applies torn pieces of newspaper dipped in wheat paste to his sculpture of an antelope, inspired by a Bambara headdress.

Fig. 2-39. Nick applies a final layer of paper to his face mask, and Scott covers the twine-wrapped horns of his antelope mask with a layer of paper. The twine will give the horns the appearance of being carved in ridges.

Fig. 2-40. After painting a base coat of black, Tamar paints the eyes and geometric designs on her mask, which is based on her drawing of the Baule mask in the gallery.

paper toweling, it is easier to make sure each layer is complete.

To make a mask that can be worn: fold one opened sheet of newspaper into a strip 2 x 29", or use a strip of flexible cardboard. Clip the ends of this strip together to form a circle, or collar, a little wider than your face. In masks based on animal figures the collar is not round but taped into a different shape, as was done in the antelope mask in Fig. 2-41. Scrunch up newspaper and fill in this collar. The stuffing should not be packed in flat; it should rise in a gentle curve from the sides (see Fig. 2-37). After applying one or two layers of papier-mâché to this form and letting it dry, tape on tubes or cut

cardboard shapes to create horns, noses, ears, eyes, mouths, or other protuberances. Secure and integrate these with the rest of the sculpture by adding two more layers of papier-mâché. In Fig. 2-39, students are adding the final layers of papier-mâché to their masks. For the antelope mask, the tubes have been wrapped with twine to form ridges on the horns, which will still be visible under one layer of papier-mâché if it is carefully smoothed. After the mask is dry, the paper stuffing is removed from the collar. Eye and mouth holes can be cut into the mask with sharp scissors or a mat knife.

When the mask or sculpture is dry, it may be painted with tempera paint. Apply a basic

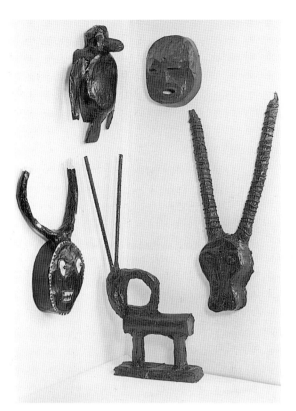

Fig. 2-41. Five papier-mâché sculptures based on drawings made in the art gallery by sixth-grade students. Clockwise from top left: sculpture based on a Senufo flying bird, by Monique; interpretation of a Dan mask by David; antelope mask based on a Bambara mask, by Alex; antelope sculpture based on a Bambara headdress, by John; mask based on a Baule mask, by Tamar.

coat of one color. Geometric designs or other color areas can be added after the base coat is dry. (See Fig. 2-40.) Other materials may be added for hair or decorations: yarn, grasses, shells, twine, stones, metal, beads, seeds. The mask or sculpture will be more durable if given a protective coat of shellac.

You can get ideas for many other art projects based on African arts by looking through the books listed in the bibliography, or by visiting art import shops or galleries. Jewelry, pottery, basketry, and weaving are all possible creative projects for the classroom.

Fig. 2-42, 2-43. A sixth-grade antelope mask, bottom, and the Bobo mask from Upper Volta, top, that inspired it.

Fig. 3-1. *The Young Shoemaker and the Lion Before Bahram,* detail from the manuscript of Firdausi's *Shah-Nameh.* Anonymous Iranian (Shiraz School and Timurid School), c. 1460. Opaque watercolor and gold leaf on paper (10½ x 7"). When the Shah's lion became loose, the shoemaker ran and climbed on his back, holding him by the ears until the keeper came. (Fortunately, the lion had just been fed!) Courtesy of the University of Michigan Museum of Art. 1963/1.69.

3 ARTS OF THE MIDDLE EAST

The rich cultural heritage of the Middle East is represented by arts that cover a span of 4,000 years: twenty-fifth-century BC hieroglyphs carved in sunken relief on an ancient Egyptian tomb; sixth-century mosaic floors from recently excavated temples in Israel; the Persian miniature paintings of the fifteenth century; and finally, in twentieth-century Egypt, the contemporary tapestries woven by the children of Harrania.

EGYPTIAN ARTS

Five thousand years ago a civilization grew up along the Nile River, developing and flowering over a span of 3,000 years. It was a peaceful culture, living on a narrow strip of very fertile land and protected from invasion by deserts on either side. Over these many centuries, a great range of magnificent art and architecture was created, and because of the dry climate and the Egyptian desire to preserve everything for the afterlife, we are still able to enjoy many examples of these arts.

Most of the art that survives from ancient Egypt was created to provide continuity between life and death. The ancient Egyptian word for sculptor means "he who makes to live." The Egyptians believed that earthly life was merely a step people took before entering a spirit world, a world in which people would need their bodies, and would want all the things they had enjoyed in life. Therefore, bodies were carefully preserved and sculptors and craftsmen were set to work reproducing replicas of servants, animals, and domestic furniture, which Egyptians believed would become real in the spirit world. Portrait sculptures of the kings and persons of high rank were also made, so that the spirit would have a place to go if it could not inhabit its own body. By the same token, the beautiful wall paintings on the tombs depicting hunting along the Nile, servants dancing, and other domestic scenes were to provide after death the things loved in life.

Beautiful objects were also created for the living, however: jewelry, vases, small sculptures, elegant hand mirrors, cosmetic containers, fine furniture. All these things were created by well-trained, anonymous artisans. There is no evidence that individuals became known as artists in their own right.

This high civilization came to an end with the occupation of a succession of invaders after 300 BC. Many tombs were plundered, and temples destroyed. Eventually the language was no longer spoken, and the ancient writing could no longer be read.

Hieroglyphs

For many centuries the meaning of the ancient Egyptian hieroglyphs was a mystery. Then in 1799, French soldiers, digging trenches at Rosetta after Napoleon's conquest of Egypt, came upon a stone with three different styles

Fig. 3-2. Egyptian sunken relief of the Courtier Biu, Sakkarah, Egypt, circa 2500 BC. Courtesy of the Oriental Institute, The University of Chicago. The hieroglyphs, part of a speech by the noble, were cut into limestone in the chapel of his tomb. The vertical lines are the speech, and the horizontal line at the bottom serves as a label and reads, "The sole companion (of the Pharoah), Biu." Guided by the sounds given for hieroglyphs in Fig. 3-3, can you find the name Biu?

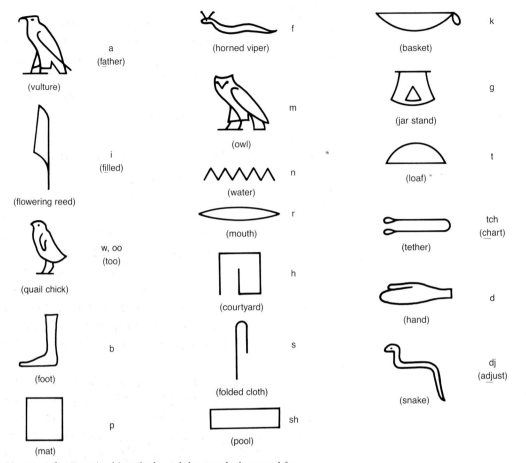

a (father)
(vulture)

i (filled)
(flowering reed)

w, oo (too)
(quail chick)

b
(foot)

p
(mat)

f
(horned viper)

m
(owl)

n
(water)

r
(mouth)

h
(courtyard)

s
(folded cloth)

sh
(pool)

k
(basket)

g
(jar stand)

t
(loaf)

tch (chart)
(tether)

d
(hand)

dj (adjust)
(snake)

Fig. 3-3. A few Egyptian hieroglyphs and the sounds they stand for.

of writing engraved on the surface: hieroglyphic; demotic, a popular handwritten form of hieroglyphic; and Greek. It was realized that all three might say the same thing and that the inscription in Greek might provide clues to the two forms of the Egyptian language. Two years later, the stone was surrendered to the English and taken to the British Museum in London. Scholars there went to work on the problem immediately. The task was difficult, because part of the text was missing, and it was hard to match words. The most brilliant work was done by a French scientist, Jean-

François Champollion. He had decided at the age of ten that he wanted to decipher the Rosetta Stone and pursued studies that would help him toward that end. By the time of his death in 1832, he had made great progress in understanding the hieroglyphs and Egyptian grammar. The work of studying Egyptian writing is ongoing, however, and words are still being added to the known vocabulary.

Some hieroglyphs represent a single sound. For instance, an owl represents the sound *M* because the ancient Egyptian word for owl begins with that sound. However, some

Fig. 3-4. Debbie, age ten, cuts hieroglyphs into plaster with a linoleum cutting tool after drawing them first with a pencil.

sometimes for the sake of symmetry they read from left to right. The hieroglyphs, whether on flat surfaces or engraved in stone, were usually colored. Often the colors were the same as the object they represented, but sometimes hieroglyphs were painted a single color.

Carving Egyptian Hieroglyphs

Plaster is a perfect medium for carving hieroglyphs. (The directions for mixing the plaster are given in the appendix. *Please note cautions in preparing and using plaster.*) Pour it into Styrofoam meat trays or small shallow boxes. Styrofoam works nicely because it is easily removed when the plaster dries. Other containers will need to be coated with petroleum jelly before the plaster is poured in, so that it won't stick. Pour in ½" of plaster. Set it to dry overnight.

Draw the hieroglyphs on the plaster with a pencil. Run the plaster slab very quickly under water to make carving easier and eliminate

hieroglyphs represent a group of sounds, and some stand for an entire word. There are many hundreds of hieroglyphs.

There are two forms of hieroglyphic writing: the monumental form used on statues and in paintings and the cursive script form used for keeping records. Viewed aesthetically, the former is sometimes a beautiful fine art, enjoyable just for the skill of execution, grace of form, and balance. These hieroglyphs were carved and written so they would fill the space properly, not just to follow the necessary sequence. For instance, instead of simply stringing hieroglyphs in a line, one low symbol might be placed on top of another to balance a tall one next to them. They usually read from right to left (in the direction they face), but

Fig. 3-5. Debbie's hieroglyphic tablet.

plaster dust. Cut the hieroglyphs into the plaster with linoleum cutting tools. Be sure that the hand holding the plaster is *behind* the one that is using the cutting tool. (After use, wash the tools; the plaster corrodes metal.) Fig. 3-3 shows how some of the ancient hieroglyphs looked and sounded. Students may want

Fig. 3-6. Winged scarab amulet of blue faience c. 18th Dynasty (1580–1321 BC). Modern stringing. 1971.2.4 Courtesy of Kelsey Museum of Archaeology, University of Michigan.

to combine them to make an approximation of their own names. Although there were no symbols for vowel sounds as we know them, some sounds came close. A few more hieroglyphs, some of those commonly used in Egyptian jewelry, are shown in Fig. 3-8.

Jewelry

No jewelry has ever surpassed that made by the ancient Egyptians. Its beauty is breathtaking—and what has survived the millennia is only a small fraction of what was created. Jewelry was perhaps the most valuable property of the royal families and the wealthy. It was enjoyed in life and then put in the grave with the deceased so that it could be enjoyed in the afterlife. A few tombs escaped the grave robbers active throughout Egypt's history, and from these we have a glimpse at what was made and how it was worn. Both men and women wore jewelry: necklaces, pendants, bracelets, crowns, anklets, rings, and pectorals (ornaments men wore on the chest). The earliest jewelry, from prehistoric times, was made of stones, ivory, bone,

shell, and clay. Around 4000 BC, gold and silver had begun to be used. Faience (a glazed clay-like material) in shades of green and blue and sometimes red and yellow, was also used in jewelry. Throughout the span of Egyptian culture, not only these materials but also lapis lazuli, carnelian (a red stone), turquoise, and many other semiprecious stones and colored glass were used in jewelry.

Jewelry was made in workshops by artisans whose families had been employed at the craft for generations. Beads were strung in many designs, perhaps the best known being intricate, broad collars. Pendants were sometimes made in animal forms: lions, crocodiles, frogs, flies, hawks, ibis, vultures. These were usually symbolic in nature. Serpents were frequent motifs, and so were flowers, especially lotus buds and papyrus. The scarab, the sacred beetle associated with the sun and worn as a protective amulet symbolizing immortality, was frequently used in rings, pectorals, and other settings. See Fig. 3-6.

Fig. 3-7. Blue and blue-green Egyptian faience beads from the New Kingdom, c. 1580–525 BC. These have been restrung based on examples in which the original arrangement was preserved. The outside string is of lotus flowers, small and large; the next string alternates cylindrical with fluted half-round beads; the inner string is of lentil-shaped beads. Courtesy of the Oriental Institute, The University of Chicago.

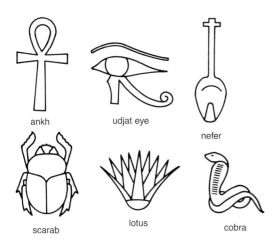

ankh

udjat eye

nefer

scarab

lotus

cobra

Fig. 3-8. Hieroglyphs and designs commonly used in jewelry.

Hieroglyphs were used as design elements on jewelry. Fig. 3-8 shows some that were commonly used: *ankh*, symbol of life; the *udjat* or Horus eye, source of health and happiness; and *nefer*, symbol of goodness, beauty, and joy. But hieroglyphs of stars, animals, birds, lizards, and fish were also employed.

Making Clay Beads

If possible, inspire students with a museum trip to see ancient Egyptian beads, scarabs, and other jewelry. Most of the jewelry found in the tombs is made of gold, blue lapis lazuli, turquoise, red carnelian, and beads of glass. Faience, with a blue or blue-green glaze, was used extensively. We don't know exactly how it was made, but many believe that it was a paste of ground quartz and some kind of adhesive, with a glaze containing copper. Clay handles very much like the ancient paste. If students make beads of a clay that fires to a white or buff color, they can paint them to approxi-mate a turquoise or blue faience. Fired red clay can approximate the color of carnelian.

Beads of clay may be rolled or patted into many shapes. To make cylindrical beads, form long rolls of clay about ¼" in diameter and cut in equal sections. Roll round beads between the palms of the hands. Make lentil-shaped beads by rolling a round shape and then flattening it. Egyptian necklaces often follow a pattern of alternating shapes or sizes, small and large or cylindrical and round. The beads will have more interest if students use at least two different shapes. Pass a finishing nail (one without a head) completely through the bead and out the other side to form a hole for stringing. (If the nail is merely poked in and then removed from the same side, the hole tends to close up.) Make the hole while the beads are still soft. Use a nail of eight penny size or larger. This may seem large, but the holes shrink during firing. The beads themselves shrink, so make plenty if the necklace is to fit over the head.

Fig. 3-9. Kathy presses a ball of clay into a hieroglyph carved in her plaster tablet to make a raised design on a bead. She has made a simple clay pot to hold the beads during firing.

Fig. 3-10. Kathy passes a finishing nail through the top of her clay bead. If it is put through parallel to the flat surface of the bead, the bead will lie flat when strung.

Fig. 3-11. Clay beads by (from top) Kathy, nine, Debbie, ten, and Alec, ten.

If the students have first made plaster hieroglyphic slabs, they can create beads with fine raised designs. Roll out a marble-sized sphere in the palm of the hands, and then press this ball of clay into the hieroglyph. When it is lifted, an impression of the hieroglyph remains in the clay (assuming the hieroglyph is engraved deeply enough). Any number of impressions may be taken. The Egyptians made faience beads uniform by pressing the material into pottery molds in a very similar manner. If the bead is to lie flat when strung, be sure the hole is run through parallel to the flattened surface of the bead. This means that the bead cannot be pressed too thin, or there will not be room for the hole.

Fire the beads in a kiln. The easiest way to keep one student's beads separate from another's is to make very simple clay pots to fire them in. Roll and pat a fist-sized portion of clay into a round ball. Then hold the ball of clay in the left hand, press into the top with the right thumb, and pinch in against the clay with the fingers. (Reverse if left-handed.) Keep turning the clay against the left hand and pinching the sides until it opens up into a bowl shape. Write the student's name on the bottom of the pot with a pencil or nail so that it can be identified after firing. If the pots are made first, the students can store their beads while they are making them. The pot will be fragile before firing, so handle it with care.

After firing, the beads may be left in natural clay colors, usually white or brick red. If the clay is white, the beads may be painted with watercolors: a turquoise blue tint looks very much like Egyptian faience. If the painted bead has a raised hieroglyph on it, children can bring out the design by wiping some of the color off the raised figure with a damp cloth, creating a little more contrast with the rest of the bead. If painted, the beads should be protected with a coat of polymer medium applied with a light touch.

Nylon fishing line is a very strong material for stringing beads. Because it is stiff, it can be pushed through the bead holes easily. Although heavy thread can be used, the holes may not be straight enough for a needle, and thread alone is not stiff enough to push through. Make strings of beads long enough to go over the head, or make a catch by forming a loop in one end of the nylon line and tying a paper clip to the other. You can make better looking catches by twisting heavy copper wire into hook and eye shapes with hognosed pliers, or you can buy inexpensive commercial catches.

Fig. 3-12. A tapestry woven by Reda Ahmed, age fourteen. She began weaving in Harrania at age ten. Courtesy of Middle Earth, Ann Arbor, Michigan, and the Ramsis Wissa Wassef Centre.

Fig. 3-13. A young weaver at the Ramsis Wissa Wassef Centre brings her own ideas to life with colorful wool. Photo by Gretchen Whitman.

The Tapestry Weaving of Harrania

In the village of Harrania, fifteen miles from Cairo, the children make very beautiful tapestry weavings that are now known and valued as far away as Europe and America. Work in this craft began fifty years ago, when Professor Ramses Wissa Wassef and his wife Sophie introduced the young children to the art of tapestry weaving. The Wassefs supplied the looms and wool and taught the children weaving techniques.

Weaving a tapestry involves working a picture into the design (unlike a rug of solid colors or stripes, for instance). It is done on a simple frame loom ab6ut which the warp (vertical threads) can be stretched in a way that keeps them taut. The weaver creates the picture by weaving colored wools over and under alternate threads of the warp.

The children of Harrania (beginning at age 8–10) learned to weave directly on the

Fig. 3-14. *Palm Pruners* by Soad Radouan, age thirteen. A tapestry woven at the Ramses Wissa Wassef Centre, Harrania, Egypt. Courtesy of Middle Earth, Ann Arbor, Michigan.

loom without first making a drawing of their idea. Through long hours of practice—for even a small tapestry takes many hours—the children became excellent weavers. They learned to make their ideas visible and to keep very complex designs in their minds. The Wassefs, who had strong faith in the innate artistic ability of children, were careful not to influence their designs. Their faith was well rewarded, for the tapestries are fresh and original. They often reveal close observation of natural surroundings: marvelous tree designs, animals, birds, fish, and the life of the people in the village. Sometimes the subject matter is portrayed realistically, and sometimes it is transformed by a whimsical imagination. The tapestries show a fine sense of balance and rhythm. Each is an individual expression. Copying is discouraged, and the work of each weaver can be distinguished quite easily from that of the others.

Using natural dyes, the weavers themselves dye the wool for the tapestries. The slight variations of hue in batches of hand-dyed wool add richness to the very colorful designs. See Fig. 3-14.

Professor Wassef died in 1974, but the creative work continues in Harrania under the direction of Fouad El Awadley. Some of the first "children" are still weaving, and have children of their own, who are weaving also. There are currently eighty adults and children at the workshop. Their fine work is much sought after by museums and art collectors.

Making a Tapestry Weaving

Children in public school do not have time to weave large individual tapestries. However, a community project can both result in a large tapestry and introduce the art to many people.

One school decided to make a large tapestry to install permanently in their auditorium. This was a cooperative art project, and parents, teachers, and children worked together. Because many people were to work on it, the tapestry's design had to be made first. The students saw photographs of the Harrania tapestries and of designs from other countries so they could understand the range of possibilities. They were encouraged, however, to use their own ideas. A great variety of designs was

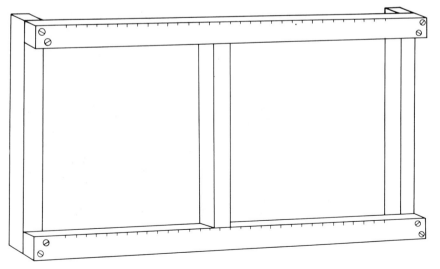

Fig. 3-15. A simple tapestry loom of 2 x 2" wood, screwed together at the corners. It may be made any length or height desired. The brace in the center is simply wedged in, without screws or nails, after the loom is warped.

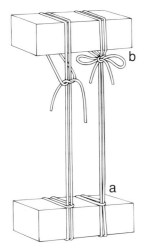

Fig. 3-16. How to tie the warp to the upper and lower beams of the frame.

submitted, and it was difficult to make a choice, but a committee of parents selected one that they thought would work well. (They looked for bright color areas and not too many fine lines that would be difficult to execute.) A simple loom was constructed of 2 x 2" wood, screwed at the corners, measuring 3 x 5'. A 2 x 2" brace was inserted in the middle of the loom to keep it from sagging with the weight of the tapestry. The loom was marked off every half inch, top and bottom, as a guide to warping (see Fig. 3-15).

The warp was tied to the frame. For this size loom, a piece of yarn ten feet long was doubled. The doubled end was wrapped around the bottom of the frame, and the two single ends were pulled through the loop (see Fig. 3-16a). The ends were carried up and around the top frame and tied in a bow knot over the warp (see Fig. 3-16b). This formed two warp threads, and the procedure was repeated until the whole frame was filled all the way across, with two warp threads every half inch. Since very young children were going to learn to weave on the loom, every other warp thread was dyed red to help them pick up alternating threads as they wove the weft into the warp. (This was an afterthought. It would be much easier, in tying on the warp, to use two colors instead of one. Tie two pieces, one of each color and each five feet long, together. Place the knot at the bottom of the loom and proceed to tie on as before.)

Before weaving began, the original drawing was enlarged to the size of the loom (in this case, into a semicircle that fit the contours of an area in the auditorium) and placed underneath the warp on a flat surface. The outlines of the design were transferred to the warp with a black marker. (This is a bit difficult. Because the warp may turn during weaving, each thread must be separately marked completely around the strand.) An inch or so of extra-heavy yarn was woven in at the bottom to space out the warp threads, which start out clumped together in twos. This was to be turned under when the tapestry was finished. The drawing was left taped to the back of the loom as a color guide.

The loom was placed in a hallway. The school was fortunate to have several parents who were weavers. A schedule was set up, and most afternoons found parents and children weaving together. The parent-teacher organi-

Fig. 3-17. Lois Kane, parent and weaver, supervises second-grade students working on a tapestry. This tapestry, *A Sea of Fish,* was designed by Sarah, age ten.

zation paid for some wool, which was supplemented by leftover wool brought from the students' homes. The original weavers taught other parents, who supervised in their turn. Children who had completed their classroom assignments took turns weaving. The loom was big enough for four people to weave at the same time.

All together more than 100 parents and children worked on the tapestry for three months, watching it grow into a beautiful addition to their school environment. Many children, ages six through eleven, were introduced to a new art form. Through this work they gained a great appreciation of the much more complex work of the children of Harrania. A companion piece to the first tapestry was completed the next year.

Some Weaving Techniques

Heavy, four-ply yarn is best for tapestry weaving. If the yarn comes in skeins, roll it into balls. Then twine it into "butterflies" for weaving. Fig. 3-19 shows how to make a butterfly. Hold the end of the yarn (a) between the first two fingers. Wrap the yarn into a figure eight around the thumb and little finger. After making two or

three dozen turns, cut the yarn from the ball, remove the yarn from the thumb and little finger, and wrap end (b) around the middle of the figure eight. Tie by putting end (b) through the last turn around. Take it around once more and tie again in the same way. Pull the yarn out at end (a) to weave with the butterfly.

Pick up a group of warp threads of one color (every other one). Holding them in one hand, pass the "butterfly" of wool through the "shed." Do not pull the yarn straight across, but leave a "hill." This is very important. Because the wool goes over and under each warp thread, it must be longer than the distance across the weaving. Pat the hill down flat with a fork (see Fig. 3-20a). At the end of the row, the yarn circles the last warp thread and

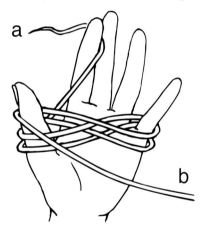

Fig. 3-18. Fifth-grade students Jon, Julie, John, and Angie take a turn at weaving a tapestry.

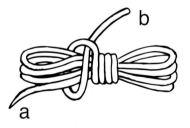

Fig. 3-19. Making a "butterfly" of yarn.

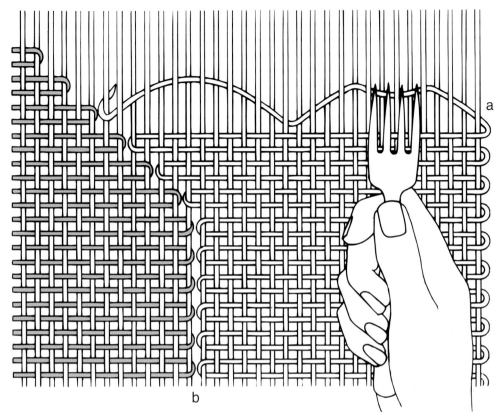

Fig. 3-20. The yarn should not be pulled straight across but left in "hills," which are then beaten down with a fork (a). When one color reaches another it turns around and goes back (b).

comes back, this time going under every thread it went over on the previous row (and over every thread it went under).

When starting a new color area, pull weft that is ending through to the back, and let it dangle there. You do not need to tie any knots. Start the new yarn in the same place, letting the end hang in the back also. If the tapestry is woven face forward, the children can see the work as it progresses. Traditional tapestries are sometimes woven with the back facing the weaver.

When one color area meets another, the weft can turn around and go back, building up that area, so long as there is always solid weaving underneath to beat against with the fork. (In other words, a pyramid area could be woven in the warp to completion without weaving surrounding areas of a different color until later, but a funnel shape could not be done until surrounding areas were done first.)

There are several different ways to weave adjacent color areas. The easiest for beginners is for each color to turn and go back, as is shown in Fig. 3-20b. Although this forms a vertical slit in the tapestry, unless the slit is very long, it does not cause a problem and is com-

Fig. 3-21. Overhand knot. Push the knot close to the weaving.

Fig. 3-22. *Tree of Animals* designed by Jenny, age eight, was woven by more than 100 parents and students. Because the tapestry was designed to fit an alcove in the auditorium, it is mounted on semicircular heavy cardboard, with warp ends tied and stapled to the back.

monly seen in tapestries. If it does cause a gap, it can be sewn together on the back after the tapestry is completed.

As the weaving progresses, the warp may become loose. If it does, untie the knots at the top one by one, pull the warp tighter, and retie.

When the weaving is finished, tie the warp with an overhand knot (see Fig. 3-21). Cut two strands loose from the loom and tie them up close against the weaving before progressing to the next two. When the tapestry is hung, the tied warp may hang down as a fringe, or it may be taped up against the back.

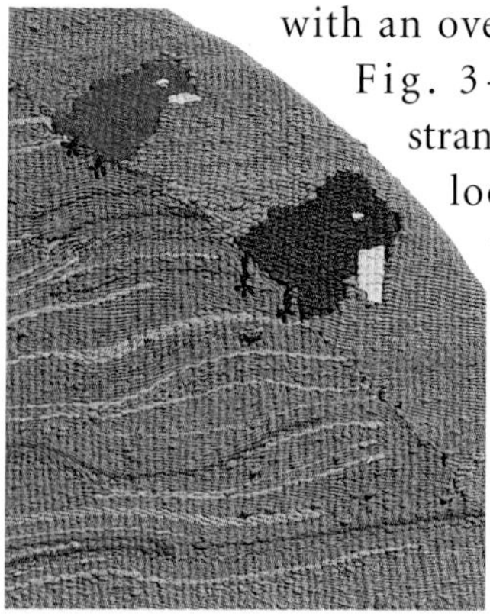

Fig. 3-23. A detail of the tapestry. A few fine lines—such as the birds' feet—were embroidered on after the weaving was done.

Many tapestries are woven with the design running parallel to the warp—on the loom it looks like a picture turned sideways. When such a piece is off the loom, the fringe will appear at the sides instead of at the top and bottom (this is shown in the Harrania tapestry, Fig. 3-12). Beginners find it easier to weave with the design parallel to the weft, just as it will look when taken off the loom. The fringes are at the top and bottom.

THE ANCIENT MOSAICS OF ISRAEL

Israel is rich in arts that reflect the many religious and cultural groups that have lived in this tiny but historically significant land. Judaism, Christianity, and Islam have their roots in this area, and synagogues, churches, and mosques have been carefully preserved over many centuries. History is piled upon history, and the architecture and arts of early times are continually being brought to light. Sometimes this is by accident, and sometimes it happens through the efforts of archaeologists.

In the early twentieth century collective settlements (kibbutzim) were begun in many parts of the country. The people worked very hard to raise crops and dug irrigation ditches to bring water to the arid land. In 1928, while digging such a ditch, people from a settlement at Hefzibah in the valley of Jezreel unearthed some ruins. They realized they had made an important discovery. The site was carefully excavated by Professor E. L. Sukenik, an archaeologist from the Hebrew University in Jerusalem. When the earth was removed, the foundations of an ancient synagogue named Beth Alpha were revealed. The synagogue, which was probably destroyed by one of the earthquakes that devastated the area in ancient times, had a beautiful mosaic floor, the most complete to be discovered in Israel. An inscription in Aramaic (a Semitic language) states that the floor was laid down in the reign of the Roman Emperor Justinian, who ruled from AD 518 to 527.

The art of making mosaic floors was developed by the Greeks in the Mediterranean area as early as the fourth century BC. In Greek and Roman times, it was widely used in public and private buildings. However, the design of the floor at Beth Alpha is very unusual, because it is unrelated to classical art styles of the time. It is signed by two craftsmen, Marianos and his son Hanina, and is a refreshingly original and touching expression of these two artisans, about whom we know little else. A childlike directness and simplicity imbues the mosaic with a spirit of joy and reverence. It is believed that the craftsmen were not trained in mosaic

work but were unusually gifted folk artists of that rural area. The floor is divided into three panels that include designs relating to religious services, signs of the zodiac adapted from Greek figures, and a depiction of the Biblical story of Abraham and Isaac.

Another beautiful mosaic floor from the fifth-century synagogue of Ma'on was discovered at Nirim, a kibbutz founded in southern Israel in the Negev Desert in 1946. This mosaic, which includes brightly colored birds and animals in its design, was discovered during

Fig. 3-24. Detail of a servant from the panel of Abraham and Isaac, part of the mosaic pavement of Beth Alpha Synagogue, Hefzibah, Israel. Early 6th cent. From *Israel—Ancient Mosaics*, produced by the New York Graphic Society and published by Little, Brown and Company. Reproduced by permission of UNESCO.

Arts of the Middle East   **43**

Fig. 3-25. *Hen with Chickens.* A detail from the border of the mosaic pavement of Beth Alpha Synagogue, Hefzibah, Israel. Early 6th cent. From *Israel—Ancient Mosaics*, produced by the New York Graphic Society and published by Little, Brown and Company. Reproduced by permission of UNESCO.

the plowing of a field and was excavated in 1958. (See Fig. 3-26.)

Mosaics were often used on floors and walls in ancient times. They made a decorative and durable surface in homes and public buildings. Small cubes of stone, called tesserae, were cut and set in cement mortar. The range of colors was usually limited to the limestones available locally and ranged from white and cream to red-brown, browns, and black. In some areas artisans used marble and brick. Sometimes blue, yellow, and green glass cubes added to the colors.

Since the color range was limited, the designs depended on value, the range from light to dark, for effectiveness. Usually, a craftsman set off a figure from the background by using dark colors against a light background, or occasionally the opposite. Another common way to make the design stand out was to outline the shapes in a very dark color. The small squares that make up the mosaics create a very pleasing pattern and give unity to the designs.

In all, over 500 mosaic floors have been found in Israel. Discovered in ancient churches, synagogues, Roman palaces, villas, and baths, they reflect the long history of the area and the many peoples who have lived there.

Fig. 3-26. Detail of a leopard from the pavement of the Synagogue of Ma'on at Nirim, Israel. Late 6th cent. From *Israel—Ancient Mosaics*, produced by the New York Graphic Society and published by Little, Brown and Company. Reproduced by permission of UNESCO.

Paper Mosaics

Lower elementary students can make very lovely mosaic designs using paper tiles. Cut half-inch strips of construction paper in many colors (including white), and then cut these strips into half-inch squares. Make the mosaic designs on pieces of 9 x 12" colored paper. Brown and dark blue make good backgrounds.

At each table, put trays of tiles sorted out by color (frozen-dinner trays that have separate compartments are excellent for this). Students select their colors and work directly on the background paper, pasting each tile down with white paste. The best method is to make one large central figure and then fill in the background with a contrasting color. The spacing is difficult for young children—explain that the tiles should not touch but should not be too far apart either. Make a sample to show them.

When the mosaic design is finished and dry, you can enhance it by brushing on a coat of shellac or polymer medium. This gives a glaze-like sheen to the paper tiles. Attach the mosaic design to a slightly larger piece of colored construction paper (one that repeats a color used in the design) and then to a larger piece of black or dark brown paper that extends 2½" beyond the design. (See Fig. 3-28.)

Making Tile Mosaics

Older elementary students can use ceramic tiles in place of the stone and glass cubes used in ancient mosaics. Tile can be purchased from ceramic tile dealers or building contractors. Occasionally tiles left over from jobs or in discontinued colors will be donated to a school. Tiles are available in two thicknesses. It does not matter which you use, as long as you don't mix them in one mosaic (irregular height makes the final step of grouting very difficult). Small 1"-square tiles are a little easier to handle. The color range of ceramic tiles is somewhat limited (just as it was in ancient

Fig. 3-27. Becky, six, works on a paper mosaic design.

Fig. 3-28. *Flower*, paper mosaic by Rachel, age eight.

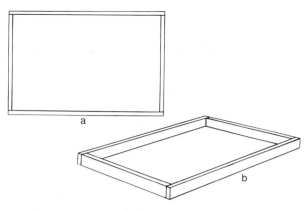

Fig. 3-29. Diagram of a tray for a tile mosaic. (a) Top view. The screen molding is glued around the outside of a plywood base. (b) The two shorter pieces of molding are the same length as the sides of the base, so the other two pieces must be longer in order to overlap them.

times, although for different reasons)—they tend to be quiet, muted colors. In selecting tiles, think more of value than of color. Be sure that there are some very light and some very dark colors. Imported glass tiles (tesserae) are made especially for mosaic work and can be purchased at art supply stores and some tile supply stores. They come in a wider range of colors, but can be expensive.

First make a wooden tray to hold and frame the mosaic (¼" plywood works well). A size of approximately 7 x 10" is ample for a sixth-grade student. Older students may have the patience for a larger piece. Frame the plywood with ¼ x ¾" pine molding. A common mistake is to cut all the pieces the same size as the sides of the plywood. Two must be longer so they can overlap (see Fig. 3-29). Glue the molding to the plywood with white glue, applying glue to the plywood edge and the corners where the molding joins.

Work out a design with charcoal on a piece of paper the size of the plywood. The charcoal will help the students think in terms of bold designs with thick lines and solid color

areas. Very fine lines and details cannot be made in an area this size with tile fragments.

It is very important to explain the concepts of color and value before students begin. They often find the concept of value difficult. You may have tiles in several different values of the same color, for instance, from light blue to dark blue. Because a mosaic is made up of pieces, a design does not show up unless it contains contrasting values. For example, if a figure is made of light blue tiles and the background is made of light green tiles, the figure will tend to disappear into the background. No matter what the color, if the figure is to stand out from the background, it must be very different in value—either much lighter or much darker.

Tiles must be broken up into small pieces. It would be too time consuming for students to

Fig. 3-30. Tamar, eleven, breaks tiles into smaller pieces for her mosaic. She places the tiles between a folded newspaper and hits them with a hammer. It is important to wear goggles to protect against flying fragments.

Fig. 3-31. Tamar puts white glue on a piece of tile with a brush. She will then fit the tile into her mosaic design.

cut the tiles into precise shapes. Fortunately, fine mosaics can be made from irregular pieces. (Even the small 1" tiles should be broken up. They are not only too large for this size mosaic, but they are also too mechanical and regular in appearance. All ancient mosaic stones were hand-cut and quite uneven.) To break the tiles, place them between several layers of newspaper or between the pages of an old magazine and hit them hard with a hammer. *Always wear protective goggles*, because the newspaper often tears and the fragments of tile can fly a good distance. Replace torn papers immediately with new papers.

After working out the design in charcoal, draw it directly on the plywood. Glue small pieces of tile to the plywood, filling in the design. Use a white glue, and leave a space of approximately ⅛" between pieces. Occasionally it may be difficult to fill a space with the accidental shapes of the broken tiles. In this case, shapes can be cut to fit with tile clippers. Tile clippers look a bit like pliers, but the cutting blades do not come completely together. Place the clipper blades so that they just nip the edge of the tile, and press the handles together. A cleavage will form straight across the tile from the point of pressure (see Fig. 3-32). *When you cut tiles, always keep both the tile and the hand holding the clippers inside a clear plastic bag. This prevents fragments from flying, and still allows you to see what you are doing.*

When the tile pieces have all been glued to the plywood, let the mosaic dry overnight before filling it with grout. Grout is available at art supply stores and wherever tiles are sold. *There are elements in dry grout that may be toxic to breathe, so use pre-mixed white grout.* The mixtures with a base of acrylic polymer are best—do not use a ready-mixed grout that has petroleum spirits listed in the ingredients. Spread the grout over the mosaic, forcing it down into all the cracks with a straight piece of cardboard. Scrape the surface as clean as

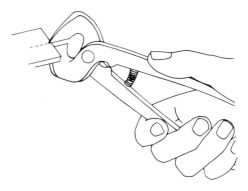

Fig. 3-32. Place the tile clippers so that the blades just nip the edge of the tile. The dotted line shows where a cleavage will form when the handles are pressed together.

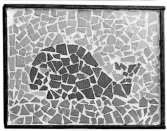

Fig. 3-33. Tile mosaics by sixth-grade students. Clockwise from upper left: *Duck on Pond* by Ellen, *Pot of Plants* by Elizabeth, *Abstract Design* by Steve, *Whale* by Marie.

possible and wipe it gently with a damp sponge. After the grout has dried, clean the surface more thoroughly with the sponge. Clean the wood frame, too. When the frame is dry, use fine sandpaper to remove any remaining traces of grout on the surface.

The mosaic will look more finished if you stain the frame. A walnut stain goes well with most colors. To protect the mosaic surface, place masking tape around the edge where it meets the frame. Apply the stain with a brush to the inside and outside of the frame. Wipe off any excess. Let it dry before removing the masking tape. If some stain seeps under the tape you can scrape it off the grout with a knife or remove it from the tile surface with paint thinner.

The sizes suggested for the mosaic panels are for individual student projects. Several students working together might want to make a large mosaic for permanent display in their school, public library, or other civic center.

PERSIAN MINIATURE PAINTINGS OF IRAN

Present-day Iran has its roots in ancient Persia. The miniature paintings for which Persia is so well known were a late development. Much of the early art was on a very grand scale—great carvings in rock and huge wall paintings. There was also work in bronze, other metals, and fine ceramics with decorative brushwork. In the early thirteenth century, the Mongol invasions of Persia opened the way for Chinese influence on painting styles. By the late thirteenth century, this influence combined with Persian concepts to give new impetus to Persian artists, who for a period of over 300 years, created manuscripts illustrated with small paintings of great purity of color and fine detail.

Schools of manuscript painting developed under the patronage of the shahs, the rulers of Persia. Fine books were traditionally held in great respect. Because they were meticulously made by hand with expensive materials, only the very wealthy could afford them. Workshops were set up, and specialists were hired for every aspect of book making. Very fine paper was made of linen and brought to a glossy finish by careful burnishing. Calligraphers, who did the writing, were held in very high esteem. Some artisans specialized in sewing the pages together and others made elaborate leather covers for the books.

Artists trained for years to become painters. To begin with, there were long hours of lessons in drawing. Before they used color, the students had to learn to make their own brushes. They raised white Persian cats just for this purpose and plucked especially fine hairs, which they bound to a pigeon quill. At first they filled in the colors after a master had drawn the outlines. Gradually, if they showed

Fig. 3-35. *Siyawush Displays His Prowess Before Afrasiyab*, detail from the manuscript of Firdausi's *Shah-Nameh*. Anonymous Iranian (Shiraz School and Timurid School), c. 1460. Opaque watercolor and gold leaf on paper (10½ x 7"). In this polo game, a test of strength and skill, Siyawush drove the ball "out of sight, to see the moon," which pleased King Afrasiyab. Courtesy of The University of Michigan Museum of Art. 1963/1.49.

Fig. 3-34. *Asfandiyar Slays a Dragon*, detail from a manuscript of Firdausi's *Shah-Nameh*. Anonymous Iranian (Shiraz School and Timurid School), c. 1460. Opaque watercolor and gold leaf on paper (10½ x 7"). Courtesy of The University of Michigan Museum of Art. 1963/1.61.

talent, they were given more responsibility, until they too held positions of honor. Artists of exceptional ability could rise to a high position in the shah's court, even if they were of humble birth.

The paintings illustrate traditional stories of action, both historic and romantic. Because the painters used contemporary settings (rather than setting the stories in their actual earlier historical period), the paintings show life in the Persian courts of the time. They are so detailed that we can learn much about the clothing, customs, and occupations of the people in those days. They are not realistic, however. The people and their surroundings are arranged to make a flat, balanced design in a mosaic of bright color and decoration. Gardens bloom; every surface of wall and courtyard is decorated with geometric or floral designs, and clothing, saddles, and tents are richly patterned. Gold was used lavishly—for the sky or mountains and in clothing and ornaments. Silver was used for pools and streams (although it now looks black, having oxidized over the centuries).

The Persian pigments have never been rivaled for purity and intensity of color. Such stones as lapis lazuli, for blue, were pulverized and mixed with special binding materials. Some minerals were brought by camel from thousands of miles away. The workshops kept their formulas secret, and we still do not know the exact methods that produced the paints. Brilliant reds, pure yellows, many shades of green, and intense blues glow like jewels on the paper.

The paintings were bordered in gold, and the page was often further embellished with a wide margin that was flecked with gold or painted with decorative birds and animals or golden arabesques (flowing flower and vine designs).

These great manuscripts are treasured and kept in museums in many parts of the world. We are fortunate that present-day methods of reproduction can bring some of their beauty within everyone's reach.

Figs. 3-1, and 3-34 and 3-35 are paintings that were made to illustrate the *Shah-Nameh* (*History of Kings*). This great Persian epic poem of some 60,000 verses was written by the poet Firdausi, who finished it in 1010 after working on it for thirty years. It is a legendary history of the Persian people, full of heroic adventures and the rise and fall of empires and leaders. Many illustrated editions of the *Shah-Nameh* were commissioned by princely patrons of the arts.

Miniature Painting

Most students have been told in painting classes for many years to "make it big" and are delighted to have a change of pace and work on a small, intimate scale, painting tiny details to their heart's content. A piece of white drawing or construction paper about 7 x 10" is a good size. Draw a ¼" border around the edge with a ruler.

If the painting is to have the feeling of the Persian miniatures, three things must be emphasized: action, color, and surface decoration. Although there were a few ancient portraits and animal paintings, most miniatures told a story. The Persian miniatures seem to come from a land of eternal spring, with flowers always blooming amid scenes of battles, dragon slayings, and duels. Students may want to paint a scene typical of a Persian painting, or they may want to use familiar subject matter. They may want to illustrate historical stories, legends, or narrative poems from their own heritage. Longfellow's *Hiawatha*, the story of Daniel Boone, and the legend of Paul Bunyan are only a few of many possible inspirations to the student.

Have students make a careful drawing in pencil before they begin painting. Surfaces in the miniatures are richly patterned. A tree is not just an expanse of green; it has leaf patterns in great profusion painted in different shades of green or gold. The ground is decorated with tiny flowers. Our buildings do not have the elaborate surface designs found in these paintings, but a pattern of bricks or shingles can add a design quality. If an area of grass or a wall or clothing is to be embellished with flowers or a pattern, first outline the area and paint it with a background color (say, green for the grass). Let the paint dry, and then draw the flowers or patterns that will be painted on top of this basic color. Paint with a fine detail brush, using tempera paints in bright reds, yellows, blues, greens, and gold. White, too, plays an important part in most of the paintings. Keep everything on a small scale. Although some of the Persian paintings illustrated rather large books, they are still miniature, because the figures are small and the paintings filled with action and detail.

Paint the border gold. Mount the painting by first gluing it to a white or cream-colored piece of paper that is ⅛" larger all around than the painting. Then mount these two pieces on a mat of decorative paper that extends 1" or more beyond the painting. Wallpaper sample books often contain many gold designs—flecked, flowered, or marbleized—that are very much in keeping with the Persian miniatures. (The artists who painted the miniatures did not usually make the page margins themselves; they were painted by students who were trained to do only that job.)

Fig. 3-36. Miniature paintings by sixth-grade students. Clockwise from top left: *Deer* by Chris, *Unicorn* by Eileen, *Hunting by Horseback* by Saskia, and *Man Playing a Lute* by Fred.

Fig. 4-1. *Housewarming.* Straw inlay panel, Zhlobin, Belarus. Collection of the author.

4 EUROPEAN ARTS

Although this book associates a particular art with a certain country, the art may not be unique to that country. This is especially true of the arts and crafts of Europe. Cookie stamps, here associated with Sweden, are made in many parts of Europe for decorating cakes and sweets. The art of pressing and arranging flowers is probably just as common in Switzerland as it is in Germany. Although craftspeople in Poland excel in the art of wycinanki, or cut-paper designs, artists in Germany also create intricate cutouts, which are called Scherenschnitte. In several European countries it is the custom to decorate eggs for the holidays, although many different methods are used. Straw decorations in great variety are created in rural areas throughout the continent.

However, while the general idea may be the same and similar materials used, arts and crafts are usually distinctive to a particular cultural area. The traditional designs, patterns, and styles of one country or region distinguish artworks from similar items made elsewhere.

To begin this chapter we go back to some of the earliest extant art in Europe.

THE PREHISTORIC CAVE PAINTINGS AND ENGRAVINGS OF FRANCE AND SPAIN

The Vézère river valley in southwestern France is lovely in the spring. Along the hillsides the great limestone outcroppings hover over the little town of Les Eyzies. Imagine, if you can, climbing a hill and entering a long, narrow, uneven passageway that leads deep into the cave of Font-de-Gaume. It is dark, damp, and mysterious. After some distance the guide shines her light onto the cave wall and you see a reindeer painted with such grace and accuracy and loveliness that it takes your breath away. This overwhelming experience immediately convinces you that the painting was made by people like us; people who, 15,000 years ago, also appreciated beauty and had a desire to understand and comment on their world through creative activity.

During Paleolithic times, from two million to 10,000 years ago, the earliest hunter-gatherers roamed the earth. By 40,000 years ago, the time of the most recent ice age, they were anatomically identical to modern human beings, and we call such people on the European continent Cro-Magnon. A number of different Cro-Magnon cultures rose and developed from about 40,000 BC to 10,000 BC.

For more than 10,000 years the art made during Paleolithic times was hidden and forgotten. In the mid-nineteenth century, collecting and studying ancient artifacts became popular. In France and Spain entrances to

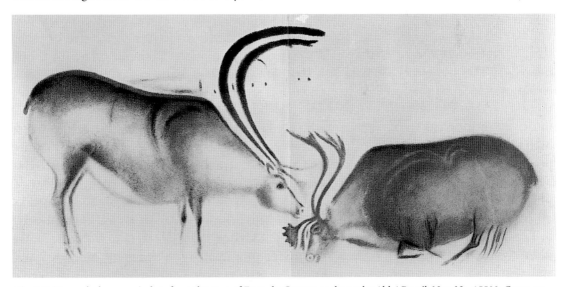

Fig. 4-2. Two polychrome reindeer from the cave of Font-de-Gaume, as drawn by Abbé Breuil. Neg. No. 15509, Courtesy the Library, American Museum of Natural History.

Fig. 4-3. Cave painting of bison, 12,000 BC. Altamira Cave near Santillana, Cantabria, Spain. Photo courtesy of R. Frerck/robertharding.com.

caves in limestone cliffs were found to be rich in evidence that prehistoric people made shelters there—stone and bone tools, and even small engraved sculptures were found.

Some of the first discoveries of paintings, however, were made by curious and observant children. In 1879, near Santillana in northern Spain, Don Marcelino de Sautuola, an enthusiastic collector of prehistoric artifacts was digging at the entrance to a cave near his home. His eight-year-old daughter Maria, going farther into the cave, called, "*Papa, bueyes!*" ("Daddy, oxen!"). There on the cream-colored limestone ceiling were enormous paintings of bison, four to six feet long, in rich red ochres and black. The figures had been engraved, drawn with charcoal, and then painted on natural swellings in the limestone, which gave them a three-dimensional quality. They were all different—some were standing, others walking or lying down, and one was bellowing. There were paintings of other animals—deer, a wild boar, horses, hinds, ibexes, and aurochs (ancestors of oxen). In addition, Sautuola found pigments that had been used in making the paintings. He was convinced

that the paintings were from Paleolithic times, and in 1880 published a booklet describing them. Unfortunately, the world was not ready to believe that Cro-Magnon people were capable of such art. It was called a hoax, and Don Marcelino de Sautuola did not live to see his belief upheld some twenty years later by scientists. These paintings, in the cave now known to the world as Altamira, have been radiocarbon dated to about 15,000 years ago.

Other caves with paintings were found, and in 1940, the great cave of Lascaux in southwest France was discovered by three boys who were walking in the woods. With homemade lamps, the boys explored the chambers and long passageways. They found a large central hall decorated with many beautiful paintings of bison, aurochs, deer, and horses, most in motion, some seeming to gallop along the wall. In the passageways leading further into the cave they found more paintings. When the boys' discovery became known, a great number of people then came to see Lascaux, and the cave eventually had to be closed to the public, because the paintings began to suffer from the changes in humidity. The 600 paintings and 1,500 engravings in the cave were created over a period of several generations, about 17,000 years ago.

The walls in painted caves are often engraved, but there are some caves that are devoted almost exclusively to engraved figures, often in great profusion. They were incised into the walls with flint tools. In addition, many of the most skillful engravings by Cro-Magnon people were not on cave walls, but on small items that could be carried and were made of bone, stone, and ivory. These engravings often decorated tools, but other, sometimes exceedingly beautiful items, have no apparent useful purpose. (See page ix.)

Well over 300 decorated caves have been discovered in Europe, mostly in France and Spain. Moreover, archaeologists are studying paintings and engravings on rocks and in caves all over the world. They are on every continent except Antarctica, and seem to testify that art has been an innate activity of human beings from the very beginning.

The cave paintings in Spain and France were created with paint made from the local earth pigments—red hematite (iron oxide), red and yellow ochre, and manganese. Charcoal was also used. These pigments were ground between rocks and mixed with such binders as animal oils or calcium-rich water that helped to fix the pigments. The paint was applied with brushes made of animal or human hair, or frayed sticks, or daubed on with pads made of fur or moss. Handprints on the cave walls were probably created by making a blowpipe of animal bones or reeds, and then spraying paint around the hand. The

Fig. 4-5. Engraving of a reindeer, Grotte des Combarelles, courtesy of Musée National de Prehistoire, Les Eyzies de Tayac, Dordogne, France.

people painted by the light of lamps that were filled with oil from animal fat.

Of the large number of animal species depicted, three dominate. Bison, which were used as a vital resource, prevail in many of the larger halls. Aurochs—a very dangerous animal, rarely hunted—were also frequently painted. The most commonly painted animal was the horse, several species of which are accurately shown. Other animals that occur less frequently are deer, reindeer, ibex, rhinoceros, lion, bear, boar, mammoth, and fish. People were very rarely depicted.

The paintings show an understanding of perspective and shading. Legs on the far side of an animal were separated from the body by a small space to make them appear to recede. Some animals were shaded or left bare in such a way as to create

Fig. 4-4. Cave painting of horse, c. 15,000 to 10,000 BC, Lascaux, Aquitaine, France. Photo courtesy of robertharding.com.

roundness in form on the backs and bellies. (See Fig. 4-4.) Many animals are painted over previous paintings, over a time span of several generations. There is no concern for consistency in size—enormous aurochs and tiny horses co-exist. The animals are not static—they walk, gallop, and sometimes fight. They appear alone on some walls, and sometimes in herds.

Why were these paintings made? The people did not inhabit the caves—bears and cave lions lived in these dark, cold, and dangerous places. The earliest theory, that the paintings were made as magic to help with hunting, is now disputed. The evidence shows that the most commonly eaten foods—reindeer, and much smaller animals—were not those most frequently depicted in the caves. It seems possible that the mystery of the deep caves and the care taken in making the powerful paintings point to a spiritual purpose. Perhaps shamans came to the caves to repeat the history and beliefs of their culture. It may be that these places were used for initiation rites. There is evidence that music (flutes and, possibly, drums have been found) may have been part of these ceremonies. We may never know the answer, but one thing is certain—the people who lived in upper Paleolithic times were not like the cartoon stereotypes of brutal cavemen. We are grateful for these paintings that give us a glimpse, however mysterious, into the minds of prehistoric people. The skill and sensitivity shown by artists who lived so very long ago underscore these valuable and continuing parts of the human spirit, essential qualities to be cherished and fostered.

Making a Cardboard Cave with Paintings

A cave large enough to be dark and mysterious can be made using refrigerator boxes. The fourth-grade students who made the cave in the accompanying illustrations had the advantage of using a vacant room at their school. The size and shape of the cave you make will depend on how much space you have available and on your imagination. It can be as simple as a box on its side, strengthened with papier-mâché, or you may make a large cave that may need as many as five refrigerator boxes. Since every cave will be different, the following are only general instructions.

Often, the paintings in prehistoric caves were concentrated in a large main "hall," with other art scattered through tunnels leading to and away from it. In order to simulate this, first build the central hall. This can be done with two boxes. To open up a box, use a utility knife to make one cut down the side, at a corner. (Do not allow students to handle the knife.) Release the flaps at top and bottom. Fold the flaps at the bottom in, so they will be on the inside of the cave. Fold the top flaps in also to form part of the top or dome. Open this four-sided wall, and join it to the other box which has been opened in the same way. This makes an eight-sided structure. You may want to protect the floor by laying cardboard down inside the cave walls. Make one of the entrance holes and then use papier-mâché—two or three layers on both the inside and the outside—to connect the walls.

If possible, the entrance and exit tunnels should be well separated from each other. You can make them out of smaller boxes (as long as they are big enough for an adult to crawl through), but refrigerator boxes are best because

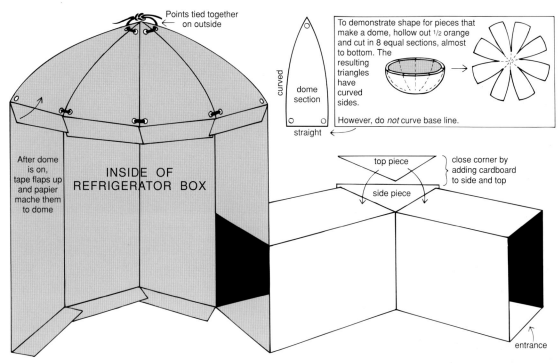

To demonstrate shape for pieces that make a dome, hollow out 1/2 orange and cut in 8 equal sections, almost to bottom. The resulting triangles have curved sides.

However, do *not* curve base line.

curved

dome section

straight

After dome is on, tape flaps up and papier mache them to dome

INSIDE OF REFRIGERATOR BOX

top piece

close corner by adding cardboard to side and top

side piece

entrance

Fig. 4-6. A cross-section showing the construction of a domed cardboard cave and an entrance tunnel.

they have enough headroom for painting. Place a box on its side up against the central hall. Cut a hole in the hall the size of the end of the box, and connect the two with papier-mâché. Depending on how much room you have, you can add another box to the entrance end of the tunnel at an angle. The outside angle will need to be filled in with extra cardboard (see Fig. 4-6). This will increase the mystery because you can't see directly into the main hall, and also less light will enter the cave.

The cave will look much more realistic inside if you disguise the squareness of the boxes. Loosely crumple newspaper and tape it into the angles between floor and wall at the base of the tunnels and central hall. Papier-mâché over it with large pieces of newspaper. (See Fig. 4-9.) This will also strengthen the cave. Do the same for the angles between the ceilings and walls of the tunnels.

The roof can be made with flat pieces laid across the top—but it may sag. A stronger, rounded dome can be made by cutting slightly curved tall triangle shapes from other boxes, one for each of the eight sides. If the shortest side of the triangles are the exact length of the top of each wall segment, the dome will fit well. To understand the shape of these triangles, clean out half of an orange. Make eight evenly-spaced cuts from the edge to 1/4" from the center, and flatten the peel. You will see that each resulting triangle has a slight curve on the two longer sides. These pieces are the shape you will need. (See Fig. 4-6.) In length they should be 3/4 of the height of the walls for a high dome, or 2/3 of the height for a lower dome. After you cut out the triangles, they need to be bent, one at a time. Hold a triangle by the base, with the tip on the floor. Step on the tip, bending the cardboard. Move your foot up, stepping and bending the cardboard all the way to the end. Then tie the triangles

Fig. 4-7. Sitting in the entrance tunnel, Anna grinds red ochre and oil together between two stones to make paint.

Fig. 4-8. Sarah paints a bison on the domed ceiling of the cave, using the light of a battery powered lamp.

together to make the dome. With a nail, punch holes in all three points of each triangle, about 1" in from the edges. Tie adjacent holes together at the bottom, and tie all eight points together at the top. (See Fig. 4-6.) Put papier-mâché over the seams. The triangles may overlap and be uneven—but real caves aren't perfect either! Make the dome separately, and with the help of several people, lift it onto the top of the cave and apply papier-mâché along the seams on the outside. Inside the cave, add more papier-mâché to attach the top flaps of the wall to the dome for added strength.

When you have done enough papier-mâché work to make a solid structure, paint the outside a dark earth color, or paint grass, flowers, and trees on the cave. (Many European caves are underneath the rolling countryside.) The inside should be painted a light gray, or golden-cream limestone color, which will contrast nicely with the animal paintings. This requires a lot of paint. Leftover white latex house paint can be used; tint it with a little black tempera paint for gray, or brown and yellow-orange for cream.

After the students have had a chance to see resource books that show a variety of cave paintings, they should sketch their ideas in charcoal on newsprint. Encourage them to think about the kinds of animals that lived thousands of years ago—some that are extinct, such as mammoths and woolly rhinoceros, others that are still with us, such as horses, deer, lions, and bison—and their importance in the life of these people who were such fine artists so many millennia ago. The size of the drawings does not matter. In the prehistoric caves the artists mixed large and small figures together in the same areas. When the students are satisfied with their sketches, they can go into the cave and draw on the walls with charcoal. Black curtains hung over the entrance and exit can make it very dark inside, and they will need a battery powered light to work by. *Under no circumstances should real fire, in any form, be used for illumination!* Obviously, this work will have to be done in small groups, while the rest of the class is working on related projects.

Students can make their own paint. If you live where colored earth is available (such as red or yellow ochre—and there are many such places), you can collect your own pigments. They need to be dried and pulverized with a hammer. They can be washed so that impurities rise to the surface and can be removed, then dried again, pulverized, and put through a screen or sifter. See *Color from the Earth: The*

Fig. 4-9. The entrance tunnel to the cave with paintings of ponies and a mammoth. Note the rounding of the corners at the floor and roof with papier-mâché.

Fig. 4-10. A cardboard cave with the main hall in the center, an entrance tunnel to the right and an exit tunnel at the far left. Apple branches gathered from spring pruning at a nearby orchard were brought in and forced into bloom to give a country feeling.

Preparation and Use of Native Earth Pigments by Anne Wall Thomas for complete directions. Otherwise, for red, you will need to buy some iron oxide (the pigment that colors the natural ochres) from a pottery supply source.

Place these pigments on a grinding slab or palette. The students pictured had a supply of smooth stones. They used a large flat stone as a palette. About one teaspoon of iron oxide was placed on the stone. A half teaspoon of vegetable oil was added slowly, while the oxide was ground to a smooth paste with a smaller stone. A little more oil was added to the paste until the mixture became the consistency of cream. Alternatives would be to use a mortar and pestle, or a flat tile, piece of slate, or sheet of plate glass, and a metal spoon. Water can be used instead of oil. Always add the water to the dry material, not the reverse. Oil turns the red ochre into a beautiful deep brick red, whereas water creates a paint that dries to light orange. The water paint will dry very quickly, but can be easily brushed off. The oil paint will dry more slowly, over several days (safflower oil dries quickest), but will become waterproof and will not brush off.

Brushes can be made by binding dog hair or human hair to sticks with string. Waterproof glue can also be used to attach the hair. (The Cro-Magnon made a strong glue.) Be sure any hair cutting is done only with parental permission! You might get some hair from a hairdresser. Students should take the paint on their brushes directly from the palette after the pigment is ground with oil or water. Remind them

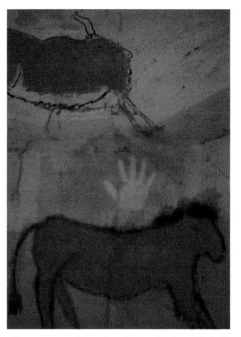

Fig. 4-11. Fourth-grade paintings in the main hall glow in lamplight—a bison, horse, and a hand print.

Fig. 4-12. Mandy and Sarah use a spray bottle with a mix of water and iron oxide to create a hand print on a tunnel wall.

Making Stone Engravings

The Cro-Magnon people made countless beautiful engravings on small pieces of stone, bone, or ivory as well as on the limestone cave walls. Bone, an extremely hard substance to engrave, is not suitable for young students. Limestone and sandstone are fairly soft and easy to work with, but difficult to obtain for a school project. However, it is sometimes possible to get broken slate roofing or floor tiles from contractors or stores. Use a hammer to break slate into small pieces for students. *Be careful of sharp edges.* If it is not possible to obtain slate, you can make plaster pieces resembling stone. Pour plaster (see Appendix for directions) into shallow foam trays. When it is dry, you may want to break the plaster into irregular, more natural shaped pieces. Then paint them a light golden brown or gray.

Place the slate or plaster pieces on newsprint and trace around them. With a pencil, work out a satisfying drawing that fills the shape before beginning the actual engraving. It is difficult to make corrections once one begins on the stone. The shape of the piece may suggest to the students an appropriate

when painting that some areas can be left bare to help round the form (see Fig. 4-4). More charcoal can also be added over the painting for shading or defining features. Figures should be painted in the tunnels, and in the central domed hall, including on the ceilings.

Prehistoric artists frequently left prints of their hands on the cave walls. This was probably done by using a blowpipe made of bones or reeds. An easy way to do this now is to mix some of the iron oxide with water and place it in a spray bottle. One student places a hand on the wall and a fellow student sprays over it. A mixture wet enough to spray causes dripping—be prepared with a paper towel!

When the cave is completed it is fun to give tours to other classes or parents. One class learned a few French phrases, and students acted as guides. Everyone, from the principal and parents down to the littlest kids in the school, crawled through the tunnels on their hands and knees to enter the great hall of the cave and admire the wonderful paintings. They felt a little bit of the mystery and surprise of the real thing.

Fig. 4-13. Fourth grade engravings on slate. Clockwise from top left: *Deer*, by Melina; *Rhinoceros*, by Fred; *Deer*, by Dan; and *Fish*, by James.

subject, such as animal, bird, fish, or hunter.

Use a large sharp nail to engrave the stone or plaster. A fine pointed finishing nail is best used for plaster. For slate, use a 3" (called a 10d) common nail, which is easier to grip when applying strong pressure. On both plaster and slate the lines will be white. Engraving on stone will of course require much more pressure than engraving on plaster. Keep the nail sharp by using a whetstone. This project takes persistence but is satisfying. Some students might work on their engravings while others take turns painting the cave.

ANCIENT GREEK SCULPTURE

Greece is a beautiful country, a mountainous peninsula bordered by the Aegean Sea on the east, the Mediterranean on the south, and the Ionian Sea on the west. Several forms of art were being created in this area as early as 1900 BC. The earliest temples were built at that time; relief work was carved in stone, pottery and painting were practiced, and art objects were created in gold and ivory. From this early time on the arts flourished and continued to develop. The height of artistic accomplishment was reached between 450 and 375 BC during what is often called the "golden age of Greek art."

Greece, in the fifth century BC, was made up of independent, self-governing city-states. The strongest and most influential of these was Athens, whose government fostered the arts, especially the building of temples to their gods, during times of peace.

The Greeks believed in many gods. Zeus was the supreme deity, and there were many such lesser gods as Poseidon, god of the sea; Ares, god of war; and Aeolus, the wind god. In Greek myths the gods often interacted with people, and the people felt very close to them. The city of Athens is dominated by a hill, the Acropolis, and here the citizens raised public buildings and temples. The most important of these was the Parthenon, a temple built in honor of their patron goddess, Athena Parthenos (Athena the Maiden), the goddess of wisdom and patron of the arts and sciences. Athenians held that the things of the mind—philosophy and the search for truth and beauty—were the greatest of human values.

The Parthenon, built of white marble, is considered to be one of the most beautiful buildings in the world. Although ravaged by time and wars, enough of it remains that peo-

Fig. 4-14. *Lowing Heifer,* from the Parthenon frieze. 442–438 BC. © British Museum.

Fig. 4-15. Greek relief of Prancing Horses. c. 400 BC on the Lycian Sarcophagus in Istanbul, Museum of Archeology. © Loyola University Chicago, 1989: Photo by R.V. Schoder, SJ.

ple still feel its power. It was completed in 432 BC, after fifteen years of work.

Sculpture was often integrated with architecture in Greek temples. The Parthenon's pediments were filled with magnificent sculptures of the gods, showing the birth of Athena and other mythological events. On the outer wall of the temple's cella (the enclosure that housed the statue of Athena) was a long frieze of sculpture in low relief. This represented the procession that took place each August in honor of Athena. Forty inches high and extending for 500 feet, it depicted the citizens of Athens—young men on horseback, musicians, people bringing offerings and leading animals for sacrifice, maidens with a new robe for Athena, and, at the end, a gathering of gods to receive the offerings. There were 600 figures in the procession. (See Fig. 4-14.) The sculpture was overseen by the most famous artist of the day, Phidias. It is not known how much of the sculpture was done by his own hand. He may have created the drawings and perhaps some clay models, but the work was probably carried out by trained anonymous artists.

To make a statue or relief carving, an artist first made a clay model. A copy of the model was then created from marble. First the form was roughed out with a chisel and hammer. Then, as the form got close to that of the model, the artist used a bronze rasp to craft the final shapes. Polishing stones and powders were used to rub the marble to satiny smoothness. Clothing was left a little rough to suggest texture.

The Greeks excelled at all forms of sculpture: sculpture in the round (a statue that can be walked around and seen from all angles); low relief, in which the figure rises from but remains attached to a background; and high relief, in which the figure is attached to the background but some parts are sculpted almost into the round (such as the muzzles of the horses in Fig. 4-15).

When we look at Greek sculpture today we take pleasure in the play of light and shadow on the white marble and in the quality of the smoothed or roughened stone. It is hard for us to visualize, but originally the classical Greek sculpture was brightly painted. Over the centuries the sculpture that remains has lost its paint from exposure to the elements. Without color to distract us, our attention is drawn even more to the purity of the forms themselves. For this reason, sculptors of our day prefer to let the surface quality of the natural stone be part of their design.

Homes in ancient Greece were kept very simple. But beautiful work was done in gold jewelry, glassware, painting (little of which has survived), gem carving, and engraved coins. Pottery reached high artistic levels. Clay vessels, called amphoras, were used for storing wine and oil, and these were decorated with paintings of people and gods. Some sculpture was done for the tombs of Greek citizens. A fine example of such a monument is shown in Fig. 4-15, a detail of horses from a sarcophagus found in the ancient country of Phoenicia at Sidon, where there was once a Greek settlement. The sculpture, in high relief, shows hunting scenes, including four horses drawing a chariot in pursuit of a lion.

Carving a Sculpture in Low Relief

Carving a relief in marble would be much too difficult for young students, but they can carry out a similar process using a plaster slab. Twenty-five pounds of plaster will make enough slabs for thirty children. *A note of caution: although plaster has been used in artrooms for many years, inhaling plaster dust is potentially dangerous.* Mix it according to directions on page 269, or use a commercially available nontoxic sculpture medium.

Pour the plaster or substitute into shallow boxes or Styrofoam meat trays to a depth of ¾" to 1". A size of approximately 5 x 8" will probably provide ample challenge. For a

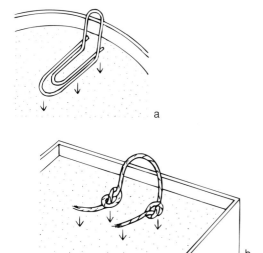

a

b

Fig. 4-16. Two ways to make hangers for the plaster relief sculptures. The bent paper clip (a) and the 6" of knotted picture wire (b) are sunk ¼" into the half-set plaster.

round shape use a flexible plastic bowl.

Now make a hanger for the sculpture. It must be added after the plaster has begun to set, but while it is still soft. Cut a 6" piece of picture wire and tie a knot near each end. Bend the wire to form a loop, and insert the knotted ends ¼" into the plaster, centered well down from the top of the piece. A bent paper clip can be substituted, but makes it more difficult to lay the piece flat later when carving the other side. (See Fig. 4-16.) The plaster should dry for several days before being carved.

Work out a design in pencil on paper cut to the size of the plaster. First draw a ¼–½" border around the edge which will give the piece a more finished look. One or two figures that fill the remaining space will be more effective than many small shapes. The Greek artists excelled in portraying the human figure and many animals: horses, dogs, lions, owls, herons, fish, deer, snakes, dolphins, and even elephants. They also created decorative friezes of geometric designs and stylized leaf and flower shapes. Students may want to work out a decorative pattern based on floral or geometric forms. Whatever their subject matter, the students should think in terms of a low relief (sometimes called bas-relief). Plaster is not strong enough for high relief. The design should be drawn on the plaster with a pencil, or transferred with carbon paper. *Be sure the hanger is at the top of the back before applying the design.*

A note of caution about carving: *Keep the plaster damp to help eliminate plaster dust which can be a problem for a child prone to asthma.* It will also cut more easily. The piece should be run under water *very quickly* before carving. It should be damp, not wet. Work on doubled newspapers and stop frequently to

Fig. 4-17. A dolphin design before rounding. It has been drawn on the slab and plaster has been cut away from exterior outlines of the form and border, down ¼" to a flat plane. Penciled letters label the parts to remain high (H), those to be medium high (M), and those to be lowest (L). This design is loosely based on a 15th cent. BC seal from the tomb of Vaphio, near Sparta. It is now in the National Museum, Athens.

Fig. 4-19. Low-relief plaster sculptures by fifth grade students: *Lizard*, by Emilie; *Standing Bird*, by Zoe; *Dolphin*, by Virginia; *Polar Bear*, by Florencia; and *Flower*, by Eva.

dump the accumulated chips into a wastebasket. As the plaster dries, dampen it again. The piece should be gently cleaned with a dry soft paintbrush as the work progresses.

The first step is to cut away plaster that surrounds the design. Cut down to a level ⅛–¼" below the exterior outlines of the design

Fig. 4-18. Emilie begins to cut down to a flat level around her lizard relief sculpture, using a wire clay-cutting tool. She uses the brush to gently remove plaster dust into a pile on the newspaper.

and border. (In other words, create the background for the figures.) The tools with wire ends that are made for shaping clay can be used, and are effective and safe. Linoleum cutting tools may also be used. Follow the safety rule of always cutting *away* from the hand that holds the plaster.

Occasionally a student will cut too deeply into the plaster and break through the background. This can be mended by mixing plaster and applying it to the broken area. Wet the plaster slab thoroughly before adding the new plaster, or the new plaster will dry suddenly on contact, becoming extremely hard, and thus difficult to carve. Smooth the added plaster with a wet finger. Allow to harden before carving again.

The next step is to work details into the surface of the figure and curve it down toward the edges so that the figure begins to have a natural rounded form. Proceed slowly and carefully. This is best done by scraping with a flat blade or knife, or rubbing with very small pieces of fine grade wet/dry silicon carbide sandpaper, or a fine damp sanding sponge.

It may help in rounding the form to first study the figure and, with a pencil, mark the places to remain the highest with an H, the medium highs with an M and low parts with an L. (See Fig. 4-17.) Rounding the form is the most difficult part but when it is done successfully, it gives great realism to the figure. The ancient Greeks have never been surpassed at creating the illusion of depth and roundness of figure in what is really a very shallow surface. It is helpful while carving to refer frequently to photographs of a relief sculpture. If possible, let students see and especially feel a plaster reproduction. (They are sometimes available at museums.) It is easier to learn about the subtle curves of low relief by such direct observation than through verbal instruction.

From the highest point of a rounded form, the surface is gradually curved down to the edge. It is rarely flat anywhere. The beginning student tends to round the edges only where the form meets the background. Ask students to observe their own arms and hands—is there a really flat surface anywhere? All human (and animal) surfaces tend to have a rounded form, either convex or concave. On the other hand, the background surface from which the figure rises should be as flat as possible. This enhances the illusion of a fully rounded form in the figure. Geometric designs, however, can successfully incorporate both flat and rounded surfaces.

The final step is to give the sculpture a very smooth surface. With light pressure, use a very fine grade wet/dry sandpaper or a damp sanding sponge to remove any scratches or dents. The edges of the cast piece may crumble somewhat during carving. These should be smoothed with sandpaper also. A coat of matte acrylic medium will protect the sculpture from stains.

Fig. 4-20. "The Sower on Stony Ground," (Bible window nXV, Panel 19), Canterbury Cathedral, 1178. Photograph by Miss Mary Tucker. © Dean and Chapter, Canterbury.

THE STAINED GLASS OF GREAT BRITAIN[1]

Stained glass originated thousands of years ago, probably in the Middle East. Glass was made from natural materials—sand (silica), seaweed (for soda ash), brushwood (potash), and lime. It is speculated that glass was probably discovered when these materials were accidentally combined in a campfire on a beach. In the beginning, opaque glass was used

[1] In writing this project I have relied heavily on *Glass, An Inspirational Portfolio* by Jera May Mortin. New York: Watson-Guptill Pub., 1999.

Fig. 4-21. Bird stalking a spider, 14th–15th cent., Zouche Chapel, York Minster. Yorkshire, UK/Bridgeman Art Library.

Fig. 4-22. Sunflower window (summer), one of four symbolizing the seasons, 1877. Artist unknown. St. Nicholas' Church, Brockenhurst.

Stained-glass windows were used in churches as early as the sixth century AD, but the art reached its height in medieval times, especially during the thirteenth and fourteenth centuries. By this time the pointed arch had replaced the half-round Romanesque arch, churches had grown higher and slimmer, and with the support of flying buttresses, walls became lighter, and immense stained-glass windows were possible. This was the time of the great age of cathedral building in France, Germany, Spain, Italy, and England. Soon after William the Conqueror arrived in England in 1066, work began on seven new cathedrals. The building continued through the seventeenth century, during the Gothic and Renaissance periods. Some of these great cathedrals are at Winchester, York, Salisbury, Canterbury, and London.

The stained glass in the Gothic cathedrals is breathtaking—the natural light shining through the brilliant reds, blues, yellows, and greens created a glorious, awe-inspiring atmosphere that enhanced the spiritual feeling of the place of worship. The windows themselves usually depicted Biblical stories, so they were instructive as well as beautiful. Lines on the figures were painted in dark blackish brown on colored glass and fired in a kiln to fix the paint.

Most stained glass is not clear glass that has been stained. The colors are created in the molten batch while the glass is being made. Metallic oxides create the color: for instance, blue from copper oxide and cobalt, red from selenium, and yellow from cadmium. However, in the fourteenth century a yellow stain was developed. Silver oxide was painted on white glass, and when heated in a kiln it

to make colorful beads, and then by 1500 BC, bottles, inlays, and windowpanes were being created. These were all cast pieces. Phoenicians were the first to blow glass, around the first century BC. Blown glass, which was translucent, could be spun out into a flat disk, and the Romans began using it to make window glass. Later, in Islamic lands, pieces of stained glass were inserted into alabaster screens that were set into windows.

fused with the glass and produced a range of yellows. From this stain came the name used today for all colored glass. Fig. 4-21 shows a delightful bird painted on a small pane of glass in York Minster. The stain is used for the beak and border. By the fifteenth century glass was decorated in many ways—it was etched to reveal the white glass beneath an overlay of colored glass; painted and then scratched through with a sharp tool to create designs; and enameled.

During the Renaissance, medieval glass fell out of favor, and often windows were

Fig. 4-23. Detail of a heron and other birds. Gilbert White Memorial window depicting Saint Francis preaching to the birds, 1920. Designed by Alexander Gascoigne, painted by Horace Hincks. St. Mary's Church, Selborne. White, a noted naturalist, wrote *The Natural History of Selborne* in 1789. The window depicts all the birds in that book.

created by painting very detailed figures on white glass, using only a small proportion of colored glass. It wasn't until the early nineteenth century that there was a revival of interest in medieval stained glass and the old techniques were studied. By the end of the nineteenth century William Morris and Edward Burne-Jones were creating masterpieces in stained glass as part of the larger Arts and Crafts movement. These windows were created not only for churches, but for private homes and businesses.

In Scotland, Charles Rennie Mackintosh created work in Art Nouveau style without any painted lines, using only the lead lines to outline forms. In the early twentieth century Alfred Walmark took this further and created the first non-figurative stained-glass window in England, a radiant design of reds, blues, oranges, and green.

In the mid-twentieth century, a British firm invented float glass, a process which made large sheets of colored glass cheaper and more available. Glass is now a popular artistic medium, incorporated into the architecture of homes and public buildings and used for sculpture. Techniques include etching, photo transfer, sandblasting, and manipulation to enhance the play of light.

In traditional stained-glass making, a drawing, called a cartoon, is placed under the colored glass as a guide, and the pieces of glass are cut out with a special tool. The small pieces are joined together with lead came. A cross-section of a length of came looks like an **H** lying on its side. The glass fits into these channels. To finish the piece the lead is soldered, and cement is forced into any remaining crevices. However, some modern artists use glue to secure the glass, and an adaptation of this method can be used with children.

Making Stained Glass Designs

Consider arranging a field trip to see stained glass in a church or public building. Experiencing its magical beauty firsthand can be very inspiring.

This project requires a lot of work by the teacher, and is best done with mature students. The teacher should first prepare small pieces of colored glass. Many artists who work in stained glass accumulate scrap pieces that they are only too happy to give or sell to schools for a small fee. These scraps should be further cut down, following carefully the methods

Fig. 4-24. An employee of the English stained-glass company, Goddard and Gibbs, Stoke on Trent, demonstrates how to use the glass-cutting tool. Photo by Richard Waite. Courtesy of the Ivy Press Ltd.

described on page 119 and page 268. *Be sure to wear goggles when cutting glass pieces, and, if using tile or glass clippers to modify pieces, do all of the cutting inside a plastic bag, as tiny fragments fly a long distance.* Frosted glass is cut on the smooth clear side. After cutting, sort pieces by color and place them flat on shallow trays lined with white paper. *Caution the students to pick them up with a very light touch.*

The teacher should also prepare a small matched pair of clear glass rectangles or squares for each student. Most glass companies will give a teacher pieces of clear scrap glass. These are usually long and narrow and easily cut into duplicate sizes. They may have traces of oil, so clean the glass thoroughly after cutting it.

Have students choose between a full stained-glass design, or a design with a stained-glass border surrounding a drawing on frosted glass. (See Figs. 4-29 and 4-30.)

For a full stained-glass design, students should draw around one of a pair of clear glass pieces, and work out a simple design that fits this space. Using a broad black marker will keep the design bold and not too detailed. See Fig. 4-25a.

Then tape the design under a piece of glass, and using the design as a guide, fill in the shapes by laying pieces of stained glass on top. The glass pieces will only approximate the suggested design. Being angular, they cannot conform exactly. See Fig. 4-25b. An alternate method is to work without a drawing and simply create a design with selected pieces of glass. Either way, the design will be most effective if students restrict the number of colors rather than using a sampling of all available.

a

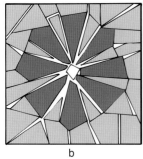

b

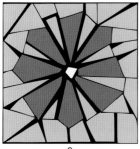

c

d

Fig. 4-25. Making a stained-glass design using glue and grout.
(a) Create a design with a wide marker. Place it under a piece of glass.
(b) Glue stained glass on the piece of glass using design as guide.
(c) Fill all cracks with black grout.
(d) Place matching piece of clear glass on top. Draw lines with black glue to define form. Tape edges together.

When satisfied with the design, students should glue each piece in place with a clear-drying, non-flammable, no-solvent glue (such as Elmer's Probond China and Glass Cement). Squeeze the cement into a small dish, and supply small brushes or cotton swabs to spread it evenly on the entire back of each piece, placing them as close together as possible.

This is a slow-setting glue—the pieces slide around, so the glass should be stored where it will not be disturbed before the glue sets. It should be allowed to dry overnight. Any glue that dries on the top surfaces of the glass can be scraped off, after it dries, with a table knife.

The next step is to fill the cracks with black grout. See Fig. 4-25c. Filling cracks forces all light to enter through the stained glass, making it glow. Use smooth, not sanded, grout. Dry grout may be toxic to inhale, so it is best to use a pre-mixed black grout. The mixtures with a base of acrylic polymer are best—do not use a ready-mixed grout that has petroleum spirits listed in the ingredients. If black grout is not available, white grout can be colored to a dark gray with tempera or acrylic paints. Add the smallest possible amount of paint, so the grout doesn't become too wet, and mix well. Apply grout to the glass, forcing it down with a stiff piece of mat board, into all the cracks between the pieces of stained glass. Pay attention to the edges. Warn the students

Fig. 4-26. Stephanie brushes glue on a piece of stained glass for her star design.

Fig. 4-27. Emily D. has made her design for a frosted glass panel and is working on a border of blue stained glass.

Fig. 4-28. Zoe sponges the excess black grout from her stained-glass design, *The Sun.*

that are self hardening. They are available from school supply catalogues and can be tinted dark gray with tempera or acrylic paints. Plaster of Paris can also be used, but should be prepared by the teacher, using precautions to avoid breathing the plaster dust. (See appendix.) Add water to black tempera paint, and then add enough plaster to create a mixture that is stiff enough to hold its shape. It must be used quickly before it hardens. Wipe clean with a damp cloth when the plaster has set.

When the grout is dry, place the second

not to use their fingers to force the grout in. Clean off the surface with a second piece of cardboard. After twenty minutes wipe off the surface of the glass with a damp cloth or sponge. Let the glass dry overnight. After it is thoroughly dry, the glass can be cleaned more carefully by scraping with a table knife.

Alternatives to grout are nontoxic clay products or acrylic polymer clay substitutes

Fig. 4-30. Three frosted glass designs by fifth-grade students: *Mountain Scene,* by Inga; *Glass Cat,* by Eva; and *Visit to the Antarctic Zone,* by Emily D.

piece of clear glass over the first piece, sandwiching the stained glass between the clear glass. Use a little tape to temporarily hold the pieces together.

The shapes are then defined more carefully with lines that resemble lead lines. See Fig. 4-25d. Use white glue, in 8-ounce bottles (with a round hole, not a slot under the cap). Remove the glue from the bottles and clean out the bottles thoroughly. In a bowl, stain the glue by mixing it with black tempera paint. If this mixture is too runny to maintain a line, mix in some powdered black tempera paint as well. Let this sit long enough to dissolve the

Fig. 4-29. Fifth-grade stained-glass pieces, clockwise from top left: *Blooming,* by Emily F.; *Stained Glass Heart,* by Leeya; *Bird of Paradise,* by Christina; and *Star,* by Stephanie.

powder and stir again. Test the glue: it should flatten a little but maintain a line. Return the glue to the bottles and using them as drawing tools, outline the shapes that determine the forms in the design. This eliminates sharp angles and brings the design into focus.

The final step is to run black vinyl electrical tape around the edges to bind the glass "sandwich" together. Placing the glass ¼" over the edge of a table acts as a guide to making a straight line with the tape. (See Fig. 4-70.) The finished stained-glass panel may be leaned against a window, so light can show through, or make a hanger for the piece with a second strip of tape. Starting across the bottom, go up one side, and at the top fold the next 5" in on itself by thirds, which eliminates the sticky surfaces and narrows and strengthens the tape. This forms a loop. Then continue down the other side and across the bottom again.

A student may choose to make a design that incorporates a drawing on a central panel of frosted glass (see Fig. 4-30). The procedure is much the same, with a few differences. Start as above by placing one of a pair of clear glass pieces on paper and drawing around it. Create a design in this space that includes a ½" border and place it under the glass. A rectangle of frosted glass is then glued to fit inside this border on the piece of clear glass. To make the border, create small square or rectangular pieces by cutting long strips of stained glass and then clipping off square pieces. These are glued on as described above. See Fig. 4-27. Before applying grout to the cracks, protect the frosted glass with masking tape, as it is hard to clean. After grout is applied and the surface cleaned and dried (as above), have students remove the tape and clean any grout

that seeped under it with a damp cloth or by scraping with a table knife. When dry, use a very fine pointed brush and make the drawing on the frosted glass with India ink or sumi-e ink; or use a fine black felt-tipped pen, which is easier to control. Then proceed as above with the second layer of clear glass, define the border with black glue, and tape the pieces together.

Students can work together on a large stained-glass panel that can be placed against an existing window in the school. It can be held in place with small strips of wood secured with brads to the window frame. It will give pleasure for many years. (See Fig. 4-31.)

Fig. 4-31. *Fish,* a detail of one of three stained-glass panels made by sixth-grade students working together. Installed, 1975, in windows at Burns Park School, Ann Arbor, MI. In place for over ten years, they were removed and lost during renovations.

Fig. 4-32. After practicing on newsprint, Laura applies glue to the pencil lines on black paper. She is careful to break up large areas of color into smaller segments.

Fig. 4-33. Gina, nine, made a colorful border around her butterfly design. She fills in the areas between the dried glue lines with dense application of colored chalk.

Stained-Glass Project for Younger Children

Younger children can make a stained-glass design on black paper using white glue for the lead lines. When the glue is dry it is transparent and the black paper makes the raised lines dark. Colored chalk will represent glass.

After showing the students pictures of stained-glass windows, have them pencil designs on black construction paper. These should be simple forms because small details are difficult to make with glue. If there is to be a border, it should be made first. It gives the piece a more finished look, but may be difficult for the youngest children.

Using small glue bottles as drawing tools, go over all the drawn lines with fairly thick lines of glue. Large areas of color need to be broken up with lines: explain that early stained glass was made in small pieces and was held together by the lead. For the border, draw one glue line directly on the edge of the paper, and a second line about ¼" in from that. Then, every 2" or so, draw lines at right angles to these lines, making a ladder-like effect. These segments will later be filled with color. (Note the red border around the sunflowers in Fig. 4-22.)

If the students stand up while using the glue they may be less likely to smudge the lines

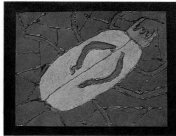

Fig. 4-34. Glue-and-chalk stained-glass designs by fourth graders: *Flowering Stars*, by Laura; *Short Life (Beetle)* by William; and *Dinosaur under a Tree*, by Sam.

with their arms. Very large blobs of glue can be wiped off with a tissue. Assure the students that the glue lines do not have to follow the pencil lines exactly.

After the glue has completely dried, have students fill in the areas within the raised lines with colored chalk, applied so that no black paper shows through. Smooth the chalk with a finger or cotton swab. If it is to have a medieval look the emphasis should be on bright primary colors—red, blue, yellow, and also green. Modern stained glass uses a wider range of colors.

Lightly spray the pictures with a fixative. They look especially fine mounted on black paper, particularly if there was no border in the design.

SWEDISH COOKIE STAMPS

In the old days, the interiors of Swedish farmhouses were brightened with many decorative arts. During the long, dark winters people spent a lot of time indoors, and they passed the time making clothing, furniture, tools, and decorations for the home. Fine linen wall hangings were woven to hang from the rafters on special occasions; clothing, cushions, and coverlets were embroidered; mittens were knitted in fancy patterns; wooden boxes and kitchen utensils were richly carved; chests, boxes, and bedsteads were painted in floral patterns. Gifts of beautifully carved spoons and other household implements often showed a young man's serious attentions to his

Fig. 4-35. Carved wooden cookie stamps from Småland, Sweden, 19th century. Courtesy of the Nordiska Museet, Stockholm, Sweden.

beloved. If they married, the implements were used and treasured throughout their married life. A young girl began filling a chest with her handwoven and embroidered linens long before her marriage took place.

One of the items made for cooking was the cake or cookie stamp. It was the custom for each family to have a set of beautifully carved stamps to use for special holiday celebrations, weddings, and funerals. Guests were given small cakes stamped with their host's designs to take home. At Christmas piles of little cakes or cookies were made for all the members of the family, each cake impressed with its own special stamp. A girl's fiancé would carve a stamp and give it to her as a token of his love, and she in turn would make him some cookies, decorating them with the stamp. They were called fiancé buns.

The stamps were round, square, or diamond shaped, and cut into them were geometric patterns or figures of birds, animals, or hearts. Some designs became traditional to a particular province, especially if it was isolated from other areas. There were several different cookie recipes. One favorite cookie still being made is called the pepparkaka. It is a spice cookie much like a gingersnap.

The custom of making cookie stamps is believed to have begun sometime in the early sixteenth century, and it reached its height during the eighteenth and nineteenth centuries. In some rural families, stamps handed down for generations are still being used in Sweden today.

With industrialization home crafts began dying out, but when this trend became apparent, Sweden made an effort to foster its country crafts. Organizations were formed to market products, and linen, wooden articles, baskets, and rugs were commissioned. The heritage of fine craft work has not been lost. Sweden is famous for its contemporary arts and crafts as well as its traditional home crafts.

Making Cookie Stamps

Swedish cookie stamps were made of clay or carved in wood. Clay is an easier and safer medium for young children. Make a ball of clay by rolling a walnut-sized piece between the palms of your hands. Then place the ball on the table and flatten it to a disk about ½" thick—no thinner, or there will not be room to carve in designs. If you make several of these, you will have a set. Also experiment with square and triangular stamp bases. Next roll out some clay under the fingers and palms in a back-and-forth motion against the table to make a long "snake." A ½"-thick roll is about right. Cut this roll into sections about 1½–2" long. Each section will be a handle. Place the handle in the center of a disk and join by smoothing away the crack where the handle joins the base. This may be easier to do if you slide your finger down the side of the handle, bringing a little clay with it, to fill the crack at

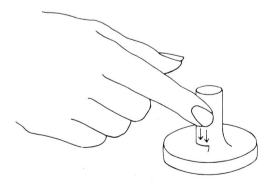

Fig. 4-36. Push a little clay down the handle to fill in the crack at the base.

Fig. 4-37. The classroom teacher joins Megan, Rachel, and Jane in stamping cookies for the party.

Fig. 4-38. Cookie stamps made by fourth-grade students and the decorated cookies.

the base (see Fig. 4-36). Rotate the stamp, smoothing all the way around the handle until the joining is complete.

Before the design can be cut into the bottom of the stamp, the clay must dry to the leather-hard stage. This is dry enough to be firm and hold its shape but still damp to the touch. (If the clay reaches this stage before you are ready to cut the design, place it in a tightly closed plastic bag to prevent further drying.) Cut a design into the bottom of the disk, using linoleum cutting tools. Geometric patterns, flowers, snowflakes, heart shapes, animals,

leaves, birds, and holiday symbols are all good designs. Thin lines will not show up when stamped on the cookies. A simple design cut in deep, wide lines is most effective. Stamping reverses images, so initials or words must be carved in mirror image (reversed in both order and direction) if they are to read correctly. The stamps must dry thoroughly for several days before being fired in a kiln.

After firing, the stamps are ready to be used, although they will look fancier if the handle and the top side of the disk are glazed. Commercial glazes come in powdered form. Mix to a creamy consistency and apply with a brush. *Do not glaze the part that presses into the cookie dough.* Fire again at the specified temperature.

Now all is ready for a cookie stamping party! The two recipes below work well.

Swedish Pepparkaka

⅔ cup brown sugar
⅔ cup dark syrup (Karo or molasses)
½ tsp cloves
1 ½ tsp ginger
1 ½ tsp cinnamon
¾ T baking soda
⅔ cup butter or margarine
1 egg
5 cups flour

Heat the sugar, syrup, and spices to the boiling point. Add baking soda, stir, and pour the heated mixture over the butter. Stir well until the butter melts. Add the egg and flour and mix well. Chill for an hour, roll out, and cut into rounds with a small juice glass. Press with a stamp. (If dough is handled too much, it gets tough.) Bake for 8 to 10 minutes at 325°. Makes 5 dozen cookies.

Almond Butter Cookies[2]

1 cup butter or margarine
½ cup sugar
1 tsp almond extract
2 cups flour
¼ tsp salt

Cream the butter and sugar. Add almond extract, flour and salt, mixing after each. Chill the dough. Form 1" balls and roll them in sugar. Stamp with cookie stamps. Bake at 350° for 12 to 15 minutes. Makes about 3 dozen cookies.

POLISH WYCINANKI: PAPER CUTOUTS

In the early nineteenth century in Poland, the farming families decorated their homes with beautiful cut paper designs called wycinanki (pronounced vî-chee non-key). Each spring, just before Easter, people whitewashed the walls of their homes and glued colorful wycinanki designs to them for decorations. These intricate cutouts show how a distinctive new art can develop from the most basic materials. The designs were cut out with the best tool available—sheep shears. It seems incredible that such lacelike designs could be created with these mammoth scissors. They are cut out freehand with no preliminary sketching.

Traditionally in Poland, men did the heavy craft work (carpentry, pottery, and blacksmithing); women decorated the men's work with painted designs and did such lighter craft work as weaving and embroidery. Although men now cut wycinanki too, the designs were originally created by women who would sometimes gather together, young and old, to make them. This work was done not for money but for the satisfaction of making the home beautiful and for the pleasure of excelling in an art form.

The wycinanki are cut from folded paper, so that when the paper is opened up and spread flat, the design is symmetrical. The subject matter reflects the countryside: trees, flowers, roosters, birds, stars, and sometimes, men, women, and religious symbols.

Many different regional styles developed. The Kurpie (*koorpy-eh*) designs from the area around Ostroleka (north of Warsaw) are cut from one-color, glossy paper. There are two main types, the leluja (*le-lu-ya*), which is cut from a piece of paper folded lengthwise, and

Fig. 4-39. Kurpie leluja wycinanki design from Poland, early 20th century. Signed by Czeslawa Konpka. Originally a bright color, it has faded with age to almost white. Collection of the author.

[2]From Eleanor and Carroll Rycraft, *Rycraft Scandinavian Cookie Stamp Recipes* (Corvallis, Oregon: Rycraft, 4205 S. W. 53rd St., 97330, 1971).

Fig. 4-40. Contemporary Kurpie gwiazdy design. Collection of the author.

the gwiazdy (*g-vee-azda*, meaning star), which is a circular design. Leluja designs usually include a central treelike form and one or more pairs of roosters or birds, although each design is different. Gwiazdy designs, cut from a round piece of paper, are folded to make patterns that repeat eight, sixteen, or sometimes even thirty-two times. They are often incredibly intricate and lacelike.

From the Lowicz area west of Warsaw come very colorful wycinanki made from layers of symmetrical paper cutouts. Basic shapes of peacocks, roosters, and flowers are first cut out and opened up. Then differently colored smaller shapes are cut out and glued one on top of another, each shape smaller than the preceding one. There are two types of Lowicz cutouts. One is a collage of birds, flowers, and leaves. The other, with the same subject matter, is cut in black from a folded circle, and additional colors are pasted to this base. (See Fig. 4-41.)

Other regions have also developed distinctive styles. In Opoczno they specialize in tree designs; in Lublin the wycinanki resemble embroidery. The Sanniki area specializes in peacocks and wedding scenes.

All the cutouts show a fine and joyous sense of design. The birds, trees, and plant forms are all decorative rather than realistic, and they show the individual style and ideas of each craftsperson. The unique beauty of these designs soon created a demand for them outside the home. Although in some rural villages wycinanki are still pasted directly on the walls of farmhouses, they are more frequently made now to be framed. Many are sold to people living in the cities and in other countries. The high level of skill is still maintained. In both Poland and America exhibitions and competitions are held in which people display their wycinanki. Prizes are given for originality and fine craftsmanship.

Fig. 4-41. Lowicz wycinanki, circular design. Artist unknown. Courtesy of the Polish Museum of America, Chicago.

There are many other folk arts in Poland: wood carving (especially of religious figures), decorated Easter eggs, straw designs, painting on glass and walls, pottery, weaving, and elaborate embroidery on clothing. All these arts brightened and enriched the lives of rural people in days gone by and are engaged in today by many Polish craftspeople who decorate their homes for special occasions.

Making Kurpie Wycinanki

The Kurpie wycinanki are made in two forms, leluja and gwiazdy (see Figs. 4-39 and 4-40). Both designs are made by folding and cutting single sheets of brightly colored paper. The colored kraft paper that comes in large rolls, which is used in some schools, works well. You can also use fadeless colored papers, gum-backed papers, and origami papers, all of which are available at art supply stores. Solid color wrapping papers are also excellent, but construction paper is too thick for this project.

Fig. 4-43. Masashi has drawn his design on folded paper and is cutting it out.

Whatever the paper, choose the deepest colors, which look most effective when set off against a white background.

To make leluja wycinanki, fold a piece of 12 x 18" paper lengthwise (this is a little larger than most Polish designs but easier for beginning students to handle). Draw one-half of the design on the folded paper, so that when it is cut out and opened up it will form a symmetrical design. Keep in mind that the folded edge will form the center of the design (see example in Fig. 4-42). In the most common leluja design, a pair of birds or roosters is near the bottom, flanking an abstract treelike form. This form may also include another pair of birds. The design is enhanced with fanciful flower and leaf shapes and some purely geometric patterns. The entire design must be one connected piece. The penciled outline should be one continuous line that never crosses over itself or cuts across the fold. If students shade in the part that is to be cut away, they'll be able to make sure that the design consists of only

Fig. 4-42. The wycinanki design is drawn on folded paper (color inside). Shading in the areas to be cut away helps make the design stand out. Cut on the solid lines. The fringe (dotted line) need not be drawn. It is cut in after the basic tree form has been cut out.

one piece. The fold must be kept intact. The decorative edge to the tree form need not be drawn in. It is cut into the edge after the basic shape has been cut out.

Use small pointed scissors to cut the wycinanki. It is best to do the cutting in stages. First cut the lower part and the outline of the tree form. Next, cut a decorative fringe into the border of the tree. When students think of "fringe," they usually think of a series of parallel cuts. This type of fringe will close up when it is pressed flat. Pieces of paper must be *removed* by curved or wedge-shaped cuts (see examples in Fig. 4-44). Lastly, cut the designs within the tree. Occasionally an extra fold is made to do this. In the leluja wycinanki in Fig. 4-39, you can see that while the paper was still folded, the two large leaves at the bottom and the two at the top were folded again along a center line, and the vein patterns were cut into them.

When the cutting is finished, open up the

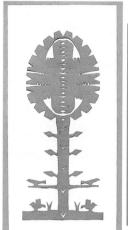

Fig. 4-45 from left. Wycinanki designs by Masashi, age eight, by Jennifer, age nine, and by Amy, age nine.

Fig. 4-44. Examples of fringe designs used in leluja wycinanki.

wycinanki and use a white glue to attach it to white paper. The wycinanki makes an especially nice display if the white paper is then glued to an even larger piece of construction paper that repeats the color of the cutout design.

Gwiazdy, the "star" designs, are cut from a round piece of colored paper. Draw a circle (6–7" in diameter for small designs, 12–14" for large) on the paper with a compass, or draw around a bowl or other round object. Cut out the circle. Fold it in half with the colored side *inside*. Fold it in half again, and then fold it in half again. This will give a pattern of eight repeats. As students gain experience (and if the paper is quite thin), they may want to fold once more for a pattern of sixteen repeats. In either case the folding will create a wedge-shaped piece with folds on both sides (see Fig. 4-46).

Before using the colored paper, students might cut some practice designs from newsprint or newspaper. Students may cut freehand, or they may wish to make a pencil drawing as a guide, based on their experiments

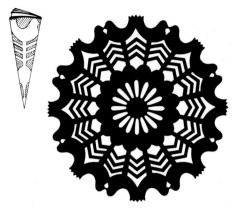

Fig. 4-46. To make a gwiazdy (star) wycinanki, fold the round piece of paper, colored side inside, three (or in this case, four) times, and draw a design on the pie-shaped piece. Shaded areas in the diagram are cut away to produce the design shown at the right. This design is based on a wycinanki by Rachel, age eleven.

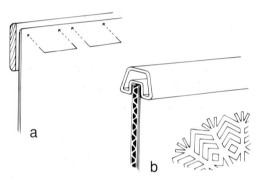

Fig. 4-47. Two ways to frame wycinanki: (a) by stapling the design to screen molding, and (b) by using plastic packaging tubes.

with the newsprint. The design is created by cutting into both edges and the curved outer edge. In most gwiazdy, the basic roundness of the edge is maintained—it is not turned into starlike points, for instance.

Completed gwiazdy look especially nice framed. Glue them to a larger square of white paper with a margin of at least ¾" at the sides and 1¼" at the top and bottom. Place this on a piece of thin cardboard cut to the same size.

The wycinanki should be protected with a sheet of acetate. The least expensive is a thin sheet that comes on a roll. It can be drawn around to the back of the cardboard and held in place with tape. A thicker acetate, which is still pliable but stiffer, can be cut the same size as the cardboard and used like a sheet of glass.

You can make wood frames similar to that in Fig. 4-40 with ¼ x ¾" flat screen molding. With a fine-toothed saw cut the strip of wood into sections and glue them to the top and bottom edges of the acetate. When the glue is dry, staple the design and the cardboard backing (shirt or posterboard thickness) into the wood from the back. (See Fig. 4-47a.)

The small gwiazdy student work illustrated in Fig. 4-48 was framed with plastic tubes that are used for packaging integrated circuits. These tubes are discarded by manufacturers of computer-related equipment. (You might find such a company by looking in the yellow pages under data processing equipment, electronic equipment and supplies, or electronic research and development.) The tubes measure 18" long. In cross-section they are hollow, but a

Fig. 4-48. Small framed gwiazdy designs by Brian, age eleven, and Alison, age ten.

Fig. 4-49. A display of large gwiazdy designs by fifth- and sixth-grade students. In the center is a round design like those from the Lowicz region in Poland.

notch pushes into the center, giving the tube an angular C shape. The tubes can be cut with a very fine-toothed saw. The wycinanki is mounted on white paper, backed with corrugated cardboard, and protected with sheet acetate. Spread white glue along the top edge of the mounted wycinanki and push it into the notch or slot of the tube, which has been cut to fit. Do the same on the bottom edge. When the frame has dried overnight, you can thread a piece of yarn through the top tube to form a hanger. (See Fig. 4-47b.)

You can also frame wycinanki by holding the cutout, acetate, and cardboard together with a border of black or colored tape.

UKRAINIAN PYSANKY: DECORATED EGGS

A few weeks before Easter every year, Ukrainian women make decorated eggs called *pysanky*. The eggs glow with bright colors in intricate designs that are made with traditional symbols handed down over generations. Although associated with Easter, this custom began long before Christianity came to the Ukraine in 988. In Neolithic times, people worshiped the life-giving sun, symbolized by the egg. Every spring when the sun's warmth returned and things began to grow again, people decorated eggs to celebrate. Using dyes made from plants, bark, and berries, they colored the eggs as brightly as they could.

With the coming of Christianity, the custom continued. Many of the same designs were used, but they were assigned new meanings. The egg, pagan symbol of rebirth in the spring, became the Christian symbol of spiritual rebirth. The villagers made two kinds of decorated eggs at Easter: the pysanky, which were too beautiful to be eaten, and the

Fig. 4-50. Ukrainian pysanky, courtesy of Mrs. Cyril Miles.

krashanky, which were dyed bright solid colors and hard-boiled for later eating. On Easter morning villagers put both kinds of eggs in a basket with other foods, especially a particular round bread called *paska* (a work of art in itself), and the baskets were blessed at the church. Then they were taken home, and the krashanky and other foods were shared for breakfast.

Many traditions were associated with the colored eggs in these farming villages. They were thought to have special powers and were used to heal, to assure a good harvest, to bring children to a childless couple, and to protect the home from fire. According to an ancient legend, making pysanky kept the world from destruction: evil, which took the form of a creature in chains, had the power to destroy the world. In years when few pysanky were made, the chains became dangerously loose; when many pysanky were made, the chains tightened, and love conquered evil.

Pysanky are now exchanged by family members and friends as a sign of love on Easter morning. Symbols are often appropriate to the person the eggs are made for: a

Fig. 4-51. Some traditional pysanky designs and what they symbolize: the sun (life and growth), evergreens (eternal youth and health), hen (fertility), another sun or star design, butterfly, wheat (good health and bountiful harvest), fish (Christianity), flower (love and good will), deer (good will, wealth), ram, and pussywillows.

chicken or other bird, a fertility symbol, may be drawn on an egg that is given to a young married couple; a rake and wheat stand for a good harvest for a farmer. A young woman might make pysanky with flowers, symbolic of love, for her fiancé. These designs suggest objects rather than depicting them exactly. There are geometric patterns and plant and animal designs.

Each egg is unique—the same exact design is never used twice—but the Ukrainians follow a particular framework. They divide the eggs into wide bands, triangles, or ovals in which further designs are made, and use traditional symbols. Thus the eggs have a quality that is easily identified as Ukrainian, even though many countries in central Europe have egg-decorating customs.

The tools and materials are simple. A smooth, fresh egg; a candle; a lump of beeswax; a tool called a kistka, and dye. The kistka, a tiny metal spout or funnel attached to a handle, is heated over a candle. The hot spout is pressed into the beeswax, and melted wax is scooped up into it. Designs are drawn on the egg with the kistka, which lets out a fine line of melted wax. (The word *pysanky* comes from the verb pysaty, "to write.") The egg is then dipped into a dye, usually yellow; the beeswax lines resist the dye, which preserves the white color underneath. After the egg has dried, more areas are covered with beeswax, this time preserving the yellow. The egg is dipped in a darker color, perhaps orange, and then waxed again, and so on, until the final color of black or red is used. Then the egg is warmed until the wax melts. The wax is wiped off, and the many-colored design is revealed. The eggs are usually lacquered, which

Fig. 4-52 *(left)*. Marianna demonstrates Ukrainian egg decorating to fifth-grade students. First she heats the wax in the kistka over the candle flame, and then she draws with the hot wax on the egg.

Fig. 4-53 *(right)*. Marianna alternates waxing and dyeing the egg. When it is finished, she heats the egg beside the candle flame and wipes the melted wax off with a paper towel to reveal the brightly colored egg.

strengthens their shells and makes them glossy.

The psyanky are made with skill and pride in a tradition that has passed from mother to daughter over many generations. A gift of a pysanky is truly meaningful. The psyanky are not only beautiful works of art but a remembrance of someone's love, and they are kept and treasured for a lifetime. (See Fig. 4-50.)

Making Pysanky

It is difficult to give adequate instructions for making pysanky in the space available here. Some excellent, inexpensive booklets are available (check the Bibliography on page 274); or better yet, find out if your community has a Ukrainian family that carries on this tradition and can demonstrate pysanky making. It is much easier for children to understand the art if they can watch a demonstration, and it is exciting to see the design grow under the hands of a skilled person. In many cities international organizations can help you contact people of different ethnic backgrounds.

Because this project uses candles to heat the kistkas, it must be done under careful super-vision. Tie back long hair, and place the candles in secure holders on metal sheets or pans. Because short, squat candles cannot tip over, they are safest.

Use fresh, white eggs that are free of bumps or blemishes. Clean and rinse them with a vinegar solution to remove any grease. (Greasy fingers will make spots that will resist dye, so also be sure hands are clean.) Check to see that there are no cracks in the eggs. Traditional pysanky are usually made with fresh eggs. As the egg dries inside, gases build up, and if there are weak places in the shell it will burst. To prevent this, some Ukrainians use blown eggs. Another reason to use blown eggs is that the yolk and white can be saved for cooking. The eggs should be blown before dyeing, because the dyes, which are not edible, may seep inside. Directions for blowing eggs can be found on page 184. Allow eggs to warm to room temperature before applying wax; cold eggs will "sweat," and the wax will not adhere.

Kits with dyes, kistkas, and beeswax can be obtained quite inexpensively at the sources mentioned in the bibliography. Alternatively, substitute other materials. You can use strong

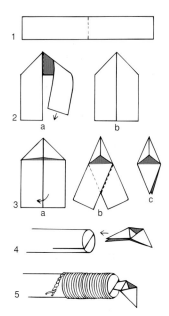

Fig. 4-54. One way to make a kistka.

solutions of fabric dyes, or you can make excellent dyes by soaking colored crepe paper in hot water. For commercial dye preparation, follow manufacturers' directions. In general, dye will be brighter if one teaspoon of vinegar is added to one cup of dye. Put the dyes in wide-mouthed jars (such as peanut butter or mayonnaise jars), and provide a separate spoon for each. Well-covered dyes can be stored from year to year if you add a tablespoon of vinegar every couple of months. Red, blue, yellow, and black will give you all the colors you need. If the dye has been prepared with hot water, do not use it until it is cold, or it will melt the wax on the egg.

You must use beeswax for making the designs. Paraffin and candle wax flake off too easily and expose the shell to the dye. A very small cake of beeswax, which you can buy at some sewing supply stores and art stores, will decorate many eggs.

Kistkas can be made in several ways; each craftsperson has her favorite. Fig. 4-54 shows one method. The directions are as follows:

1. Cut a strip of brass shim (0.005" thick) in a strip ¼" x 1½". Fold it in half, and open it up again to get a center line.

2. (a) Fold sides in and down along the center line, creating shape b.

3. (a) Turn the folded piece of brass over and cross one end over the other. This raises the spout. (b) Trim ends to a point by cutting along dotted lines, resulting in spout c.

4. Take a piece of ¼" dowel, 4¼" long, and cut a slit in the end of it. Make the slit by placing a mat knife on the end of the dowel and tapping it with a hammer. Adults should do this step. *Do not hold the dowel in your hand and force the knife in.* Insert the brass spout and bend it down.

5. Wrap the end of the dowel tightly with copper wire, covering ½" of the dowel, and twist the ends of the wire together.

To prepare the kistka for drawing with the hot wax, hold the point over the tip of a candle flame for about ten seconds. Be careful that the wood handle does not burn. Quickly scoop up a little wax into the larger part of the funnel. The wax will melt and flow into the point. Heat again if necessary. Applied to the egg, the wax will flow out in a dark line. Draw on a practice egg until you can control the flow.

Most pysanky have some formal design framework; the designs are not drawn freely on the surface. This framework usually consists of lines that go around the egg to create geometric areas. Although a practiced pysanky maker can do this freehand, it is a great help for a beginner to use ½" tape or a rubber band as a guide. Put a wide rubber band around the egg and draw light pencil lines on either side of it as a guide for the kistka.

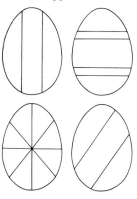

Fig. 4-55. A few basic ways to divide the egg into geometric areas.

Fig. 4-56. Some traditional ribbon designs for narrow bands around the egg.

Do not erase, which will cause smudges. The band can run around the middle, or it can run lengthwise. Two bands can cross, dividing the egg into quarters. The quarters may be further divided into triangular-shaped eighths. One design usually runs around inside this band (which is also often bordered with smaller bands called ribbon designs), and other designs are repeated inside each geometric area (flowers, stars, birds, deer, and the like). This is a great simplification of pysanky designs, which are extremely elaborate and have many fine details.

Here are the steps in making a pysanky design. The design is not meant to be copied—substitute your own variations. Although it looks complicated it is really quite easy, taken step by step. (See Fig. 4-57 a-e.)

a. The egg is still white, and everything covered with wax (black lines and areas in this figure) will remain white. First divide the egg in the middle with a wide band. Run two narrow bands above and below it. Draw a small circle at each end of the egg and draw lines down to the band, creating eight sections. Draw a sunflower petal in each section. Divide the wide band into four sections with four narrow columns. Alternate deer and pine trees in each section, or use some other figure of your choice. Draw a triangle design in the narrow ribbon bands. Fill in one line of triangles, as shown. When all this is done, dye the egg yellow. Put the egg in a spoon and lower it gently into the dye. (If the egg is blown, the holes should be sealed with wax first. It will have to be held under the dye, because it will tend to float.) Remove the egg with the spoon and blot it dry with paper toweling.

b. Wax the parts to remain yellow: the sunflower center and petals and a design drawn in the upright columns. Then dye the egg orange. (In dyeing the eggs, you will notice that successive dyes will be affected by the color previously used. A yellow egg dipped in a red dye will become orange at first. The longer it stays in the dye, the redder it will get. A yellow egg given a quick dip in blue will turn green and then deepen to blue-green. Purple can be made by combining blue and red.)

c. Cover with wax the parts to remain orange: the area around the sunflower. Then dye the egg red.

d. Wax the parts to remain red: cross-hatch the triangles in the ribbon bands, and wax

Fig. 4-57. Pysanky steps.

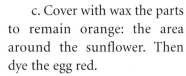

Fig. 4-58. The finished pysanky.

the columns between the deer and the tree. Next, dye the egg black. It may have to stay in the dye for fifteen or twenty minutes to achieve a good solid black.

e. The whole egg will be almost completely black with wax and dye; only a suggestion of color will show through the wax. Let it dry thoroughly.

Remove the wax by holding the egg close to the side of the candle flame until the wax begins to melt. (If it is held above the flame, smoke will discolor the egg.) Wipe off the melted wax with a tissue or soft cloth. Melt only one small area at a time. Now for the first time you will see the design revealed in full color. Fig. 4-58 shows the finished egg.

You can soften wax from many eggs at once by placing them in a warm oven. Make an egg holder by pounding sets of three nails into a board, about 1" apart in the form of a triangle. Place each egg in a triangle of nails and put the board in a slightly warm oven (150–200°) for ten to fifteen minutes. Leave the door open and watch the eggs. When the wax begins to soften and get shiny, remove them. Wipe them clean with a soft cloth or tissue.

Fig. 4-59. Pysanky by sixth-grade students.

The holes in the ends of blown eggs may be sealed again with a spot of wax.

The eggs will be strengthened and the colors made more brilliant if they are given several coats of clear lacquer or varnish. Between coats, set the eggs in the holder to dry.

STRAW DESIGNS OF BELARUS

In many parts of the world, decorative items are made from straw. It is a mark of the creative human spirit that farming people, who labor so hard in the fields, can see the aesthetic potential of their crop as well as its value for food and profit.

In Belarus, formerly called Belorussia, for generations folk artists have made items of bright golden rye straw: dolls were fashioned from it, and straw birds and spiders were hung from the ceiling beams for good luck. Many useful items were also woven and plaited from straw: boxes, baskets, and chests.

In the city of Zhlobin in the 1950s, a group of craftspeople formed an artel, or art guild, to make straw inlay designs for sale. Each item they produced was a unique, original design, although all were based on the traditional folk arts of the area. The artel sold its work in the cities of Belarus. Two of the first people in the artel were Mikhail Vasilyevich Degtyarenko and Vera Nikofimovna Degtyarenko, a married couple.

The demand for this work became so great that the few craftspeople working at the artel could not produce enough to fill the orders. In 1960, to meet the demand, the government constructed a factory in Zhlobin to make the decorative straw inlays. Many artists specializing in applied folk arts were hired. Using tra-

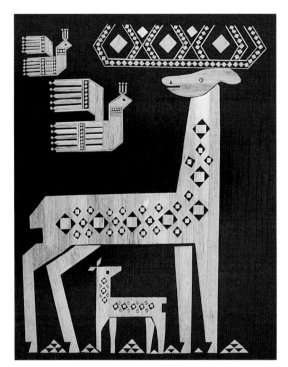

Fig. 4-60. Deer and birds. Straw inlay panel, Zhlobin, Belarus. Collection of the author.

pieces according to the design to be made and glues it to the surface of the box or panel. Sometimes the designs are composed only of the natural gold-colored straw, and sometimes they include straw that is dyed bright red, green, or yellow. (See Fig. 4-1.) The finished design is given two coats of lacquer.

The panels usually show village scenes, people in native costume working at domestic chores, birds, or animals. The boxes are covered with a mosaic of small bits of straw that form intricate geometric designs. On both the panels and the boxes, the bright straw glows against the black background. The straw inlays

ditional motifs, senior artists developed designs, which were then used as patterns. In this way many inlays are made of the same design, although they are all made by hand. This work requires considerable skill. Several hundred men and women work at the factory, and others are enlisted to make designs but do the work at home. The art of straw inlay is taught in shop classes in the secondary schools, and especially talented students work in the factory after school or during summer vacations.

The straw designs decorate both boxes and panels. The wooden article is first sanded smooth and then covered with a black dye and warmed joiner's glue. When this covering is dry, the artist cuts dampened rye straw into

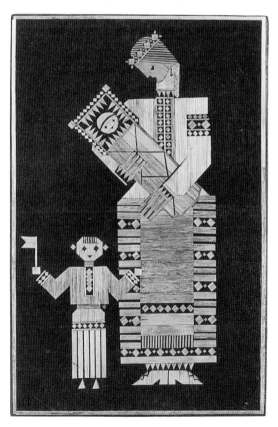

Fig. 4-61. *Motherhood*. Straw inlay panel, Zhlobin, Belarus. Collection of the author.

Fig. 4-62. Nora first worked out a design with paper. After preparing the panel, she made a frame near the edge with narrow strips of straw. Now she begins to make her design, cutting the straw with scissors and gluing it in place.

Fig. 4-63. David uses a mat knife to even the edges of the straw before the glue is completely dry.

Fig. 4-64. Fifth-grade straw designs. Clockwise from top: *Horse* by Nora, *Outdoor Scene* by Peter, *Dragon* by David, *Design* by Liz, and *House* by Katie.

of Zhlobin, which were first created for sale by a small group of artists, are now found in museum shops and import stores in the United States and other countries.

Making Straw Designs

For this project you will need new straw that has not been lying exposed to the weather (under those conditions it turns dull). You can buy a bale very inexpensively at farming and garden supply stores. It is also available at farms. If you cannot find a source, ask the parks department of your town where their supply comes from—they use it to protect newly sown grassy areas. Although the Belorussian designs are made with rye straw, oat and wheat straws can also be used. Oat straw is brighter in color, and broader, which makes it easier to handle.

Use ¼" plywood for this project. Cut a rectangle approximately 5½ x 8". Sand this piece of wood until it is very smooth. Then apply a coat of black tempera paint or India ink. When the paint is thoroughly dry, apply two coats of lacquer. Allow the first to dry before applying the second.

While the panel is drying, students can plan their designs. Give them pieces of black paper the same size as their panel and strips of yellow paper ⅛"–¼" wide. Encourage students to experiment by having them cut the paper into small squares, triangles, and various lengths and gluing them to the paper to form geometric designs, animals, flowers, people, houses, or other subject matter. Show them illustrations so they can see how the artists build up solid areas by gluing straws side by side, and how they create patterns by using square shapes. This was done in the deer's horns and the woman's dress in Figs. 4-60 and 4-61.

When the second coat of lacquer has dried, the students can begin their straw designs. To prepare the straw, peel off the dull outer covering from the larger stalks. Soak these stalks in water until they are pliable. Slit the damp straw along one side with scissors or your thumbnail so that it can be opened up and flattened out. Then cut shapes from these pieces and glue them with white glue to the panel.

It is a good idea to make a frame for the design first. Glue a thin strip of straw close to the edge on all four sides of the panel. Then proceed with the design, referring to the plan you created earlier with paper strips. In most cases the straw is cut with scissors before being glued to the panel. However, some large areas of straw can be glued on and then cut to shape with an X-acto knife, or mat knife, before the glue sets (see Fig. 4-63). As work proceeds, wipe any glue that seeps under the straw off the surface of the panel. After it dries, give the finished design a final coat of lacquer.

FLOWER-RELATED ARTS OF GERMANY

Germany has a long history of flower-related arts. Pressed flower collections and flower drawings, paintings, and prints have been made for centuries.

During the Renaissance, the artists who painted flowers as an incidental part of a larger painting were so careful that particular species can be identified by botanists today. Albrecht Dürer (1471–1528), the famous German painter, engraver, and woodcut artist, often studied plants. For one of his watercolor paintings he dug up a piece of turf and brought it to his studio. He made a painting of every detail of the dandelions, plantain, yarrow, and grasses growing in the soil. His painting (Fig. 4-65) shows a reverence for natural things and captures the freshness and beauty of even a common patch of ground on a summer's day.

Starting about the same time (the late fifteenth century), books describing medicinal plants and herbs were printed in Germany and other parts of Europe. Called herbals, these books were illustrated with woodcuts so readers could identify plants used in the treatment of illness. They were printed only in black ink, but the purchaser of the herbal frequently painted them with watercolors. The woodcuts have a simple, strong beauty. (See Fig. 4-66.)

In Germany many flowers have symbolic meanings. The edelweiss, a particularly treas-

Fig. 4-65. *Great Piece of Turf,* by Albrecht Dürer, watercolor and gouache, 1503. Courtesy of Graphische Sammlung Albertina, Vienna, Austria.

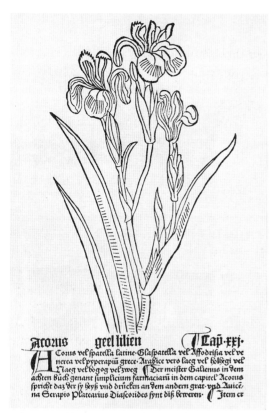

No one knows when flowers were first pressed in Germany to preserve them. For many years it had been the custom to press flowers under heavy books and then to put them under the glass around the border of religious pictures.

By the nineteenth century, it had become a fashionable leisure-time activity for young people in Europe and America to start a herbarium, a collection of pressed plants, of their area. Many flower collections were made in Germany at this time. Flowers and plants were gathered, very carefully pressed and dried, and then mounted on paper. The plants were identified and the Latin name inscribed, along with the date of collection and the location where the plant was found. Although herbaria were meant to be primarily educational, some of these very carefully pressed flowers were beautiful from an artistic point of view. Perhaps this is how the art of making pressed flower arrangements began.

Wildflowers grow in rural areas throughout Germany, but the high alpine meadows of southern Germany are especially rich in many different and very colorful flowers. Among them are blue gentians, rhododendron, wild geraniums, yellow and pink primroses, buttercups, pink and white and yellow clovers, violets, Queen Anne's lace, cyclamen, snowdrops, and bluets. The flowers are collected and pressed and made into

Fig. 4-67. A pressed edelweiss, courtesy of Karin Douthit.

ured flower, grows in the Alps, very high up at the snow line, in almost inaccessible places. In German, the name means "noble white." A small, star-shaped flower with white, velvety leaves, it is associated with immortality, purity, and courage.

A folk story concerns the origin of the wild chicory flowers that grow in profusion along the country lanes. A young girl waited for her lover by the roadside for a very long time. When he did not come, she turned into the chicory plant, her eyes the dancing blue flowers, forever watching.

Fig. 4-68. Pressed flower arrangements from Germany—on the left, framed and under glass, gentians, primulas, wild geraniums, clover, sedge, and grasses; on the right, a bookmark with buttercups, clover, wild geraniums, and sedge. Collection of the author.

Making Pressed Flower Arrangements

In gathering flowers to be pressed, several things must be taken into consideration: the places to find them, the time of day, the weather, and the kinds of flowers most suited to pressing.

Before setting out to collect flowers, do some research. Some wildflowers are so near extinction that they must never be picked (unless you cultivate them in your own garden). Others are so common that they can be picked freely. Contact your state agricultural department's Division of Natural Resources for a list of protected flowers. Obtain a field guide from the library, or go with someone who knows plants so that you are sure of what you are picking.

Most parks forbid all flower picking. Fortunately, some of the most common wildflowers make the nicest pressed arrangements, and they can be found in vacant lots and along sidewalks and roadways. The buttercup, found almost everywhere, is one of the few flowers that will keep its color a long time. Daisies, asters, clover, yarrow, Queen Anne's lace, and goldenrod are very common and can be freely picked. Even so, they are beautiful and enjoyed by other passers-by, so follow these rules: always ask permission if the flower is growing on private property, and when you do pick always leave some for others to enjoy. Do as little damage to the plant as possible so that it will bloom again.

The smaller cultivated flowers, such as violets, lilies-of-the-valley, grape hyacinth, and small marigolds, also make good arrangements. If they are not growing in your own

lovely arrangements. Sometimes schoolchildren make bookmarks from their pressed flowers. Framed pressed flowers can be found in craft shops and are exported to other countries. These arrangements combine the delicate bright flowers with grasses, sedges, and mosses in a natural way that brings to the imagination a glimpse of the fresh mountain meadows where they were gathered. (See Fig. 4-68.)

yard be sure to get permission before you pick them. Gardeners are often very willing to share their bounty—especially if you describe your project.

Gather plants, if possible, in mid-morning or late afternoon when they are dry. If they are picked in the middle of the day, the plants may wilt from the heat. Never pick after a rain because the flowers will mold when they are pressed. If possible, bring a can or jar of water with you; if the stems are in water, the flowers will stay fresh. If this is not practical, put them in a plastic bag as they are cut. You will want a 3–4" length of stem below the flower and, if the stem does not include leaves, a leaf or two. Be careful not to pull the plant up by the roots; take along a pair of scissors so you can snip off the flower.

Choose small flowers, all on the same scale. One large flower will so dominate an arrangement that the smaller flowers will be overlooked. A large flower, such as Queen Anne's lace, can be taken apart and used as smaller florets. Unfortunately, very thick flowers, such as dandelions, do not press well, nor do those that have a very thick middle, such as large daisies. Look for interesting shapes as

Fig. 4-69. A flower press made of two boards, folded newspapers, and bricks.

well as for color. The graceful line of little bells in a spray of lily-of-the-valley is very pleasing. Many of the colors will fade in time anyway, and when that happens you will still enjoy the arrangement if you have a variety of shapes.

Do not ignore interesting grasses and small leaves. Yarrow leaves look like miniature ferns, are delightful in an arrangement, and can be found almost anywhere. Small bits of moss, which grow in poor soil in both city and country, help make the arrangement look more natural.

Try to press the flowers on the same day you gather them. If there is a delay, keep the flowers in water. Professional flower pressers usually place the flowers between sheets of blotting paper, but old newspaper works very well, too. If the papers are at least one week old, there is no danger of ink being transferred to the petals.

Take one full sheet of newspaper and fold it in half along the fold that is already there, and then fold once more (as it is usually folded on the newsstand). This folded piece now measures 11 x 14". Open up the last fold and place the flowers on one side of this fold. (If the stems have been kept in water, wipe them dry first.) Try to keep the leaves and petals spread out flat. They should not overlap. Press the leaves and moss, too. Insert a long tab at the edge of the newspaper to identify each student's work. Fold over the other half of the newspaper on top of the flowers. Place the first section of newspaper with the flowers inside on a flat board. Pile the other sections on top, lining up edges and corners exactly. Place another board on top of the pile and weight it with very heavy books or bricks. This press should be in a dry location.

Fig. 4-70. Jeannie, age nine, demonstrates how to apply tape in a straight line by using the table edge as a guide.

Now forget about it for four to six weeks! It takes time for the flowers to become completely dry, and they can be spoiled by premature checking. When at least a month has passed, the press can be opened.

Meanwhile you can be gathering materials for mounting the flowers. If you like to make use of scrap materials and have the time to find them, this can be a very inexpensive project. Picture framing shops often throw away great quantities of old or poorly cut mat board. These boards are frequently in 3½–4" wide strips, which are perfect for this project. Glass companies also throw away leftover strips of glass in similar dimensions. They will often set aside a box for their scrap pieces if you promise to pick it up at a designated time. Cut appropriate sizes of glass from the scraps (see appendix on how to cut glass, page 268) and then cut mat board to fit each piece of glass. You will have a variety of sizes, which should measure in the range of 3½–4" wide by 5½–7" long. The examples of student work in this book were made from scrap materials. You can, of course, purchase a large sheet of glass and have it cut into smaller pieces.

When the flowers are dry, they are very fragile. Handle them gently. Look them over and decide which ones would make a nice arrangement. Place these on a piece of mat board that has been cut to fit a piece of glass. Arrange them so that they seem to be growing—not all spaced out in a row, but with stems somewhat grouped at the bottom. Flowers should be at different heights, usually with the tallest in a central position. Occasionally a single spray of one flower is most effective. Interesting leaves or small pieces of moss can cover the awkwardness of bare stems at the bottom of the arrangement.

When you are pleased with your composition, lift each flower or leaf gently, one at a time, and put very small spots of white glue on the back of the stem with a toothpick. Also glue behind the thickest parts of the flowers. Replace them on the mat board.

There may be oil on the glass from the glass cutting tool, so before placing the glass over the arrangement be sure that it has been washed and dried thoroughly. Bind the glass to the mat board with ¾" tape. Most colored tapes overpower the delicate hues of the plants, so white usually looks the best. If you extend the glass and mat board over the edge of the table by the exact width to be taped, it is easier to apply the tape in a straight line (see Fig. 4-70). Apply the tape to the glass first and then pull it around to the back of the mat.

Do not display the pressed flowers in direct sunlight, or the colors will soon be gone. Blues and purples (except for delphinium) fade especially quickly; yellows and oranges are longer-lived.

Making Bookmarks

Bookmarks are easy to make. Cut a strip of white paper, 2 x 7". Any heavy drawing paper will do. A slightly textured handmade Japanese paper makes an especially nice background.

Glue the flower arrangement to the paper (see previous project) and let it dry. Cut a piece of clear, self-sticking plastic film (available at hardware stores) so that it is ¼" larger all around than the paper. Peel off the protective backing from the plastic film. Starting at the bottom front of the arrangement, smooth the film down over it, letting the film down gradually with the left hand as the right thumb and forefinger press out any air pockets. It has to be placed correctly the first time; the flowers cannot be moved once they have made contact with the plastic film. Apply film to the back also. Press the edges firmly again and then trim off excess plastic. Because the arrangement will be kept closed in a book, its colors will remain fresh a long time.

Making Herbals and Botanical Drawings

If gathering flowers is impractical, students may wish to make their own herbals, each student researching a plant, writing a description of it and its uses, and making a woodcut or linoleum cut as an illustration. (See Chapter 5 for instructions on making woodcuts.) Or the teacher can bring a few flowers to school, and students can make careful botanical drawings and watercolors in the manner of Dürer.

Fig. 4-71. Pressed flower arrangements by fourth-grade students. Left by Robin, right by Geordie. Flowers include lilies-of-the-valley, buttercups, and Virginia bluebells.

Fig. 5-1. Butterfly kite handmade in Thailand c. 1975. Collection of the author.

5 ASIAN ARTS

As was the case with the European art projects, many of the arts described in this chapter are not unique to one country. For instance, shadow puppets are made in India and China as well as throughout much of Southeast Asia, and they are expressive of differing traditions in each country. Several countries are known for their lacquer ware, among them China, Japan, Thailand, and Burma. Although the art probably originated in China, each country has developed its own styles and methods. Kite making and flying, of which the Japanese fish banner presented in this chapter is one form, and the Southeast Asian kites are another, are enjoyed as an art and a pastime in many Asian countries.

Sometimes an art becomes primarily associated with a country other than that of its origin. Woodblock prints were invented in China, primarily as a method of making available multiple copies of illustrated texts. Later, in Japan, the woodcut came to be appreciated as an art form in itself and is now more often identified with that country, although beautiful woodcuts continue to be made in China. A method of decorating cloth first begun in India was developed to such a high degree after spreading to Java that it is known by a Javanese name—batik—and is identified around the world with that culture.

CHINESE ARTS

Fine artwork has been a tradition in China from as early as 4000 BC. The development of the arts was not interrupted by invasions or the rise and fall of dynasties. China has always revered its past; early skills were not lost but carried on and developed to great heights. The earliest surviving work is in bronze, clay, stone, jade, and turquoise. The art of pottery reached perfection in the porcelain vases and bowls of the Sung Dynasty. By this time, too, a new art had developed: pure landscape painting. The brushwork in these paintings shows a very close observation of nature and great skill in setting down its forms and moods. These two arts, ceramics and painting, are perhaps those best known by the Western world, but in recent years, especially with new archaeological finds, the great sculptures of the past have become widely known as well.

Three projects have been chosen for this book. Calligraphy is a unique combination of art and writing. Paper making and woodblock

printing are both Chinese inventions that have greatly affected the rest of the world.

Calligraphy

The first writing in China, in the middle of the second millennium BC, was in the form of pictographs (simplified depictions of objects) on bones and turtle shells. There were 5,000 different pictographs representing animals, plants, people, and objects. They were arranged in vertical columns and were usually read from right to left. As the language developed, the pictographs evolved into abstract characters.

The three sets of figures in Fig. 5-2 show an early pictograph (on the left) and the character that developed from it (on the right).

Two or more characters are often combined into one character to make a new symbol representing an object, idea, or feeling. For

Fig. 5-2.

sun   moon   mountain

日 月 明   木 木 林   日 木 東
sun + moon = bright   tree + tree = forest   sun + tree = east

Fig. 5-3.

kindness   peace   good luck

happiness   love   rice   long life

Fig. 5-4.

example, the character for east is made by combining the character for sun and the one for tree to symbolize the direction you would face in seeing the sun rise behind a tree in the morning. Fig. 5-3 shows some examples of combined characters.

There are 40,000 characters in the Chinese language. A well-educated person needs to know 3,000 to 4,000 of them. Chinese characters are frequently used as designs on art objects in bronze, clay, and stone and in textiles. Four of the characters in Fig. 5-4 —the characters for good luck, happiness, long life, and rice— are frequently used in decorative arts. Fig. 5-6 shows a common teacup decorated with the character for long life.

The Chinese language is used not only to communicate ideas but also as an art form known as calligraphy. The word *calligraphy* comes from the Greek and means "beautiful writing." In Chinese calligraphy, art and language are combined in a manner unknown in the Western world. To many, calligraphy is more exalted than painting, because it is a more complete abstraction of form. One of the early calligraphers was Wang Hsi-Chih (303–379). A later emperor compared his work to "a dragon leaping over the Heavenly Gate."[1] From this remark, you can understand that his brushwork conveyed tension and vigor and spirit. The meaning of the characters, therefore, fuses with the art of setting them down. The beauty of the forms themselves and the energy instilled in them by the artist are as important as the message.

Introducing Calligraphy

A calligrapher spends a lifetime studying and copying master calligraphers and developing skill with the brush. It is a difficult art to convey in a book. If you live in a large city, chances are there is someone in the community who can demonstrate calligraphy. The lesson in Fig. 5-9 can give the student at least a feeling for the art. The characters in the column on the left read (from top to bottom): "Ancient

Fig. 5-6. A porcelain teacup for everyday use decorated with the character for long life.

Fig. 5-5. Calligraphy by Chiang Shao-shen, An-hwei, China, 1971. 2' 9" x 13'. The four characters in translation read, "The Sound of the River Carries the Rain." Courtesy of Mr. and Mrs. James P. Wong.

[1] Bradley Smith and Wan-go Weng, *China: A History in Art*, (N.Y.: Harper and Row, 1976), p. 101.

Fig. 5-7. Vee-Ling Edwards shows several different styles of calligraphy to a fifth-grade class.

Fig. 5-8. Vee corrects Nora's calligraphy and demonstrates the correct way to hold the brush.

For Today Use." Before beginning, discuss the meaning of these words with the class. Two possible interpretations are: "Don't discard the past as there are lessons to learn from history," and "We build on our heritage, using what others have learned before us."

Use a 1" brush that comes to a fine point. The brush should be held straight up and down, as in Fig. 5-8. Dip the brush in India ink and practice drawing thin or heavy lines by applying more or less pressure on the tip of the brush. The lines in each character are always made in a certain order and direction. The students begin with the character at the top. The progression of strokes and the direction in which each stroke is made are shown at the right of each character. Make a large chart on newsprint so that the students can see the steps clearly. Point out to students the variation in line thickness made possible only by using a brush. Try to put life into the strokes.

When students have gained some skill by practicing on newsprint, they may want to make a final copy, either on newsprint or on rice paper from an art-supply store. Chinese calligraphers and painters sign their work in calligraphy and

Fig. 5-9. The calligraphy in the column at the left reads, "Ancient For Today Use." The steps for making each character are given at the right. They are always made in a certain order and direction. Calligraphy for this chart, and elsewhere in this project, by Vee-Ling Edwards.

Fig. 5-10. Calligraphy by Julie, age ten. She signed her name in Chinese and also with a stamp bearing her initials and mounted the calligraphy on a green scroll.

Fig. 5-11. Angie, left, and Julie glue wooden strips of screen molding to the top and bottom of their scrolls.

with a seal bearing the characters of their name. The owner of an artwork will also stamp the work, so that frequently an important scroll will carry several stamps (or seals, as they are usually called) of successive owners. The signatures are usually stamped in red ink. Students can make a seal by cutting a small cube of potato and incising their initials in it with a knife or linoleum-cutting tool. Printing reverses characters, so the letters must be made in mirror image for a correct result. Brush the seal with red watercolor and press it on the paper.

Scrolls are the Chinese way of framing a work of art. They can be rolled up for easy and safe carrying or storing. Mount the students' best calligraphy by pasting it on a longer piece of brown wrapping paper. If the school has rolls of colored craft paper, the brown paper can be pasted on a piece of colored paper as well. The Chinese often use colored silk. In Western mounting, the custom is to leave a larger space at the bottom of a mat. In the East, it is the opposite—the larger space is at the top. Glue $\frac{1}{4}$ x $\frac{3}{4}$" screen molding, painted black, to the top and the bottom of the scroll (Fig. 5-11) and glue a string hanger to the back of the top. Or, scrolls can be glued around dowels at the top and bottom.

The Invention of Paper

It is hard to imagine a world without paper! Paper, as we know it, was first invented in China around the year 105 by Ts'ai Lun. The first

Fig. 5-12. Handmade paper textured with grass is the background for the character Autumn. Calligraphy by Cho-Yee To.

paper was made by soaking rags, rope, bark, and other materials and adding glue to the mixture, which was then pressed into thick sheets. The knowledge of paper making spread very gradually to other parts of the world, not reaching Italy until 1276. Mills were not established in England until 1495.

Although paper can be made from almost any fibrous material, most paper today is made from wood pulp. Chemicals are added that maintain whiteness, stick the fibers together, and size the paper so that ink will not spread.

Making paper from most raw fibers (cotton is an exception) requires the use of caustic acids and can prove dangerous. However, used paper can be recycled into fresh new paper, and one can add new fibers to this base.

How to Make Recycled Paper

Make a frame of ¾" square pine baluster wood the size of the piece of paper you wish to make. A comfortable size to handle is 7 x 10". Nail the frame together, and nail or staple aluminum window screening to the frame. (See Fig. 5-13.)

In a blender three-quarters full of water, reduce to a pulp old paper of any kind: computer printouts, paper towels, newspaper, advertisements, old cards. Put two or three blenders full of this pulp into a pan or tub of water 3–4" deep and several inches wider than the screen.

Again, with the blender filled with water, chop up new plant fibers: grass clippings, flowers, carrots, beets, or leaves. These ingredients, separately or in combination, add color and texture to the paper. Add this to the pulp. Thoroughly mix the pulp and plant fibers with the water. Slip the frame into the bottom of the pan, with the flat screen side up. While holding it there with one hand, be sure that the pulp is equally distributed in the water by whisking it with your other hand. Then slowly, using both hands now, bring the screen straight up above the surface of the water. Keep it level so that the paper will not be thicker on one side than

Fig. 5-13. Dip the screen under the pulp and then, keeping it level, bring it straight up above the water, letting the water drain through.

Fig. 5-14. Invert the screen on a paper towel and press the back with a sponge to remove the excess water. Then lift the screen off the new paper. On the left is a sheet of new paper that is dry and ready to be removed from the paper towel.

on the other. The water will drain through the screen, leaving a layer of pulp (see Fig. 5-13).

Drain off any excess water and invert the screen onto a paper towel on a flat surface. Press on the back of the screen with a sponge to remove excess water (Fig. 5-14). Then, slowly, lift the screen by pulling up on one edge of the frame. The new paper will stay on the paper towel.

Allow the paper to dry as it is and then lift it off the toweling, or place a second paper towel on top and iron it dry. Be careful not to overdo it, or the paper may scorch. Iron one side, turn it over and iron the other side. Peel off the paper towel.

Experiment with different textures. If the paper is to be used for calligraphy or printing, it may be most effective with very subtle or no texture. (See Fig. 5-12 for an example of calligraphy on handmade paper. Students might work with one of the characters in Fig. 5-4.) If the paper is intended to be a decorative paper, beautiful in itself, consider the addition of more textured fibers.

Woodblock Printing

In the year 251 Wei Tan created an indelible ink by mixing lamp black with other ingredients. This, combined with the invention of paper, led to the invention of the woodblock for printing.

The Chinese made seals, little carved wooden or stone characters that people used to show ownership, as early as 1000 BC. They were sometimes stamped in clay tiles. Probably from this, around the year 600, the woodblock was developed. Taoist priests and Buddhist monks made impressions on paper from large seals to illustrate religious writings. In this way,

Fig. 5-16. *Chrysanthemums and Rock*, color woodcut from the *Mustard Seed Garden Manual of Painting* by Wang Kai, 19th-century edition. Courtesy of The University of Michigan Museum of Art. 1955/1.67.

they could reproduce drawings in quantity for the first time and make them available to many people. By the time of the Sung Dynasty (beginning in 960) line prints were colored in by hand, and many very fine quality woodblock books were being made. Histories, works of poets and philosophers, and a book on agriculture from this time are treasured to this day. Later, books for artists were also printed.

One book that became very famous was the *Mustard Seed Garden Manual of Painting*, a handbook of instruction in landscape painting produced in 1679 by Wang Kai. Illustrated with color woodcuts, the manual sets down general principles of Chinese painting and gives instructions for preparing brushes, colors, and inks. The woodcuts illustrate the brushstrokes used in painting a great variety of subjects: trees, rocks, people, buildings, and clouds. There are even woodcuts of all kinds of insects and a section with the delightful title, "Book of Feathers-and-Fur and Flowering Plants." Fig. 5-16, a color woodcut from a nineteenth-century edition of this manual, illustrates

Fig. 5-15. Linocut on handmade recycled paper, by Leah, age eleven.

how to paint rocks and chrysanthemums.

The art of printing with woodcuts was not widely used in Europe until the fourteenth century—900 years after the invention of printing in China.

Making Woodcuts

Because sharp tools are used, this project is best suited to students of fifth-grade level and above, when improved coordination and strength make handling the tools safer.

To make a woodcut, use soft wood (such as pine) that is free of knots. Cut the size block you want from a 1" thick board. If you wish you can use linoleum, which is a modern substitute for wood and somewhat easier for beginners to cut. Buy a sheet of linoleum and cut it into pieces on a large paper cutter or with heavy shears. A 6 x 9" piece is probably ample. (It is unnecessary to use the more expensive blocks in which linoleum has been glued to wood.) A

Fig. 5-17. Kristin, age eleven, demonstrates how to cut a linoleum block. The hand holding the linoleum is always *behind* the cutting tool.

print made from linoleum is called a *linocut.*

Work out a design on paper the same size as the block. Transfer the design with carbon paper onto the block, and then go over the design on the block with a marker to strengthen the lines.

Using linoleum or woodcutting tools, cut away the wood or linoleum, leaving the inked design uncut and therefore raised. If you are using wood, you will find it easier to cut in the

Fig. 5-18. *Curlew*, linocut by Ellen, age eleven.

direction of the grain. Linoleum cutting tools come in sets with round and V-shaped gouges and one flat blade. For woodcuts you will need to cut around the contours of the design with the flat tool or an X-acto knife and then remove wood with a gouge. For linoleum blocks only the gouges are used—round for large areas or wide lines and V-shaped for fine lines. *Always cut away from the hand holding the block.*

After cutting the block, you can print. Water-base printing ink is best for beginners because it is easy to clean up. Squeeze the ink onto a smooth surface (tile or glass) and roll it out with a brayer until it stops being slippery and has a sticky texture. (It will make a faint crackly noise as the brayer runs over it.) Then transfer the ink to the block with the brayer, returning to the tile to pick up more ink until the block is covered. Next, move the block to a clean area and make a test print on newsprint.

Fig. 5-19. Four prints by sixth-grade students. Clockwise from top right: *Seagull*, linocut by Annette; *Fish*, woodcut on blue paper by Myles; *Tree*, linocut by Eileen; *Mountains*, linocut on handmade paper by Chris.

Carefully place the paper on top of the block and rub it well with the side of your hand or with a smooth, hard object such as a wooden spoon or drawer knob.

Lift up one corner of the paper while holding the rest down to see if the block was inked well and the print is evenly rubbed. It may be necessary to add a little more ink while someone holds the paper up for you. Replace that corner, rub it down, and lift up another portion. If it is rubbed well and the paper is not too thick, the design should be visible through the paper. A woodblock absorbs ink at first, and it may take another inking to get a good print.

When you pull the test print from the block, check it to see that all the areas have been cut correctly. Usually you will find areas that need more work. You can make your design totally free of ink in background areas by carefully removing all wood or linoleum that is surface height, or you can get a textured background by letting the cutting tools leave ridges.

After the block has been corrected make prints on higher-quality papers: paper you make yourself, imported rice papers, or colored construction papers. Use a variety of ink colors, too, until you find a combination of ink and paper that pleases you.

JAPANESE ARTS

Perhaps in no other culture has art been more integrated with daily life than in Japan. This may be changing, with increased industrialization and Westernization. But for many, art was and is a way of life; the utensils used, their manner of use, and the design and order of the home are often seen in an aesthetic or spiritual light. Daily sights and occurrences are still recorded in poetry and painting by many Japanese, the object being to try and express the essence of a sight or an idea in the most succinct manner possible. This is not a shorthand but a distillation; the essence is not lost but is made more compelling.

Haiku *(hi-coo)* is a short Japanese poem with a traditional form and content. Sumi-e *(soo-me-a)* is the art of painting with ink (*sumi* means Chinese ink, and *e* means painting). Both these arts take many hours of practice—in the case of the masters, a lifetime of training. Many subtleties in haiku are lost in translation, and without knowing the Japanese language one can never fully appreciate haiku. Sumi-e is not attempted by most children in Japan, as it is thought to be successful only if the artist's mind is mature. However, students can gain a beginning appreciation of haiku and sumi-e by reading the poems, trying to write their own, making ink paintings, and putting together a booklet of their own work. Some eighteenth-century haiku writers, such as Buson, combined sumi-e and poetry on one scroll. Fig. 5-20 is such a combination by the poet-painter Baishitsu who lived from 1768–1852. A little book of one's own poems and ink paintings can be a record of one's feelings to be treasured and shared for a long time.

Haiku

Haiku were being written over 700 years ago and reached a peak in the seventeenth century. They have continued to be a part of Japanese life to this day. Haiku are short, have a definite pattern, and are intended primarily to express an emotion. They usually sketch a poignant moment in nature that stirred an emotional response in the observer, although the emotion is suggested and not stated in the poem.

Fig. 5-20. *Snail* by Baishitsu. Reprinted from *Haiku* by R. H. Blyth, vol. III, p. 245. Copyright 1952, by kind permission from the Hokuseido Press, Tokyo. The haiku inscribed on the painting reads:

The axe bites into the tree,
But the snail
     Is calm and serene.

Symbolic reference to a season—such as chrysanthemums, which bring fall to mind—is also included.

The Haiku Society of America has defined haiku as an "unrhymed poem, recording the essence of a moment, keenly perceived, in which nature is linked to human nature." The poems contain seventeen syllables: five in the first line, seven in the second, and five again in the third. (Although in the Japanese language most haiku have this 5-7-5 syllabic count, it cannot always be successfully retained in translation.) Haiku are not rhymed in Japanese, but some English translations are, in an attempt to give a feeling for the rhythm of the original language. Here are translations of haiku by two of Japan's best-known poets.

What a huge one, how splendid it was,—
The chestnut
     I couldn't get at![2]
                              –ISSA
On the temple bell
     has settled, and is fast asleep,
          a butterfly.[3]
                              –BUSON

Issa describes a situation familiar to us all: an elusive perfection just beyond one's grasp. Sometimes haiku are inspired by other haiku or by sumi-e, like the one by Oguri Sokyu of a squirrel in a chestnut tree (see Fig. 5-21). Just above him is a splendid chestnut. Could Issa have seen and been thinking of this painting (which was done 300 years before his birth)? We do not know.

Buson's poem first forms a lovely picture in the mind: massive, ancient bronze versus a delicate, ephemeral butterfly. The poem causes the reader to wonder: what will happen when

[2] From R. H. Blyth, *Haiku*, vol. IV, p. 140. Copyright 1952. Reprinted by kind permission from the Hokuseido Press, Tokyo.
[3] From Harold G. Henderson, *An Introduction to Haiku* (©1958 by Harold G. Henderson. Reprinted by permission of Doubleday & Company, Inc.), p. 104.

the bell rings? Perhaps the priest cannot bring himself to ring it. A haiku should always set one's mind to seeing and thinking.

Many different levels of meaning arise from studying a haiku by a master, and some of them are not immediately apparent in translation. For instance, read this poem by Kikaku:

> A tree frog, clinging
> to a banana leaf—
> and swinging, swinging.[4]

One sees the small frog getting a ride on an enormous banana leaf that is tossing in the wind. Is he enjoying it? Or is he holding on for dear life? Can he change his situation? This is thought to be Kikaku's comment on human life. It may also be a pun on his own poetic career. He was a student of Basho, one of the earliest and perhaps the most famous of haiku writers, and Basho means "banana leaf" in Japanese! Many haiku have these associations to the Japanese, subtleties that Westerners, unfamiliar with many of the symbols used, are unable to appreciate fully. Although we can understand part of the haiku in translation, some of the intended meanings are lost.

Student Poetry Inspired by Haiku

In helping students write poetry for their own books, remind them that haiku always include some reference to a season. It is, however, rarely necessary to use a seasonal name; the poem should be more reserved, only hinting at the season. For instance, leaves turning color, or pumpkins, both suggest fall immediately without using the word *fall*. Adjectives like *beautiful* or *sad* also lessen the quality of the haiku. This feeling should arise from the image suggested by the words but not be stated outright.

[4] Ibid., p. 58.

Some haiku do not attempt to do more than evoke a clear picture of a beautiful moment. Students should start with the idea of expressing such a moment, without trying to put too many levels of meaning into it. The image and ideas are more important than the

Fig. 5-21. *Squirrel on a Chestnut Tree* by Oguri Sokyu, 1398–1464. Reprinted from *Haiku* by R. H. Blyth, by kind permission from the Hokuseido Press, Tokyo. Notice the variety of brushstrokes, from fine fur and twig lines to broad leaves. The central point of interest (the squirrel) is darkest, and distance (the highest branch) is indicated with the lightest gray.

5-7-5 syllabic counts, and students can take some liberties to preserve a particular feeling.

Here are some examples of poems by fifth-grade American children that contain some of the principles of haiku:

The caterpillar
walking slowly through the grass—
baby butterfly. —MAREN

This expresses the wonder of transformation from a pedestrian life to flight.

Seagulls flying high
way above the roaring sea
descending slowly down. —TAMAR

This is suggestive of contrast—delicate controlled flight, destructive power below.

Praying mantis eat the fly
then stand unaware
of a lizard hunger. —JASON

The snow falls lightly.
Try to catch it on your tongue.
No luck, try again. —ADAM

The last two poems give the feeling of the transitory nature of life and beauty.

Sumi-e

Although ink painting began in China, Japanese painters adapted it to their own style. Sumi-e is the visual equivalent of haiku. The aim of the artist is to express emotion through the beauty of the forms rather than merely to reproduce objects. Through observation and practice, the artist distills the essence of the subject matter into a minimum number of brushstrokes. Usually only black ink is used and when water is added to the ink, many gradations of gray are possible. In this way a whole range of color and texture is suggested.

Fig. 5-22. Mr. Saburo Ikeuchi prepares to demonstrate sumi-e to a fifth-grade class. Seiichi Sasaki, his interpreter, stands by his side. Mr. Ikeuchi first arranges his materials carefully on a mat and then spends a few moments in quiet contemplation.

Fig. 5-23. With the brush held vertically, Mr. Ikeuchi uses the fine tip to draw delicate plum blossoms that contrast with the rugged branch. Part of the branch is drawn with a dry brush, which creates a texture suggesting bark.

Fig. 5-24. Mr. Ikeuchi creates a wider line by holding the brush at a slant.

Sometimes color is added as well, but the painting is always kept to the bare essence of the object. The white space of the paper is a very important part of the painting, taking on a positive meaning in relation to the ink strokes, becoming in the imagination sky or water, wooded hill or snow.

Japanese children use a brush when they learn to write characters. Even so, if they wish to pursue sumi-e as adults, they must spend countless additional hours learning to control the brush on a higher level. Usually they work with a master and learn stroke by stroke the way he creates a sparrow, a fish, plum blossoms, and so on. Like practicing a musical instrument, students do it by rote until they are sure enough to make their own interpretation. Sumi-e are not painted outdoors while looking at a scene, although a master painter may have spent many hours observing and sketching from life. In sumi-e many traditions are followed, down to the way one arranges the materials and prepares the mind to be quiet and contemplative before beginning (see Fig. 5-22).

Teaching Ink Painting to Students

By far the best way for students to gain an appreciation of sumi-e is to have them watch a demonstration by a Japanese painter. In larger cities try contacting international organizations, universities with Asian studies departments, or import shops that sell Japanese art supplies. If you cannot arrange a demonstration, look for books that explain the steps in sumi-e. They can sometimes be found at art museums and import shops as well as in bookstores or on the Internet.

The Japanese use a hard cake of ink, which

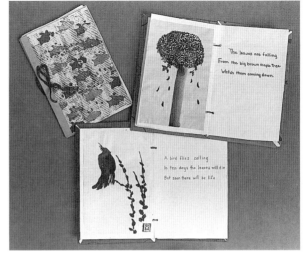

Fig. 5-25. Booklets of Japanese-style poems and ink paintings by fifth-grade students Heather, Tamar, and Paul (clockwise from upper left).

is rubbed on a stone with water to make the liquid ink. Students may use India ink. Provide water for diluting the ink to make gray and a cloth for wiping the brush. Newsprint is fine for practicing sumi-e. Paintings to be kept may be made on imported Japanese papers prepared especially for sumi-e, and these are often available in art supply stores.

Japanese artists use several different brushes. The most important is a large brush (at least 1") that comes to a fine point when wet. Brushes like this are available at art supply stores. With this one brush, students can draw many different lines. Hold the brush vertically between the thumb and the fingertips, and make brushstrokes by moving the entire arm. Draw fine lines with the tip of the brush (see the plum blossoms in Fig. 5-23) and make wider lines by applying more pressure. By holding the brush at a slant, you can make a wide, soft line. (See hand position in Fig. 5-24.)

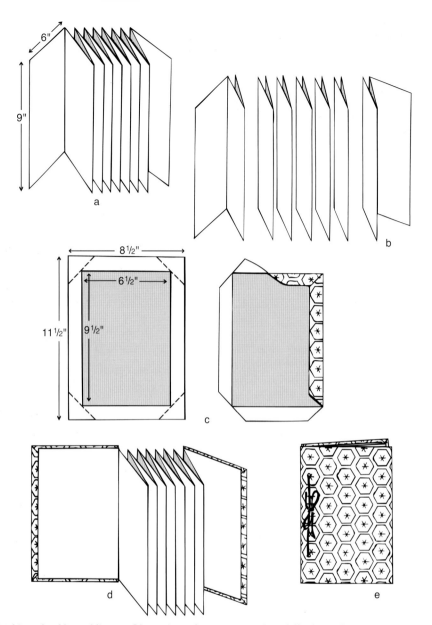

Fig. 5-26. Making a booklet. Folding a 96" long piece of paper accurately is difficult. Students may use the alternate method shown in (b).

Direct students to experiment with adding water to the ink to create a variety of grays. To get a single stroke that is graded from dark to light, immerse the brush in water and then wipe out excess moisture. Put the tip of the brush lightly into the ink and then move it up and down on a plate to mix the ink into the interior of the brush. Then dip just the tip into the ink again. When applied with the brush handle almost parallel to the paper, this will give a wide

Fig. 5-27. A variety of Japanese books with decorative covers and accordion-fold pages. The books at the back are positioned to open Japanese style, with pages turning from left to right. Two methods of binding the edges are shown. One book, on the right, is not bound at all, and can be fully spread out. The white vertical strips are for titles.

line with a gradation from dark to light, as in the tree trunk in Fig. 5-25. This gives the impression of roundness to a form.

Lead students in practicing brushstrokes with wet and almost dry brushes to see the different effects. In Fig. 5-23 the plum branches were painted with an almost dry brush. This creates a texture suited to depicting bark or fur. To obtain a dry brush, after dipping it in ink, scrub it lightly on newspaper until most of the ink is gone and the brush hairs no longer come to a point but are separated.

After practicing the brushstrokes described above, have students paint flowers, birds, animals, or other subject matter using a variety of gray tones as well as accents of pure black. Remind them of the importance of white space in their compositions and of keeping brushstrokes to the minimum necessary to convey their ideas. If their paintings are meant

to illustrate poems they have written and are to be included in a booklet, provide students with 5½ x 8½" paper.

Making a Booklet for Poems and Ink Paintings

A traditional Japanese way to make a book is by folding paper accordion style. This requires a roll of paper. White, nonglazed shelf lining paper works well. Cut the paper 9" wide, and fold the paper accordion style every 6". A piece of paper 96" long will make a book of seven pages with two extra leaves to glue to the covers. (See Fig. 5-26a.) The folding must be done very accurately if the pages are to be even, and this is surprisingly difficult for many students. An alternate method is to fold five 9 x 12" sheets in half, creating the middle pages of the book, and two sheets 9 x 18" into thirds. These last two sheets will be the first and last pages because they have an extra leaf to glue to the cover (see Fig. 5-26b).

The first step in making a cover is to decorate two pieces of construction paper, 11½ x 8½". Japanese artists make fine decorative papers by many methods: by incorporating pressed leaves in the paper when it is made, by using a batik-like method involving paste and stencils, by folding the paper and dipping it in dye to create patterns (see page 265), and also by printing. Students may decorate their cover papers by printing with forks, spools, container tops, and so forth, or with shapes cut from slices of potato or Styrofoam. (See Fig. 5-25.) Heather decorated book covers by printing fish shapes cut from a piece of potato and overlaying a water design made with a plastic object. She printed the fish in goldfish colors—red, orange, and yellow—and the wave lines in blue. In printing, an object is pressed into a pad of soft Styrofoam or paper toweling that is saturated with tempera paint. It is then pressed onto the construction paper in a pattern or design. Be sure there is a thick pad of newspaper under the construction paper, which helps to get a good impression. Push the object into the paint again each time before you print with it.

When the paper has been printed and is dry, it is glued to cardboard covers. Cut two pieces of white posterboard 9½ x 6½". Glue them to the center of the nonprinted side of the decorated paper with white glue. Cut off the corners at an angle. Fold the sides in and glue them to the cardboard (see Fig. 5-26c).

To assemble the book, place the covers on either side of the folded paper. The spine of the paper insert should be even with the back edges of the covers. (In the front of the book, the covers protrude beyond the pages by ½".) Glue the first 6" of the folded paper down to the inside of the front cover and the last 6" to the back cover (Fig. 5-26d). Next punch two holes ½" in from the spine of the book, one located 2" down from the top, and one located 2" up from the bottom. The hole punching must be done in three steps: punch the front cover first, mark the pages through the holes in the cover with a pencil, punch the pages, mark again for the back cover, and punch again. Thread yarn through the holes and tie it with a bow knot (Fig. 5-26e).

Students may copy poems directly into their books and paste their ink paintings in to illustrate them. Traditionally, Japanese books started at what is to the Westerner the back of the book, with the pages turning from left to right. Increasingly, however, they are now made Western style with pages turning right to left.

Fig. 5-28. Japanese fish banners fly from bamboo poles during the Children's Festival in May.

Fish Banners

People who live in a country made up of many islands feel a great closeness with the sea and depend greatly on it. With its teeming life, the ocean not only provides a livelihood and food for millions of people, but it figures in much of the art of Japan—in woodcuts, paintings, clay, and fabric design. Japan also has streams and

ponds in abundance, and raising goldfish has become an art form: they are bred for beauty and for pleasure. These goldfish, or carp, as they are commonly called, can be more than 1½' long. Many homes and apartments, even with

Fig. 5-29. Rebecca, age seven, finds the floor a comfortable place for painting her big fish.

Fig. 5-30. Fish banners by second-grade students Helen, Jonathan, and Tricia. Each banner is an expression of that individual.

very small yards, include a pool in the garden for goldfish, which are prized for special colors and fancy fins and tails.

May 5 is a national holiday in Japan. It used to be called the Boys' Festival; now it is called Children's Day. As part of the festival, each family that has boy children flies carp-shaped banners from a pole on their house. The carp is a symbol of masculinity, power, and determination. Carp banners are purchased by the family and friends on the first festival after a boy's birth and are flown every year afterward on the festival day. They are not made to fly free like a kite on a string. Made from two pieces of cloth, the banners form a kind of wind sock and fill out into a tube when the wind blows through them. The action of the wind in the tube makes the banner look very much like a carp fighting to swim upstream against the current. Paper carp banners, displayed indoors because they are less durable, can often be found in import shops and are painted in many different colors.

Making a Fish Banner

To make a fish banner, you need a large piece of paper, such as the 36" wide Kraft paper that comes in large rolls of many colors. Fold the paper double in a long rectangle and draw the fish so that it fills one entire side. Then, keeping the paper doubled, cut out the fish. A staple or two will keep the two pieces from shifting as it is cut. This will give two identical fish shapes. Staple the pieces together all around the edge, but leave one gap large enough so the fish can later be stuffed with newspaper. The fish can now be painted.

Japanese fish banners have a delightful pattern of scales, often painted in warm colors (red, pink, gold) or cool colors (blue, purple, gray). Students may want to make their own patterns, using stripes, dots, or shapes of their own devising. When one side is painted and dry, turn the fish over and paint the other side. When the painting is done, scrunch up a sheet of newspaper lightly (not into a tight wad, or it will become so heavy the fish will tear) and put it inside the fish to round it out as if the wind were filling it. Staple the opening together. The fish look very decorative hung by a string indoors or outdoors on a sunny day. They can swim down the corridors of a school or make a colorful contribution to an art exhibition.

Gyotaku: Fish Prints

Gyotaku (gee-o-taku) is the art of taking prints directly from fish. The word comes from gyo, meaning fish, and taku, an abbreviation of the word for rubbings (a way of making prints from stone and wood reliefs by hand). Gyotaku was first done as a method of record keeping. As part of the training of Samurai warriors in Sakai Province, the men were required to record the fish they caught by inking them and pressing paper to the inked fish. Archives exist with records of fish caught over 200 years ago.

After falling into disuse, gyotaku has been revived in the past fifty years, both as a record by fishermen and also as an art in itself. Two methods have developed. In the direct method, ink is painted on the fish and then paper is pressed carefully over it to receive an impression. In the second, or indirect method, moist paper is placed on the un-inked fish and pressed to fit all its contours. When the paper is dry, ink is rubbed gently over it. The impression is made in the same way that rubbings can be taken from engraved stones.

Both methods require a great deal of skill if they are to achieve a print that is beautiful and true to the form of the fish. The aim is to record all the fine details of scales, fins, eyes, and tail. In 1957 a traveling exhibit of gyotaku arranged by the Smithsonian Institution toured the United States. A great variety of fish, large and small, were represented in the

Fig. 5-31. Exhibition quality gyotaku of a sea bream, artist unknown. Collection of the author. Photo by David Wade.

prints—salmon, carp, halibut, mackerel, and even squid, sea horses, shrimp, and octopus—in colors from black to soft subtle shades of rose, yellow, and gray. They all brought an awareness of the beautiful shapes, patterns, and lines in fish. The prints were mounted on patterned paper or silk and either framed or made into scrolls.

Making Fish Prints

Beginning students will not be able to create the delicate, accurate prints made by practiced gyotaku artists, but they will be able to achieve satisfying results that introduce them to this art.

It is necessary to have a fish fresh from the market on the day of printing. Choose a

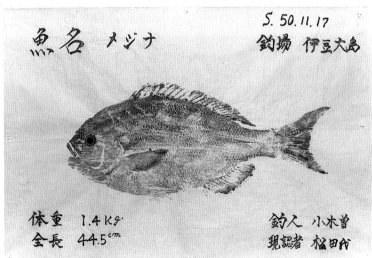

Fig. 5-32. Gyotaku by Mr. Ogiso of Takebun-do, Toyoda, Japan. This print was made as a record of a fish Mr. Ogiso caught, an opaleye, which is found only in the Japan and China Seas. Its weight, length, place caught, and the year (1975) are also recorded. Collection of the author.

fish that has a distinct scale pattern. Wipe the fish carefully to remove any mucous or excess moisture and place it on a pad of newspaper. Before beginning to print, increase the students' awareness of the fish by examining it with them. Explain how the fish breathes through its gills, how its shape is adapted to life in the water, how overlapping scales are smooth in one direction and rough in another —in sum, what a marvelous creature it is!

Fig. 5-33. A fish print by Jon, age seven.

India ink makes the best prints for beginners, but it is indelible, so the students should protect their clothing with old shirts or smocks. For the classroom the direct method of printing is the most practical. Brush ink over the fish lightly, being careful to cover every part of its body including the fins. Sometimes the fins tend to close up, but they can be fanned out and pinned to the newspaper in an open position. Place a sheet of thin paper over the fish and gently but firmly press it against the fish. Prints can be made with newsprint. However, imported papers from Japan make much better prints because they are more pliable and conform better to the contours of the fish. After pressing the paper onto every part of the fish, lift it off carefully and sign the print. Replace the newspaper under the fish frequently; ink that has spilled there will make spots on the printing paper.

BURMESE LACQUER WARE

Burma, now called Myanmar, includes over 100 different ethnic groups, the largest of which are the Burmans, the Shans, the Mons, and the Arakanese. Throughout this country there are many highly skilled artists and craftspeople working in many materials. Mandalay is noted for its fine silks; from the Shan state come brightly colored woven shoulder bags. There is artwork in gold and silver, carving in teak and

Fig. 5-34. Serafim watches as Atsushi brushes India ink over a fish. Atsushi is careful to cover every part, including fins.

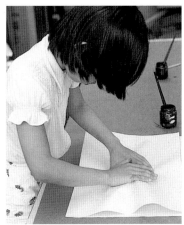
Fig. 5-35. Tomoko presses newsprint over the fish after she has brushed it with ink. She will carefully smooth the paper down onto every part of the fish.

Fig. 5-36. Tomoko signs her print.

Fig. 5-37. A gold-leafed lacquered basket made by a Khun artist in Kengtung, Burma, c. 1930. Collection of the author.

ivory, and lacquer ware in great variety.

The lacquer ware made in Burma is of very fine quality. The area around Pagan is best known for this art, but it is done in many other places as well. The art probably originated in China centuries ago, but certain types, like that with reddish-orange finish, are unique to Burma. Lacquer ware is often given as gifts, and most homes have some pieces. It is used for bowls and dishes, covered betel nut boxes with interior trays, large shopping baskets, and containers of all sizes. Some lidded containers are made in the shapes of animals, ducks, fish, and owls (the owl is a symbol of good luck).

There are several steps in making lacquer ware. First the artist weaves a basic shape using very narrow bamboo strips, and fills the uneven surface with a fine paste made from ashes. The artist sands it very smooth, then coats it with lacquer (made from the sap of the thitsi tree), allows it to dry, and sands it again. This is the first of many coats of lacquer. Some very fine pieces may be worked on for many months, as the successive coats are applied, dried slowly, and sanded.

The next step is to paint a design on the black lacquer with a vinegar-and-water solution. The artist then pats lacquer on with a cotton ball and carefully presses very fine gold leaf into the lacquer using the fingertips. (Gold leaf is real gold that has been hammered and beaten by hand until it is very thin, sometimes an unbelievable 1/200,000"!) The gold leaf will not adhere to the designs that were painted in vinegar and water. When the piece is washed, the gold leaf flakes off over those lines, revealing the black lacquer underneath. To the uninformed, it looks as though the designs had been drawn on with black ink. The owl and turtle containers in Fig. 5-38 were decorated in this manner.

Burmese lacquer ware is sometimes painted a reddish-orange inside the containers with a pigment made of cinnabar (mercury sulfide) mixed with oil. Sometimes a layer of dark green is applied under the black lacquer and then designs are incised through the lacquer to the green layer underneath.

Beautiful lacquer ware baskets are made in Kengtung by the Khun, a branch of the Shan ethnic group. They are used much like large

Fig. 5-38. Gold-leafed lacquered containers from Burma—an owl and a turtle. Collection of the author.

handbags and have intricate raised designs sculpted on the surface. Lacquer is thickened with ash until it can be rolled into fine threads. The threads are applied to the lacquered basket in floral and leafy patterns or in figures of men and women. Gold leaf is applied over this relief work to finish the richly ornate surface. A cloth handle is secured in two metal loops attached to the basket, and the interior is of either black lacquer or the orange finish (see Fig. 5-37).

Fig. 5-39. Making a papier-mâché container in the form of an animal. Newspaper is crumpled and taped into a basic form and then covered with papier-mâché. Features are added with a papier-mâché mash, and then another layer of papier-mâché is applied to the whole figure.

Making Papier-Mâché "Lacquered" Containers in the Shapes of Animals

The steps in making a papier-mâché container are illustrated in Figs. 5-39 and 5-40. First, crumple newspaper into the form of a small animal. Make a very simple shape, suggestive of only head and body. The Burmese animals are simplified, and there is no attempt to be realistic. Hold the newspaper in this form with masking tape. Apply four layers of newspaper dipped in wheat paste to this basic form. Work with small pieces to keep it smooth. (See page 267 for general papier-mâché instructions.)

Next, tear bits of facial tissue into a small container of wheat paste and mix with your fingers, kneading and squeezing until you have a kind of mash that can be handled like clay. With this mash, form beaks or ears, the curve of a wing, or the suggestion of feet by molding them onto the basic shape.

Let the papier-mâché dry thoroughly. Apply one more layer of newspaper dipped in wheat paste to the whole form. Use small pieces and smooth them down carefully, going over the entire piece, including the parts added with mash, and integrating them with the rest of the figure.

Fig. 5-40. The figure is sawed in half, the stuffing removed, and a flange glued to the inside top of the bottom piece. One layer of papier-mâché is applied to the flange. When dry, the container is painted with gold paint and India ink designs.

When the piece is thoroughly dry (after several days), smooth the surface with fine sandpaper. This will take out some of the ridges that are apt to form in papier-mâché. Saw the papier-mâché animal into two pieces so that it will make a container and a top. The best place is frequently at the neckline, but some figures may be sawed approximately halfway between top and bottom (see the turtle in Fig. 5-38). It will be difficult to replace the top properly if the top piece narrows from the point where it is separated from the body. If this is the case, make the cut lower down in a more vertical area.

Remove the loose newspaper stuffing inside, leaving a papier-mâché shell in the shape of an animal. With white glue, secure a cardboard flange to the inside of the bottom piece so that it stands up straight, about ¼" above the bottom piece (see Fig. 5-40). The top piece will fit down over the flange, and the flange will hold the top in place. Apply a single layer of paper dipped in wheat paste to the flange. Smooth it down over the rough top edge where the figure was cut. Seal the cut edge of the top in the same way.

When the piece is dry, it may be painted. Paint the inside with black tempera, the outside with gold tempera or gold polymer (the latter works especially well). After the gold paint has dried, use a tiny detail brush and India ink to decorate it with fine lines and fancy patterns. (If the gold paint resists the ink, add a few drops of liquid soap to the ink.) The Burmese owl in Fig. 5-38 has shiny black eyes, wings that look like flowers, a leaf pattern on its breast, and lots of little curved feather lines.

Paint a coat of clear gloss acrylic medium over the black tempera on the inside. Apply with a light touch to keep from smearing the paint. Paint the eye spots, too, to make them shine. The little container is now ready to hold some special treasure.

Fig. 5-41. Papier-mâché containers in animal shapes painted gold with inked designs. Left to right: *Cat*, by Dana, ten; *Owl*, by Jenny, nine; and *Owl*, by Linda, nine.

THE MARBLE INLAYS OF INDIA

In India today, skilled craftspeople do very fine artwork of many kinds. Carved ivory figures, brass sculpture, silver jewelry, pottery, woven fabrics of silk and cotton, paintings, wood carvings, and lacquer ware are some of the many beautiful things made. The great variety of artwork reflects the diversity of India's more than 800 million people. Many different religious, cultural, and language groups make up the population of this vast subcontinent.

Fig. 5-42. The Taj Mahal, Agra, India, built as a monument to Mumtaz Mahal, beloved wife of Emperor Shah Jahan.

There have been 5,000 years of continuous civilization in India. Sculpture in clay, stone, and bronze has been found from as early as 2500 BC. Architecture and sculpture were integrated in the many richly carved stone temples built throughout India.

One art for which India has become well known is stone inlay work. Craftspeople in Agra make beautiful designs by cutting and shaping semiprecious stones and setting them in marble and soapstone. This art dates back 400 years. Although the majority of Indians are Hindus and many of the arts reflect this,

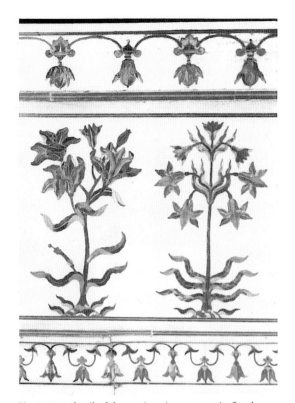

Fig. 5-43. A detail of the semiprecious stones, in floral designs, that inlay the white marble cenotaph of Mumtaz Mahal. Photo courtesy of the Government of India Tourist Office, Agra.

son, Jahangir, and his grandson, Shah Jahan, made many additions to the fort during their reigns. There were marble palaces, reception halls, baths, mosques, and formal gardens within the walls.

In Agra, also, is the Taj Mahal (Fig. 5-42), built by the Emperor Shah Jahan in memory of his wife who died giving birth to their fourteenth child. The Taj Mahal, a perfect synthesis of Hindu and Muslim arts, is so famous for its ethereal beauty and romantic origins that it has become for many a symbol of India. In this graceful memorial are combined the pointed arch of Muslim architecture and the delicately perforated white marble grilles developed by Hindu architects for their temples. They give shade from the sun but allow breezes to flow through the building.

Fig. 5-44. Marble box inlaid with lapis lazuli, carnelian, jade, tiger eye, agate, and other semiprecious stones. Made in Agra, India. Collection of the author.

successive invasions over the centuries brought other religions and diversity of culture. One of the most important of these invasions was by Muslims from central Asia. The Moghul Empire, which they established, controlled vast areas of India from the sixteenth to the eighteenth centuries. Their rule brought a strong influence on the arts. Persian ideas combined with already established Indian painting traditions to form the Moghul school of miniature painting. Moghul architecture introduced the pointed arch and Persian decorative designs, including stone inlay work.

The Moghul capital alternated between Agra and Delhi. At Agra a large fort was built by Akbar, the greatest of these emperors. His

To create it, artisans were imported from many lands, and 20,000 Indian craftsmen and laborers worked on it for seventeen years. The memorial was completed in 1647. Situated on the banks of the Jumna river, the Taj Mahal is made of white marble on a red sandstone base. A great dome rises from the center of the Taj. Inside, around the cenotaph (which is directly under the dome) is a marble screen, 6' high, carved into lacelike designs from a single block of marble. Throughout the Taj Mahal, on the wall and screens and on the tombs, is inlay work of semiprecious stones in floral patterns. Jasper, lapis lazuli, agate, and carnelian were cut into leaf and flower shapes. Holes of the same size were chiseled into the marble and the pieces inlaid so carefully that no break can be detected between the stones—they are perfectly smooth to the touch. One flower, created in an area 1 x 1", contains sixty different inlays. The colors glow against the white marble.

Inlay work is found in gateways and palaces constructed around this time in other parts of India, but none surpasses that done in Agra. The craftspeople working in Agra now are descendants of the artisans who worked on the Taj Mahal, and they are still carrying on the tradition of this beautiful art. (See Fig. 5-44.)

In a related rural craft, many villagers in India decorate the interiors and exteriors of their homes with a kind of mosaic that resembles inlay work. Where the homes are constructed by plastering stone or brick walls with a smooth layer of a mud-clay mixture, broken glass (especially from the bright glass bangles that are worn in great numbers by women and young girls) and pieces of broken china cups and saucers are pressed into the mud before it dries. Intricate flower, leaf, and tree designs and sometimes words of welcome to the home are created in the brightly colored glass.

Making Inlaid Designs

Stained glass inlaid in plaster has some of the same glow of color against a white background as do the marble inlays of India, although the method of working and materials used are very different. (This process is perhaps closer to rural art of glass and china mosaics.)

Stained glass is rather expensive, but a few small sheets will go a long way (they will be broken up into many much smaller pieces). Do not buy a textured glass for this project.

Fig. 5-45. A piece of cardboard wrapped with masking tape, sticky side up, holds the glass fragments in place while Sara, eleven, works out a design for her glass inlay.

Stained-glass artists frequently have boxes of scraps that they are willing to donate or sell inexpensively for class projects.

It is not practical for students to try to cut small pieces of glass into predesignated shapes. An adult should prepare the broken glass for them. The students then work out a design using these irregular shapes.

Begin by cutting the glass into long, thin strips with a glass cutting tool. Separate the scored lines from the pane with glass pliers. See page 268 for instructions. Strips cut in this way should then be cut into small pieces with tile- or glass-clippers. These clippers look a bit like

Fig. 5-46. A sixth-grade glass inlay of two flowers and a butterfly. Unsigned.

pliers, but the blades do not come together completely. Place the clipper blades so that they just nip the edge of the strip of glass, and press the handles together. A cleavage will form straight across the glass from the point of pressure. (See Fig. 3-32.) Crude shapes may be formed in this manner, but it is difficult to control exactly where the crack will go. Tiny fragments of glass will fly when you use these clippers, so cut the pieces with your hands and tool inside a clear plastic bag. You will be able to see what you are doing and protect yourself and others from flying fragments. *Always wear safety glasses.* A good working size for pieces is around ¼–½" in length.

To prevent injury, carefully instruct students in procedures for handling the glass. Separate the glass by color and arrange it in flat trays so students can easily see the pieces. This will minimize the amount of handling needed. Instruct students to pick up glass pieces very gently, with light pressure. If glass pieces are selected with care and not grabbed in haste, there should be no problem. Ask students to carefully replace unused pieces in the tray, not drop them from a height.

Have students choose their desired shapes and colors of glass and move them around to form a pleasing design. The shapes themselves may suggest a design. The Moghul inlays were frequently floral and symmetrical, but geometric designs were also often used. Remember that this is an inlay project, not a mosaic in which the colored pieces cover the entire area. The design should leave plenty of white space as background.

A good way to work out the design is to wrap with masking tape a small piece of cardboard the size of the inlay to be made. Put the tape on sticky side up and slightly overlapping. Pieces of glass placed on this board will stay where they are put. They can easily be removed from the taped cardboard and replaced until the design is completed.

Next you will need a small, shallow container the size of the piece you wish to make. Little cardboard boxes, large wax-paper cups (cut down to 1" from the bottom), aluminum containers, and square sections of aluminum trays can all be used. Cut pieces of aluminum foil to fit the bottoms of the cardboard containers, being very careful to keep them as smooth as possible. One by one, remove the bits of glass from the design on the

Fig. 5-47. A glass inlay of brightly colored butterflies by Annette, and one of a tree with a bird, by Monique, both sixth-grade students.

taped cardboard and glue them in position with white glue on the aluminum foil or directly to the bottom of the waxed cup or aluminum container. Do not use too much glue; a spot in the center of the glass will be enough. Wipe up glue that oozes from underneath glass onto the bottom of the container, because otherwise it will make a hole when the plaster is poured. Let the design dry for several hours.

Mix plaster and pour it over the glass to a depth of ½–¾". *The teacher should mix the plaster according to the safety precautions on page 269.* After pouring the plaster, tap the edge of the container to eliminate bubbles. As the plaster is thickening, insert a loop of heavy string or copper wire (with the ends curled to make it hold better) into the plaster to use as a hanger for the inlay. It must be done before the plaster has become hard, and you must remember which is the top of your design. Let the plaster dry for two hours and then pull the container away from the inlay. The plaster will still be weak, so do this carefully (and do not pull by the hanger). If the glass was glued to aluminum, you will find that the glue is partially dissolved; the glass should be cleaned gently with a wet paper towel before it dries again. Glass that was glued to a paper cup will need a little more vigorous cleaning with a wet towel and some scraping with a table knife or flat linoleum-cutting tool.

The glass should be nicely inlaid, level with the plaster. If there are imperfections in the plaster surface, a very small additional amount of plaster can be mixed and applied to the surface. Wet the inlay first, apply the plaster, and smooth it with the straight edge of a piece of

cardboard. When the plaster is thoroughly dry (this takes several days), you can further smooth it with a damp cloth. Scrape off plaster that has adhered to the glass surface, using a table knife. The sides of some aluminum containers impart a wrinkle to the sides of the inlay; smooth these with coarse sandpaper after the piece has been quickly run under water. Finish with fine sandpaper and by rubbing with a damp cloth.

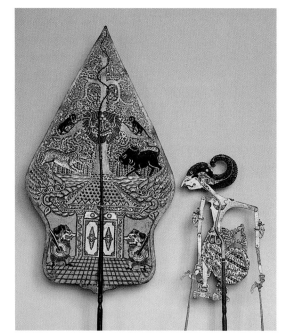

Fig. 5-48. Wayangs (shadow puppets) of a kayon and Arjuna. Courtesy of A. L. Becker and Judith O. Becker.

Fig. 5-49. Wayangs from the plays based on the Mahabarata epic showing three types: Bagong, a clown; Arjuna, a prince; and a demon king. Courtesy of A. L. Becker and Judith O. Becker.

INDONESIAN ARTS

Wayang Kulit:
Javanese Shadow Plays

Shadow plays, one of the oldest forms of theater, have been performed in Java for over 1,000 years. Java is part of the string of more than 3,000 islands now known as Indonesia that stretch from Sumatra, near the tip of Malaysia, down to western New Guinea, north of Australia.

The performances were probably an early expression of religious ideas. Hindu kingdoms were established in Java by the seventh century. During this time, the plays portrayed Hindu epics, especially the *Ramayana* and the *Mahabharata*. The legendary events and their original sequence were adapted as Javanese characters and ideas were incorporated into the stories. Later, Muslim rule also had some influence on the plays, but they remain strongly Javanese.

The plays are called *wayang kulit* (*wi-äng coo-lit*), *wayang* meaning shadow and *kulit* meaning skin. The puppets, called wayangs, are made of thin buffalo hide with a fine, carefully smoothed surface. There are over 600 distinct characters, their sizes and shapes fixed by tradition. A single performance may use as many as sixty. The puppet is traced from a pattern and cut out with a hammer and small chisels and punches. Some of these puppets are so finely cut they look like filigree work. Arms are movable, jointed at the elbows and shoulders, and are manipulated with rods of buffalo horn. A large rod runs the entire length of the puppet, supporting the thin leather figure and ending in a handle at the bottom.

The wayangs are brightly colored on both sides (Fig. 5-48). The colors are often symbolic and give clues to the puppet's character. The color of the face, which may differ from that of the body, is especially significant. A black face symbolizes inner calmness, maturity, and humility and also sometimes indicates physical strength. A gold or white face indicates a person with good qualities. Gold also often stands for youth. A red or pink face indicates a crude, violent, and uncivilized nature. The shapes of the wayangs and their clothing and jewelry also give clues to character. The puppets are not meant to look like ordinary people—they are stylized and given shapes symbolic of certain personality types. The spiritual wayangs are slim and small. Their heads are bent, and their faces look down in an attitude of humility. They have delicate noses and finely cut, inward-looking eyes. They are symbolic of the Javanese ideal character: introspective, intellectual, and refined.

The largest puppets, often portraying ogres, symbolize a violent nature and gross habits. They have heavy bodies, raised heads, big blunt noses, and round eyes. They symbol-ize great strength but lack spiritual power, and so they are always defeated by smaller but spiritually stronger heroes.

There is a third group of puppets whose nature is a mixture of these two. In general, the puppets portray humans, gods, and ogres. There are also wayang for deer, horses, armies, and such props as arrows and daggers.

All the puppets are manipulated by one person, the *dhalang* (dä läng), who speaks all the voices as well. The performance is accompanied by a *gamelan* (gämelän), which is a Javanese orchestra of twelve to forty instruments. The dhalang signals to the gamelan for tempo, mood, and piece changes. The shadows of the puppets are projected on a stretched

Fig. 5-50. Some of the instruments used in a gamelan (Javanese orchestra): gongs, bonang (pot gongs), and saron (metallophones). Courtesy of the University of Michigan.

white cloth screen by a flickering coconut oil lamp, which, added to the lifelike movements created by the dhalang, bring the shadows to life. Today, electric lightbulbs are often substituted for the oil lamps.

Performances are held outdoors or on a porch. They begin at sundown and last until early morning. Before the performance, the puppets are stuck upright by their handles into a porous banana log that lies at the base of the screen and extends to either side. The performances begin and end with a tree-shaped wayang called a *kayon* (kä yôn) placed in the center of the screen. The kayon represents all forms of life; during the play, it can also represent powers of nature: fire, water, and storms.

The plays are performed at births and marriages and at other religious rites. They are also given on many festival nights. Meant to be much more than entertainment, they preserve traditions and are a medium of instruction for both young and old. They deal with the forces of life, human nature, and its relationship to the natural and the supernatural order of the universe. People watching are believed to be protected from evil. Serious problems of good and evil are enacted, relieved occasionally with the humorous episodes of clown characters. There is no simple solution to the problems presented. Characters rarely are so bad that there is not some redeeming quality, and the good are prone to occasional mistakes or dilemmas that force them into unfortunate actions.

The epics are long and very complicated. A brief synopsis of the *Rama Cycle* may give some idea of their content. Although based on the Hindu epic of the *Ramayana*, the Javanese play does not conform to it exactly:

The aging King Dasarata, of Ngayoja, wants to abdicate and give his eldest son, Rama, the throne. However, through trickery, the king grants his second wife's wish to have her son, Barata, succeed him instead.

Rama goes into exile with his faithful wife, Dewi Sinta, and his brother, Leksmana. They live in the Dandaka forest and fight the Raksasas, who are giants that trouble the ascetic hermits living there.

The king of the Raksasas, Rawana, abducts Sinta. (One of his demon servants changes himself into a golden deer to distract Rama, leaving Sinta unguarded; and Rawana, disguised as a hermit, seizes her, and carries her off to his palace in a chariot.) Rama allies himself with Hanoman, general of the white monkeys, and with the aid of the monkey armies wages war on King Rawana. Rama wins, Sinta is rescued, and they return home. Barata gives up the throne, and Rama is crowned as rightful heir. (See Figs. 5-51, 5-52, 5-53, and 5-59.)

This is an oversimplified thread of one of the stories. Only a small segment of the plot would be presented in one evening. The shadow plays have many levels of meaning, the subtleties of which are very difficult for a non-Javanese observer to comprehend; but the beauty of the shadows, the great skill of the dhalang, and the sounds of the gamelan combine into a very moving experience for anyone fortunate enough to attend a wayang kulit performance.

Fig. 5-51. This and the next two illustrations are from a sixth-grade shadow play based on the Ramayana epic. Here, a demon, disguised as a golden deer, leads Rama away into the forest, leaving his wife, Sinta, unprotected.

Fig. 5-52. Sinta is abducted by the demon king, Rawana. Jatayu, the vulture, fails to save her but tells Rama of her abduction.

Fig. 5-53. "There's a ghost behind you!" (from a clown interlude).

Making Shadow Puppets and Performing a Play

A wayang kulit performance can be a fine experience in integrated studies because it brings together art, music, theater, literature, and cultural geography. A classroom teacher may enjoy working with the art and music departments in putting on a shadow play.

Students can write a play and create their own characters, or they may wish to read a translation of one of the Hindu epics and perform a simplified version of one episode. Whichever they choose to do, the basic construction of the puppets is the same. By performing one of the epics, students can identify with another country's villains and heroes and gain some understanding of a different culture. The wayangs, at first odd in appearance, become understandable when the symbolism of the different shapes is explained. They begin to convey to the students some of the meanings conveyed to the Javanese audiences. Students enjoy making the refined and gracious heroes, the rugged giants, and the inept clowns.

The brief clown interludes that relieve the serious epic are often original to the dhalang doing the performance. Dhalangs sometimes make wry comments on contemporary events. These parts will not be found in the Hindu stories and can be written by the students, using puns and the slapstick comedy that is found the world over.

Several books listed in the bibliography can help students design wayangs like those made in Java. If the particular character they wish to create is not illustrated, they can make one up by choosing body shapes, attitudes,

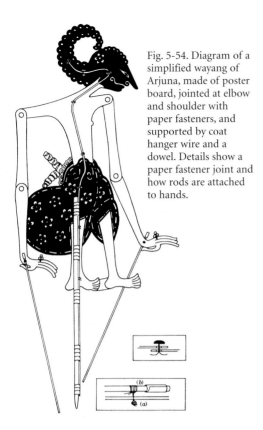

Fig. 5-54. Diagram of a simplified wayang of Arjuna, made of poster board, jointed at elbow and shoulder with paper fasteners, and supported by coat hanger wire and a dowel. Details show a paper fastener joint and how rods are attached to hands.

The puppets should be colored appropriately, taking into account the symbolic meanings of the color. Clothing is multicolored. Markers work best. A water-based paint can be used, but might weaken the thin cardboard. Puppets will be more durable if you laminate them with plastic on both sides. Alternatively, two coats of varnish will strengthen them somewhat. Test the varnish first on a scrap to be sure the colors do not run.

After cutting out the puppets, coloring them, and giving them a protective finish, assemble them. First, hinge the arms at elbow and shoulder with paper fasteners. Punch out a hole first so that the joint will move smoothly. Spread the two fastener ends apart in a gentle curve, not hard against the cardboard. (See upper detail in Fig. 5-54 for a cross-section of a paper fastener joint.) Then sew wire rods to the hands so that the arms can be manipulated.

Fig. 5-55. A wayang of Leksmana, by Brian, age eleven.

Coat hangers, cut and straightened, work very well. (See lower detail in Fig. 5-54 for a cross-section showing how to attach the rods.) First double heavy carpet thread. Make a large knot in one end. Poke the thread through the thickest part of the hand (a) and twist the threads. Wrap the thread around near the end of the rod (b) and tie. Wrap tape around the end of the rod to prevent the rod from slipping out of the thread.

and dress that symbolize the type of personality they want to portray.

Make a careful drawing first on newsprint. Remember that size is important—heroes are usually *smaller* than more violent characters. Also make a kayon to begin and end the play and to be used as scenery. Transfer the drawings to poster board with carbon paper. Cut out the figures with scissors. Use an X-acto knife or flat linocutting tool to cut out areas and designs within the figures, protecting the table with a pad of newspaper or piece of corrugated cardboard. The more details cut in, the more elaborate the shadows will be. A hole punch can be used for some of these patterns. Cut the arm shapes separately, in two sections (one piece shoulder to elbow, the other elbow to hand).

Fig. 5-56. Sara checks her ghost against the light.

The central rod should run from the head down the body and one leg and extend for at least 6" below the foot for a handle. A very delicate figure needs only the wire, sewn to the cardboard at intervals. After the wire is sewn on, a heavier figure should be reinforced by taping a ¼" dowel to the lower half of the wire. Sharpen the dowels on the end (with a pencil sharpener) so that the puppets can be stuck upright into Styrofoam at the base of the screen when they are not in active use during the performance.

There are many ways to make a shadow screen, which is essentially a frame on which to stretch the cloth and a way of suspending a light behind it. Directions for many types, from simple to complex, are given in the books listed in the bibliography. The diagram in Fig. 5-57 is for a screen built of heavy lumber and meant to last. It can be unbolted, if necessary, for moving and storage.

The frame can be made with either 2 x 4" or 2 x 6" boards. The foot pieces are cut from 2 x 10" boards. They are 8½" high and 2' long, with a 3½" deep notch cut into them into which the lower beam is fitted and bolted with 9" carriage bolts.

The trough, which is to be stuffed with a stiff Styrofoam slab, is made of 1 x 6" boards. Build it before attaching it to the frame. Cut notches 2" deep into the bottom of the trough where it fits down over the feet, and then bolt

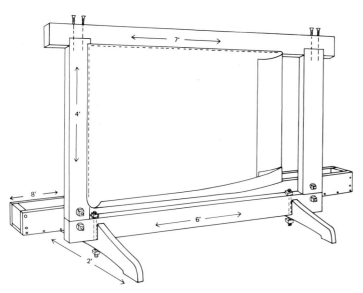

Fig. 5-57. Diagram of a shadow-play screen.

Fig. 5-58. Putting on the shadow play. Behind the screen, Fred, Michael, and Keith manipulate the puppets.

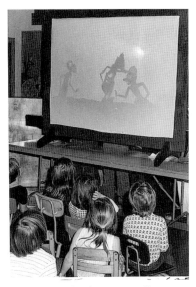

Fig. 5-59. A kindergarten audience sees Rama victorious over Rawana.

Fig. 5-60. A student gamelan accompanies the play. A metallophone, xylophone, finger cymbals, and gongs keep the beat.

it to the lower beam of the frame with 3" carriage bolts.

Notch the top beam to fit the 4' uprights and secure it to the uprights with screws as in the diagram. Secure the uprights to the trough with 3" carriage bolts.

Staple a screen of white material to the frame. Cotton or synthetic sheeting works very well. Clamp a drawing table lamp (the type that can be extended) to the top middle of the frame. When presenting a performance, elevate the screen on a sturdy table.

For a student production, it is better to have students take the parts of their own puppets rather than have one be a dhalang and do all the performing. A performance will not have the right feeling without musical accompaniment. Almost every village in Java has its own gamelan. The village instruments might be made of bamboo and iron; the large city gamelans have bronze instru-

ments, primarily gongs and metallophones set in beautifully inlaid teak supports. The music is an integral part of the performance, each character and scene having its specific type of music. There are many layers of melodies going on at the same time.

Javanese instruments are not easily available outside of Indonesia, but there is an excellent book (see bibliography) that introduces young students to traditional Javanese scales and rhythms, which are very different from those of the West. The book suggests Western instruments that can approximate some of the sounds of the gamelan.

Fig. 5-61. Musical notations for "Ricik-Ricik" ("Softly Raining").

A Javanese melody called "Ricik-Ricik"[5] (pronounced *ree-chik-ree-chik*, "Softly Raining") is approximated on our scale by the notations shown in Fig. 5-61.

Indonesian notes are designated with numbers rather than letters. In this music 3, 5, 6, 5 stands for F, A, B flat, A, and so on. The first melody (a) is played by two instruments one octave apart. For the second melody (b) an instrument plays the same note twice to each beat. Both melodies can be played on xylophones, glockenspiels, melody bars, or metallophones. In Javanese music the most important instruments are the rhythm instruments, or gongs. In this piece the large gong (G) is played only on the 8th and 16th beats, the medium gong (g) on beats 2, 4, 6, 8, 10, 12, 14, 16 and the smallest gong (g) on 3, 5, 7, 11, 13, 15. Besides gongs, use cymbals, triangles, or improvised gongs such as pot lids.

The first eight notes are repeated before going on to the second eight notes, which are also repeated before the melody is begun again. The sequence is repeated many times. The music presented here is a vast simplification of Javanese music, which even in a "simple" piece has many layers of melodies being played.

There are several gamelans in the United States. Arrangements can often be made for having students see and sometimes play the instruments. They are located at the University of Michigan, the University of California at Berkeley, Wesleyan University, the University of Hawaii, Oberlin College, the Indonesian Embassy in Washington, D.C., the University of Wisconsin, Brown University, Cornell University, Chicago Field Museum, California Institute of Art in Valencia, San Diego State College, the University of Santa Cruz, U.C.L.A., and the State University of New York at Binghamton.

Batiks

No one knows exactly when and where batiks were first made. But it is significant that the word that denotes this particular way of decorating cloth is Javanese. Batik is derived from *titik*, meaning "drop." Many centuries ago the basic method of using wax to resist applications of dye was introduced to Java from India, where wood blocks dipped in wax had been used to decorate cloth. In Java the craft of making batiks was raised to a fine art that has not been sur-

Fig. 5-62. Indonesian tjap batik. Detail of a sarong in cream, soya brown, and indigo blue, c. 1925. Collection of the author.

[5]Adapted from William M. Anderson, *Teaching Asian Musics in Elementary and Secondary Schools* (Adrian, MI: The Leland Press, Box 301, 1975), © permission.

Fig. 5-63. Contemporary Javanese tulis batik with a peacock design. Drawn entirely by hand with a tjanting. Collection of Susan Walton.

passed anywhere in the world. The Javanese invented a tool, the *tjanting* (pronounced *chanting*), which is a small copper bowl with a fine spout and a bamboo handle. This tool provides a reservoir for melted wax and is used as a drawing tool that permits the wax to be applied in extremely fine lines and dots.

Originally the art was developed and used by the women in royal families to decorate clothing, and certain patterns were allowed only for court use. Eventually, however, the making of batiks became widespread, daughters learning the techniques and patterns from their mothers. In this way, designs were passed down unchanged over many centuries. Batiks

were worn by men and by women as head coverings, shawls, and sarongs (a wrap-around skirt worn by both men and women). The original dyes, applied to a creamy, off-white cloth (a color created by soaking the cloth in coconut oil), were a deep blue made from indigo and a beautiful brown made from soya bark, a color rarely found outside of Java (Fig. 5-62). Now dyes of many colors are used.

Making batiks by hand with a tjanting is a slow, meticulous process. Fine hemp or cotton cloth is used. The cloth is prepared by careful washing, light starching, and beating with a wooden mallet to make it very smooth and supple. A special formula of resin and wax is applied to the cloth in intricate patterns with a tjanting. The wax is first applied to one side, and then the cloth is turned over and the design is applied in wax on the other side to be sure that the protection is complete. Then (if the piece is to be made in the earliest traditional colors) the cloth is dyed in indigo. All unwaxed areas will turn blue. When the cloth is dry, some of the wax is removed, revealing cream-colored undyed areas. (Where the wax is not removed, the designs will remain cream.) Those areas to remain blue are waxed with the tjanting, and the cloth is then dyed soya brown. After this final dye the cloth is rinsed in hot water to remove all the wax, revealing a completed design in cream, blue, brown, and dark navy blue where the brown combined with unwaxed blue areas.

The designs consist of both geometric shapes and shapes derived from such natural forms as flowers, foliage, birds, butterflies, animals, and fish. There are Indian and Chinese influences in some of these designs, reflecting two of the many different ethnic contributions to Javanese culture. The garuda, a mythical bird

Fig. 5-64. Sara, eleven, applies melted wax to the areas that will remain white. Always melt wax in a pot that is placed in another pan of hot water over the burner.

Fig. 5-65. Sara has dyed the cloth blue. Now she applies wax to the parts to remain blue before she dyes it purple.

placed for the design to appear continuous. Tjap batiks are less expensive than the tjanting batiks. A piece of work stamped "Batik tulis" has been done by hand. If it is stamped "Batik tangan," a tjap has been used.

The intricate beauty of the Javanese batiks has very nearly caused their extinction. As

that carried the god Vishnu, is a common motif, as are the phoenix and Nagu, the dragon. However, all these forms are very highly stylized. When Java came under Muslim influence, the Muslim religious law forbade representation of natural forms; these highly stylized and decorative forms were a way of complying with this law. Many designs have names and meanings stemming from their early use in court life. Some designs were used only by particular families, and some were made for such special occasions as marriages.

It sometimes took as long as six months to finish an especially fine sarong, measuring about 3½ x 7½'. In the mid-nineteenth century, a new technique was invented to speed up the process. Ribbons of copper formed into the desired designs are soldered into blocks called *tjaps*. The tjap is dipped in the hot wax and pressed onto the cloth. In this way, six sarongs can be made in one day. This method, done by men, still requires a great degree of skill. The blocks have to be very carefully

the cloth has become popular throughout the world, imitations made by machine methods have been mass-produced in great quantities. The copied designs do not have the beauty or wearing quality of the handmade fabrics, but their lower prices have almost eliminated the market for the real batiks. Tjanting batiks are becoming more and more scarce, and fewer and fewer women in Java learn this meticulous and demanding craft. There are artists in Java, however, who are making a great effort to keep this craft, which has contributed so much to the art of the world, from dying out.

Making Batiks

There has been a great interest in the art of batik in recent years, and many excellent books are available on the subject. It is not too complicated for upper elementary students to make simple designs, and it can be exciting for them. *Safety precautions must be carefully followed, however, in any project that involves hot plates and melted wax. It is essential to have adult supervision at every table using the hot wax.* If students are absorbed in their work, they may not notice water running low in the double-boiler or other dangerous situations. Parents will often help out in their children's classrooms for special projects such as this.

The batiking process described here is a much simplified version of that used in Java. Students should first work out a design on newsprint. They may want to make a decorative piece for a wall hanging or batik a T-shirt or an African dashiki. (Directions for making a dashiki are given on page 18.) It would be prohibitively expensive to buy enough tjantings for a large group of students, so the best way for them to begin to learn the art is to apply the wax with brushes. They must work with wider lines and broader areas of color than if they were using a finer drawing tool.

Before beginning, students must work out the sequence of colors they are going to use. This is the most difficult part of the project. They must realize two principles: First, in dyeing, one must go from light colors to progressively darker ones; secondly, a second dye will combine with the first one to produce a new

Fig. 5-66. *Llamas and Mountains—a Night Scene,* by Sara.

color. Suppose the first dye is yellow. The parts to remain yellow are waxed. Now there can be no blue areas, because adding blue to the yellow cloth will create green. Some possible sequences are: yellow to orange to red to brown or purple; light blue to medium blue to purple to black, or blue to green to brown or black.

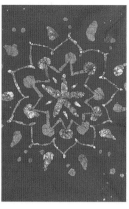

Fig. 5-67. Geometric design by Kamala, age twelve.

Cotton cloth, such as old sheeting, is excellent for batiks. New cloth should be washed and ironed before using. Avoid permanent press materials; they do not take dyes very well. Sketch the design lightly on the cloth, using a stick of charcoal (pencil lines will not wash out).

Really fine batiks use special formulas of beeswax, paraffin, and resin. Beginning students do very well with paraffin alone. Before the final dye it can be cracked easily, making the distinctive veined effect found only in batiks. (Javanese artists did not originally try for this effect, however; they tried instead to eliminate any accidental qualities in their best batiks.) Melt the wax on an electric stove burner or hot plate. Place a hot plate on a sheet of metal or metal cookie pan. It is always safer to heat wax in a pot or coffee can that is set in another pan of water over the heat source. *Never heat wax directly over the fire. It is highly combustible if it gets too hot. Be sure, if the pot has a handle, it is turned so that no one will hit it and upset the pot.* The wax is hot enough when it penetrates cloth easily. Test it on a scrap.

Fig. 5-68. A dashiki made by Jenny, age eleven. The color sequence is from white to orange to green.

Protect the work table with newspaper. Place the cloth on a piece of wax paper. The wax paper prevents the cloth from sticking to the newspaper. If a shirt or dashiki is to be batiked, open up the garment and put newspaper and wax paper inside so that the design can be done on one side without spotting through to the other side.

Once used for batik, brushes cannot be used again for painting, so you may want to use old brushes. Put the brush into the hot wax, letting it get thoroughly hot. Take it directly to the cloth and make only two or three strokes. The wax cools very quickly and will not penetrate unless the brush is filled often with fresh hot wax.

First wax any areas that are to remain white. Be sure the wax has penetrated to the other side. If it has not, turn the cloth over and wax the other side, too.

Set up a separate table for dyeing. Protect it well

Fig. 5-69. Sixth-graders Scott, Lori, and Amy wearing dashikis they decorated with batiked designs.

with layers of newspaper. Using hot water and a tablespoon of salt, mix commercial dyes ahead of time. Cool the dye before using it; warm dye melts the wax. Plastic gallon milk containers with the tops cut off make good dye pots. Immerse the cloth until it is a shade darker than desired, since it will be lighter when it dries. Remove it from the dye and rinse it gently in lukewarm water. Do not wring it out; blot it between newspapers and then hang it up to dry in a shady place.

When the cloth is completely dry, wax those areas to remain the color of the first dye. Then dye the cloth a second color, rinse, and dry. If a third color is to be used, the areas of the second color that are to be preserved are covered with wax first, and so on.

If you want a veined pattern, gently crumple the fabric (which will crack the wax) before the final dye. The last dye seeps into these cracks, creating the veined effect unique to batiks. Dry the batik for the last time.

To remove the accumulated wax, place the batik between sheets of old newspaper (newspaper less than a week old may transfer ink to the cloth) and press with a hot iron, keeping the iron in motion. When the wax melts and is soaked up by the newspaper, remove the paper and place the cloth between new papers, iron again, and continue ironing and changing papers until all the wax is removed. (Some books recommend boiling the cloth to remove wax, but this can destroy the design if the dyes are not absolutely permanent.) Some remaining wax may actually increase the brightness of the colors and may be appropriate for a wall hanging. However, an article of clothing may be somewhat stiff if all the wax is not removed. Dry cleaning will remove any wax residue.

Fig. 5-70. Peacock, owl, fish, and cobra kites made by hand in Thailand for export in the 1970s. The butterfly kites, from the same time, are machine printed but assembled by hand, and were made in Taiwan. Collection of the author. Photo by Wade Schuman.

A dashiki or T-shirt should be ironed before it is washed the first time. Use a pressing-cloth that has been dipped in a solution of vinegar and water. This helps make the color more permanent. Wash these items separately from other clothes.

A batik to be used as a wall hanging can be glued along the top to a ¼" dowel, or the dowel can be inserted in a fold sewn along the top. Hang it up with a short length of yarn tied to the dowel ends.

KITES OF SOUTHEAST ASIA AND TAIWAN

The area known as Southeast Asia that lies east of India and south of China includes Burma (Myanmar), Thailand, Cambodia, Laos, Vietnam, Malaysia, and Indonesia. It is culturally and geographically very diverse. Lowland plains cut by rivers lie beneath towering mountain ranges. There are civilizations in the plains that go back over two thousand years, and also a large number of independent tribes live in the hills. Hundreds of different languages are spoken, and there is great religious diversity, with most of the major religions of the world represented.

In the plains, where the ancient civilizations were rooted, there are long traditions of literature and art. One of these traditions is the making and flying of kites, probably introduced from China, but then developed into unique forms in Southeast Asia. This was an occupation for adults. In early times it was felt to be a way of contacting spirits of wind and sky. The kites were elaborately

Fig. 5-71. A kite maker of Kelantan, Malaysia, ready to launch his *wau bulan*—"moon kite." Note the elaborate floral patterns in red and gold, and the bow and string at the top which will create a musical sound when the wind blows over it. Courtesy Tourism Malaysia.

Fig. 5-72. A youngster runs to get his bird kite in the air at a park in Phnom Penh, Cambodia. AP/Wide World Photos.

decorated to find favor with these spirits.

In Malaysia, for generations kites have been flown to celebrate the rice harvest. Traditional kites are still being made in the Malayasian states of Kelantan and Trengganu. There are many quite abstract designs with names such as bird, cat, fish, peacock, frog, and moon. Each kite has a head, a waist, wings, and a base or tail piece. The moon kites, which have a crescent moon for the tail, are the most popular. (See Fig. 5-71.) Some of these big kites measure seven feet, tip to tail, and about six feet across. They are made with a bamboo frame, tied together with string. There are three layers of paper over the frame: one complete cover; a second with the main decorations, drawn by

hand and cut from folded, colored paper; and a third of colored paper that is folded and cut into additional symmetrical, leafy ornaments. Great importance is attached to the beauty of the kite. Each kite maker creates an individual design but uses a combination of traditional ideas. The kites are brightly colored, often with green leaves and red and gold designs, and are completed with the addition of bright paper tassels. It takes about two weeks to make a kite.

The Malays frequently add a special bow to the head of the kite that makes a humming noise when the kite is flown. Traditionally it was constructed of bamboo with string made from the leaf of the mulon tree, or from strips of rattan. Now the bow string is sometimes made of a typewriter ribbon or tape from a cassette, as these materials are more durable and have a louder hum. The big kites are very carefully balanced and two people are needed to launch them. They rise about 500 to 1,500 feet high.

In the old days matches were held between villages for the kite that flew the highest, for the most musical, and for the most ornamental kite. Now international kite festivals are held annually in Malaysia.

In Thailand, contests included maneuvering a kite through a large hoop attached to another kite. Kite fighting was favored by the kings of Thailand for centuries and contests are still held in Bangkok in March and April. There are two teams and they try to force each other's kite to land in their half of a field. These are giant kites and require several people to fly them. There are many different very colorful designs that often represent animals. All but the butterfly kites in Fig. 5-70 were made by hand in Thailand. These small kites (two feet across) were made for children and for export in the 1970s.

In Cambodia, there were also kite-flying festivals. These were royal events for entertainment and in celebration of the rice harvest, especially during the Angkor Empire of the ninth to fifteenth centuries when the kingdom covered not only present-day Cambodia, but much of Thailand and Laos. During the full moon festival, little lamps attached to the kites were carried up into the sky!

Some of the old arts and traditions in Southeast Asia—including kite flying—were disrupted during long years of war. However, kite flying has become a passion again in the parks of Phnom Penh, Cambodia. First it was children engaged in flying small kites imported from Vietnam, where they were still flown, but then the Cambodian Ministry of Culture put an emphasis on reviving lost traditions. In December 2000 a national kite-flying competition brought traditional handmade entries from all twenty-three provinces. There are now annual contests.

Many kites are made in Indonesia, both traditional and contemporary in design—birds, fish, butterflies, and flowers, as well as some in the shape of boats, trucks, and rocketships. Perhaps most unusual are the simple leaf kites made in Bali and in villages along the coast. They were developed to use in fishing, a 2,000-year-old tradition still in use today. A large leaf is rigged as a kite with a line and hook attached to the base, and it is flown out over the water so that the fisherman can reach fish away from the shadow of his boat.

Kites are made in other parts of Asia as well, such as China, Japan, and Taiwan. Fig. 5-70 shows two butterfly kites from Taiwan. Now most kites are made of plastic or nylon.

Fig. 5-73. Jack, ten, draws symmetrical designs on his owl kite with a black marker.

Children enjoy making and decorating the kites inspired by all these examples.

Making Paper Kites

It is difficult now to find paper kites. A teacher can use the photographs and diagrams shown on these pages as inspiration, or purchase some plastic or nylon kites as a springboard for the children's designs. Most kites produced for sale in Asia now are not based on traditional kites. They come from Taiwan or China, and a very few from Southeast Asia. It is sometimes possible to find imported kites from Bali, Indonesia. These brightly colored kites, some very large, are made of a nylon fabric,

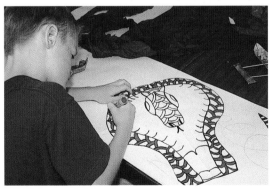

Fig. 5-74. Scott, nine, uses colored markers to fill in the designs he drew on his cobra kite.

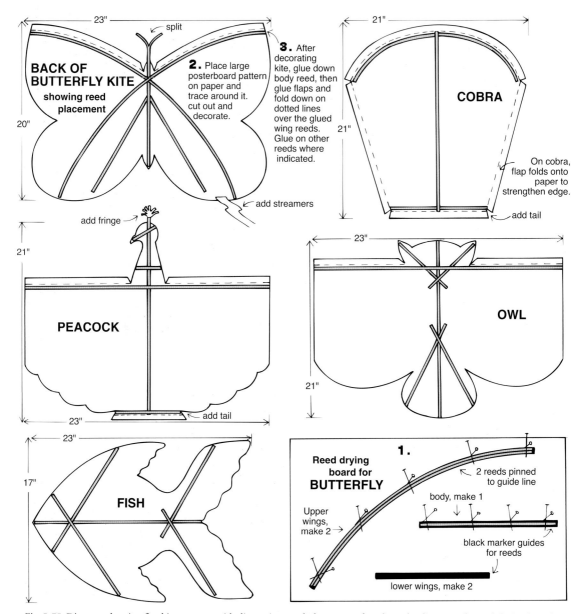

Fig. 5-75. Diagram showing five kite patterns with dimensions and placement of reeds, and a diagram of a reed drying board.

and come in many forms such as dragons, butterflies, bats, and parrots. And as the sport grows in popularity, more sources may become available. Look for them on the World Wide Web.

Whether you are working from actual kites or from photos, trace the outlines of several different designs onto poster board for the students to use as patterns. (Children can also create their own kite design—it should be symmetrical, and about 20 x 24".) If using a real kite as a pattern, examine it to see where the reeds are placed, and add an extra inch of paper (as shown in Fig. 5-75) for flaps that will be glued down over the reeds that run along the edges.

On a large piece of corrugated cardboard, use a black marker to draw lines that are the same length and shape (straight or curved) as the bamboo sticks used in the kite you are copying. Use a different board for each type of kite to be made and mark them—butterfly, cobra, etc.

Soak a one-pound coil of #4 or #5 round reeds for several hours. This is more than enough for a large class. Each student chooses a kite design and cuts the reeds into pieces the same lengths as the lines drawn on the corrugated cardboard. Pin the soaked reeds into place over the lines, making a tent shape, so that the pins cross over the reeds and hold them in place. When dry, they will retain the shape in which they have been pinned. Several reeds can be pinned together over the same line. (You can use bamboo slats from old window shades for straight pieces, instead of straightened reeds.)

Next use one of the patterns to trace the outline of a kite onto white Kraft paper, and cut it out. Draw patterns on the kite with a pencil, and then go over this with permanent black markers. Remind the students that traditional kite designs are usually symmetrical, but in all other respects the students should be encouraged to create their own decorations—the fancier the better. They may want to make feather, scale, or other overall patterns. Fill in the outlines with colored markers or watercolor. If using watercolor, demonstrate how to make the colors bright and deep, avoiding a pale, washed-out effect.

Apply white glue to the reeds and place them on the back of the kite. Their position will differ with each design. Put glue on the flaps and fold them down over the reeds.

Add peacock and cobra tails of crepe paper, colored Kraft paper, or ripstop nylon (sometimes available at places that sell recycled materials). The Thai peacock kite has a tail 5' long, and the cobra tail is 25' long! But students will be satisfied with much more reasonable lengths. Additional feather or scale designs may be drawn on the tails. Streamers of colored tissue paper can be added to the bottom of butterfly wings. The butterfly feelers are made by splitting the tip of the reed with a mat knife. (Only the teacher should do this.) If this is done while the reed is damp, the feelers can be pinned into outward curves.

Fig. 5-76. Fourth-grade kites: *Butterfly* by Samantha, *Rainbow Peacock* by Athena. Photos by David Wade. *Cobra* and *Fish* kites by sixth-grade students.

Attach a string for hanging the kite from the ceiling or a wall. In Malaysia today, some highly decorative kites are made exclusively for display. The emphasis in this project is not on balancing and flying the kites, but on their colorful design and symmetry. However, there are books available that show how to make simple kites that do fly. (See the bibliography.)

The following project was developed and written by Pat Jackunas.

Making Kites with Younger Children

The children should see examples of real kites if possible, or colorful photographs of them. Talk with them about symmetry and what animals or birds would be good subjects for kites.

Give each student a piece of thin white paper (such as Kraft paper), 12 x 18", and ask them to fold it in half like a book. They should begin their kite design by making a pencil outline, starting at the top of the fold and working out toward the open sides of the paper, ending back on the fold at the bottom of the paper. This creates half of an animal. After the outline is done, check to be sure the fold is still intact (the line for a neck, for instance, shouldn't go all the way up to the fold, or the head will be cut off when the design is cut out). They then draw other designs on that half of their animal, such as feathers, scales, or abstract patterns. When the pencil design is finished, have them go over it with a black marker.

Next, the students take their still-folded designs to the window, turn them over to the blank side, and using the light from the window, trace the other side with a marker so that when the kites are opened up the designs will be symmetrical. The kites can be cut out now, while they are still folded.

Open up the kite and use colored markers, tempera, or watercolors to fill in the design. When all the color has been applied, turn them over and tape basketry reed, strips of bamboo from an old shade, or thin strips of cardboard to the back for support. Add streamers of tissue or crepe paper for tails on birds, butterflies, and other creatures.

Fig. 5-77. Second-grade students, from left, Lilly, AJ, and Allie, take their still-folded paper and place the side with designs against the window so the lines can be traced onto the blank side of the kite.

Fig. 5-78. Henry, eight, uses markers to make bright, symmetrical designs on his butterfly kite.

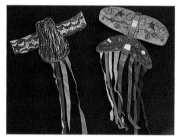

Fig. 5-79. Two second-grade kites—*Owl*, by James; *Butterfly*, by Avery.

Fig. 5-80. Saddle cover, 400 BC, from Pazyryk (46 x 23"). This beautiful felt was designed to fit on top of a saddle. Courtesy of The State Hermitage Museum, St. Petersburg, Russia.

THE FELT RUGS OF CENTRAL AND NORTHERN ASIA

Felt is made when wool, usually from sheep, is gently worked with water and soap. During the felting process the individual wool fibers, which have microscopic scales, begin to move together and form a fabric that with further movement shrinks into a very sturdy thick material. Felt is a natural insulating fabric, warm in winter, and providing protection against the sun in summer. Made in ancient times, it is thought to have originated in Central Asia, and later spread to the Middle East, Scandinavia, and Russia. In 1929, scientists excavated a burial site in Pazyryk, Siberia, and found numerous felt objects preserved in permafrost, dating back to 600 BC: wall hangings with intricate designs in rich dyed colors, boots, hats, clothes, decorations, saddle blankets, and tents. Archaeologists have also found fragments of felt made in prehistoric times that may be 5000 to 8000 years old.

Felt was essential to the nomadic people of Central Asia and still is to many groups. The nomads lived on the vast deserts and plains, herding their sheep, goats, and horses. They used fleece from their sheep to make utilitarian and beautiful felts. Their houses, called yurts, were constructed of felt over lattice frames, and could be taken apart and rolled up when they moved on. They also made hats and coats and boots of felt. Children had felt toys. Some older people in Europe and Asia today remember childhood experiences making their own felt balls from animal hair (mostly cow hair). They made the balls using a unique method—they kept spitting on the hair as they rolled it in their hands, until the ball became hard. These days, in many parts of the world, felted balls are made with wool, warm water, and soap, in colored patterns.

And they made rugs—especially rugs! Felt rugs are still being made today in Central and Northern Asia. Different regions have their own rug-making techniques and traditions. Mongolian felt carpets have a quilted design sometimes combined with appliqué. In Kyrgyzstan, cut felt designs are sewn onto a

Fig. 5-81. An alakiiz rug being laid out in Kyrgyzstan. The colored wool designs are laid on a felt backing. (Turkmen artists do the opposite, laying the design first, on a straw mat, and then layering wool on top of the design.) Photo by Mary Badcock.

Fig. 5-82. Kyrgyzstan women have rolled up and wrapped the wool, and are getting ready to roll it back and forth on a reed mat. Photo by Mary Badcock.

Fig. 5-83. Members of a Turkmen nomad family displaying a beautiful rug with traditional designs in front of their yurt. Photo by Mari Nagy.

felted backing. Then cording is sewn onto the felt where the colors join, and designs are sometimes edged with braid or decorative stitches. These rugs are called *shirdak*. The Kyrgyz also make rugs called *alakiiz* employing a method similar to the Turkmen rugs described below. (See Figs. 5-81 and 5-82.)

The method used by the Turkmen people is one of the easiest to adapt for young students. Turkmen people are descended from Turks who left Mongolia in the tenth century. They now live in the southern part of Turkmenistan and in Iran and Afghanistan. Their beautiful rugs are family treasures saved for generations. The rugs are designed with

Fig. 5-84. A Turkmen rug with ram's horn and running wave designs. Courtesy of Beth and Larry Beede. Photo by Larry Beede.

Fig. 5-85. Laying out a traditional Turkmen carpet design at an international workshop in Kesckemet, Hungary, under the direction of Turkmen artist Ogulsirin Gurbangulieva. Photo by Mari Nagy.

the straw mat and rug are rolled up together into a bundle. The bundle, with the wool inside, is then tied closed. Then another rope is wrapped around it so that two people can roll it back and forth to start the felting. Periodically the roll is opened, the rug turned, flipped and re-rolled. Eventually the rug is felted enough that it can be rolled without the mat. The women kneel and roll the rug with their forearms. The whole process can take one to two days to create a beautiful, sturdy rug.

traditional inlaid geometric patterns that have been passed down from mother to daughter. Each rug, however, is unique in the way in which the dots, curves, spirals, and lines are placed within the border. Some of these design elements have names such as wave design, ram's horns, and tree of life.

In designing their rugs, the Turkmen use both natural wool (gray, black, white, and brown) and dyed wool (mostly blue, red, and yellow). The rugs are made only by women for their own use. (In some countries, such as Turkey, felt making is done by men.) The raw wool is combed first to separate the fibers, using a plank with rows of metal spikes. The design is then outlined in colored wool on a straw mat. Next, the pattern and background are filled in with colored or white wool. Layers of white wool are then placed on top, covering the design. The last layer will become the back of the rug. The wool is sprinkled with water, and

There is a worldwide resurgence of interest in the art of making felt. Rugs, clothing, and many other practical items are now being made. Felt artists also create wall hangings and sculptural works that have no purpose other than to please the eye and the sense of touch.

Fig. 5-86. Contemporary felt half-mask of wool and silk by Elisabeth Schuman. 1990. 10 x 9½". Photograph by Kevin Shields.

Fig. 5-87. Four kindergartners, from left, Kya, Allyson, Travis, and Taylor, enjoy dipping wool into the warm soapy water.

Fig. 5-88. Janet Cathey, felt artist, shows (from left) Garret, Sarah, Molly and David how to gently cup the wool in their hands.

Fig. 5-89. Amanda and Tucker roll the almost-finished felt balls between their palms.

The following projects were written and field tested by Janet Cathey, art teacher and felt artist.

Making Felt Balls and Mini Rugs

If there is an artist in your community who works with felt, he or she may assist with this project. However, using these instructions, anyone can make simple felt items.

Wool from Merino, Corriedale, or Romney sheep will felt faster than wool of other breeds. If you have wool from some unknown breed, perform this simple test to tell whether it will felt well: pull out a small handful, squeeze it in your fist, and open your hand. If the fleece stays compacted, it will felt quickly. If it springs back easily, it will be slower to felt. Sources for felting wool can be found on page 270. In general, natural colors are less expensive and fine designs can be made in brown, black, and white.

Children who are allergic to wool should wear rubber gloves while doing these projects.

Felt Balls

The easiest way for children aged 4–6 to make felt is for them to mold wool three-dimensionally in their hands. Felt balls are a satisfying and quick project with a fun result. In fact, for all ages, making felt balls is the best introduction to the felting process.

Start with cleaned and carded wool fleece. Carded wool has been processed so that the fibers are separated and aligned in the same direction. For a class of twenty students you will need approximately ¾ lb. of mixed colors. Each child needs one quite large handful of wool. Wrap a piece of *wool* yarn around their handful in all directions to hold it together during the felting. Then gently thin another piece of fleece by pulling it apart a bit, and place it around the outside of the wrapped wool. For multicolored balls use overlapping colored wool for these last thin pieces.

Prepare a dishpan ⅓ full of hot soapy water. Use a skin-friendly liquid soap. Holding the wool ball in two cupped hands, place it underwater. Carefully lift it out, and *without squeezing*, roll the ball gently from hand to hand, over the dishpan, to catch the dripping water. Maintain the round shape of the ball by keeping the hands cupped at all times. Continue to gently dip into the water and roll the ball from hand to hand. After a few minutes the ball will become a little firmer. At that

Fig. 5-90. A colorful array of felt balls made by kindergartners.

point have the children begin to gently roll the ball between their hands: take the ball in the palm of one hand, place the other hand on top of the ball, and move the ball by making circular movements with both hands. After a few more minutes, they can lightly squeeze the balls, and roll them more vigorously as long as the round shape is maintained. Throughout this process, the wool is becoming more compacted, and the ball will shrink. The ball may be finished at any point, depending on the student's preference for a larger, soft ball, or a smaller, firm ball that will bounce. When the ball is felted to the preferred density, rinse and squeeze it under running water to remove the soap, reshape it by hand, and let it air dry.

Making Mini Felt Rugs, Turkmen Style

Older children, second grade and up, will have the dexterity to make small felt rugs using the Turkmen inlaid technique to create designs. This project is best done in three sessions: the first for studying traditional Turkmen rugs and creating their own design, the second for laying out the wool patterns, and the third for felting the fibers to create the mini rug. For a class of twenty students you will need approximately ¾ of a pound of colored (natural or dyed) roving,

and 1¼ pounds of white batting. (Roving and batting are described below.)

Show the students some rugs (or pictures of rugs) from Turkmenistan and discuss the typical design elements. Provide 9 x 12" paper so they can draw a design for their rugs. Keep in mind that the final product will shrink an inch or two in both dimensions. Most Turkmen rugs have a border. Encourage the students to draw a border around the inside edge of their papers. Using wide markers will help them to make simple, large designs. (Intricate designs will be too difficult for students of this age.) They can use traditional Turkmen patterns such as dots, spirals, waves, or tree of life, and symbols of their own to create a design that is pleasing to them.

Fig. 5-91. Some traditional Turkmen rug designs.

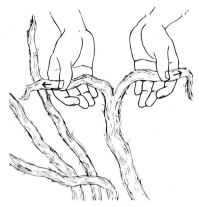

Fig. 5-92. In separating roving, always start at the top. These lengths will each be divided at least once more to create pencil-thin roving.

Place the paper with the rug design under the center of a piece of muslin, cut to about 15 x 30". (Old sheets or pillow cases can be used instead of muslin.) The marker design and border from the paper should show through the cloth. Trace the design, in permanent marker, on the cloth. (If the design does not show through, hold the paper and cloth up against a window to trace.) Discard the paper pattern and place a small towel under the muslin. This creates friction on the tabletop for easier rolling later.

The Turkmen use an inlay technique with wool fleece when creating their felt rug designs. First, they lay out the surface pattern and then they add layers of backing. This surface pattern is most easily accomplished with wool fleece that is in roving form or tops form. Roving

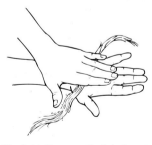

Fig. 5-93. Dampen the hands slightly and roll the pencil roving just once or twice, gently, between the palms to reduce frizz and impart a very slight twist.

is wool that has been combed so that all the fibers run in one direction. It comes rolled up in a skein, and is like very thick unspun yarn. The teacher should separate the colored roving into long pencil-thick lengths. (See Fig. 5-92.) Place the lengths of wool on the cloth along the drawn designs. If the students dampen their hands slightly and gently twirl the roving just once or twice between the palms of their hands it will be easier to put it in place. (See Fig. 5-93.) It will be most in keeping with the spirit of Turkmen rugs if the colors used are

Fig. 5-94. Dillon places colored pencil roving over the designs on the cloth.

the traditional red, yellow-orange, black, brown, and dark blue. Fill in between the colored designs with white wool. Fitting white wool snugly on either side of the designs will create a more distinct pattern on the finished piece. This completes the first layer of the rug.

The second and third layers of the rug are most quickly and easily laid down if white wool batts are used. Wool batts (usually used for quilting) are wide and flat. The thick batts will need to be peeled apart into thin ¼–½" layers. (See Fig. 5-96.) Lay one layer of white

Fig. 5-95. Caleb fits white wool snugly around his colored wool rug design.

batting on top of the patterned layer. Then cover it with a second layer of batting with the fibers aligned at right angles to the first. Finally, fold the edges of the cloth in toward the center, over the wool, making a packet. Be sure the cloth is folded snugly at the edges.

There are alternate ways to prepare the design for felting. In the accompanying photos you can see that the students have drawn their designs on a piece of cloth only a little larger than their rug designs. The edges of the cloth were brought up over the batting as far as they would go, and a piece of flexible nylon screen-

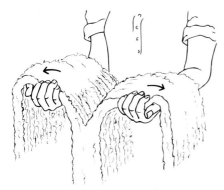

Fig. 5-96. Dividing a batt into two layers that may need further division to create thin, fluffy, ½" layers.

ing of the same size as the wool was placed on top. This is fine too, though the edges of the finished piece may be a little uneven.

Fill a plastic squirt bottle with one tablespoon of dishwashing liquid and hot water (but not so hot as to scald children's hands). Squirt the soapy water onto the packet. With your hands press down gently but firmly. When the whole packet is wet through, but *not dripping*, tightly roll it up (including the towel). You can place a 1" dowel inside the roll as an aid for the first few rollings until the pattern stabilizes. Then remove it, since it slows the felting process.

Fig. 5-97. Brooke put two layers of white batting over her design, folded the edges of the sheeting over the wool, and placed screening on top. Then she wet the wool with hot soapy water from the soap bottle, and rolled it up. She now rolls it back and forth. A piece of screening on the tabletop adds friction.

Now you can begin to felt. If the table surface is slippery, extra towels, screening, or pieces of rubber such as bathmats placed on the table will create more friction for easier rolling. Roll the felt using gentle pressure, back and forth on the tabletop about twenty times. Unroll the felt, then rotate the whole packet ¼ turn, roll up from the new edge and roll again. Periodically unroll the packet and again re-roll from a different side each time. Unroll, flip the piece over, and roll from all four sides, one at a time, ten to twenty times each. If puffy areas are noticed during

Fig. 5-98. Billy finds that the cloth peels easily from his mini rug. He will remove the cloth and continue to roll the rug in the towel until the felt becomes sturdy.

the rolling, squirt a little more soapy water on those spots.

The rug should be felting! That is, its fabric should start to hold together. If some of the wool is sticking to the cloth rather than to the rug itself, then more rolling is needed. It is important to continue to roll very *gently* until

Fig. 5-99. Second-grade felt mini rugs inspired by Turkmen design elements. From top left, lattice design by Kasey, spiral and dot designs by Dillon, *Tree of Life* by Josh, and *Sun Wheel* by Caleb. The edges were left untrimmed.

none of the wool sticks to the cloth. Once all the wool peels easily from the cloth, remove the cloth. Check to see if design elements or borders have shifted. If they have, carefully pull them back into place, squirt on a little more soapy water, and rub gently on that area with a flat palm. At this time, if you wish, you can use scissors to trim off any uneven edges from the partially felted rug. Then continue to roll the rug in the towel, using a bit more pressure, until the felt is holding together well, and feels like a sturdy fabric.

All together, the rolling may take half to three quarters of an hour. You can tell if it is "done" by pulling up gently on the surface fibers with thumb and finger. If it pulls up easily, more rolling is needed. Once the desired firmness is reached, gently rinse and squeeze the rug under warm running water, until it is free of all soap. Stretch it into the desired shape, and lay it flat to dry.

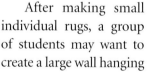

Fig. 5-100. Three felt mini rugs by fourth-graders: from top, Grace, Marion, and Jodi.

After making small individual rugs, a group of students may want to create a large wall hanging or rug for the school library or classroom. This is probably best done with the help of a professional felt artist. Minimize the cost by using less dyed wool and more natural colors.

Fig. 6-1. An old and intricate model of a double-hulled canoe made in Fiji. It has a platform with a small shelter. These canoes were used for traveling long distances between islands, for exploration, and for colonizing newly discovered islands. © Peabody Essex Museum/Photograph by Mark Sexton.

6 THE ARTS OF OCEANIA

"Where there is artistic excellence, there is human dignity."
—Contemporary Maori proverb

The area in the South Pacific that is called Oceania contains the somewhat arbitrarily grouped islands of Polynesia, Micronesia, and Melanesia, and is also sometimes extended to include Australia.

There is evidence that by 35,000 years ago the peoples of Australia and New Guinea began to colonize the islands to the east of New Guinea—part of the group of islands that includes the Solomon Islands, and is now called Melanesia.

Polynesian and Micronesian islands were settled still later, from approximately 1500 BC to AD 1000, by people from mainland China called Austronesians. There were, during this time, continued cycles of colonization, growth, and overpopulation, which would lead to more exploration and settlement of newly discovered islands. The exact dates of arrival at the different islands are still being researched by archaeologists. On the long trips between islands, voyagers navigated with incredible accuracy by observing the positions of the stars, sun, and moon and using their knowledge of the prevailing winds and ocean currents.

The islands of Oceania have varied climates, depending on their elevation and the prevailing winds and ocean currents. Earthquakes and volcanic eruptions are frequent. Geologically, there are four types of islands: volcanic (such as the islands of Hawaii), sea-level coral reefs (as in the Marshall Islands), elevated reefs (such as Makatea in the Tuamotu Archipelago), and islands of continental origin (such as New Guinea and Fiji). Some islands are mixtures of these types.

The societies that evolved on these islands varied considerably because they were affected by different climates, resources, sizes, and degrees of isolation. Many arts were developed, often reflecting the unique resources available on a particular island. Most pieces were created to be *used* as meaningful and integral parts of their societies—for religious purposes, often secret or sacred; for chiefs and other powerful people in the community; and for ceremonies such as marriage or rites of passage. Household objects and clothing were also decorated, and items were made for personal adornment. Many of these arts were charged with a spiritual power called *mana*, a concept widespread among the peoples of the Pacific islands. These works vary from the monumental stone statues on Easter Island to the exquisite craftsmanship of brilliant feather cloaks for royalty and men of high rank in Hawaii. Fine work in wood was done on many islands, such as the carved bowls and figures of black wood inlaid with mother-of-pearl in the Solomon Islands. Intricate carved and pierced wood designs were used for canoe prows and in the architecture of buildings made by Maoris in New Zealand. Powerful carved masks were made by people of the Sepik region of Papua New Guinea. Extremely fine woven textiles were created in the Caroline Islands. Pottery was also made on some of the islands, and beautiful items were carved of bone and tortoise shells. Plant fibers were plaited into mats or made into baskets. Tattooing developed into a fine art in the Marquesas. On most of these islands clothing was created from a bark cloth called *tapa,* and many different beautiful methods of decorating it were devised.

Many of the traditional arts of Oceania ceased after the arrival of Europeans in the South Pacific, and today they can be seen only in museums. Quite a number, however, are still engaged in after all these years. In addition, many non-traditional contemporary artists have a renewed interest in their heritage, finding inspiration in the old arts and referring to them in their paintings and sculpture. The arts continue to flourish throughout this area today.

From such a rich store it is very difficult to select just a few projects for this book. Two arts have been chosen that were of necessity common to most of the island peoples: the art of canoe building, and the art of tapa cloth making. In addition, representative of the many arts created in smaller areas of Oceania, the inlaid shell work of Belau in the Caroline Islands has been included.

HAWAIIAN CANOES

The exploration of the Pacific and the colonization of the islands would have been impossible without the development of outrigger canoes and double-hulled canoes (two almost equal-sized canoes connected with booms). They were used for colonization, and these amazing vessels crossed as many as 2,000 miles of ocean. The double canoes incorporated a raised platform in the middle, secured to the cross booms, that was roofed over to protect from sun and rain. These large canoes carried many people, with their chickens, pigs, dogs, supplies for many days at sea, and plants for cultivation. The travelers even cooked at sea on stone fireplaces placed on the platform.

The Hawaiian islands were one of the last archipelagos to be settled. The double canoes that first reached these islands in about AD 500 may have looked much like the model from Fiji shown in Fig. 6-1, but the settlers probably arrived from the Marquesas Islands and a little later from Tahiti. Until the islands were brought under one rule in 1810 by King Kamehameha I, there were a number of individual chiefdoms. These were thriving communities, with farmers raising such crops as bananas, yams, and taro. They had fine shelters and made clothing of tapa cloth. There were musical instruments and storytellers and the religion was one of respect for nature and for their common ancestors. It gave strength and meaning to their lives.

Canoes were as much a part of daily life as cars are today. People used them for fishing, for visiting, for exploring, and for recreation. Surfing (riding in on the front of a great wave) with outrigger canoes was at first a necessity—people had to go out beyond the breakers to

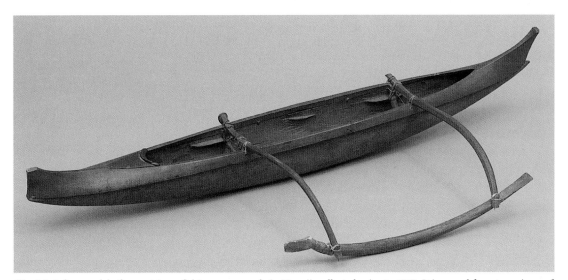

Fig. 6-2. A fine model of an outrigger fishing canoe made in Hawaii, collected prior to 1913. It is carved from two pieces of wood: a hull, painted black, and a lighter gunwale. The outrigger is lashed to the hull. Carved cleats can be seen where seats would be placed. Parts of bow and stern pieces are missing. © Peabody Essex Museum/Photograph by Mark Sexton.

Fig. 6-3. Sepia/watercolor of outrigger sailing canoes off Niiau, Hawaii, by John Webber, an artist who traveled with Captain Cook in 1778–79. Courtesy Bishop Museum. (Three small discolorations have been removed from this image.)

fish and return—and then it became a popular sport also. Races were frequently held—even the chiefs participated. The canoes could be paddled up to a speed of eleven miles an hour. Surfing with carefully crafted boards of wiliwili wood, stained black with preservative and rubbed with coconut oil, was also very popular in old Hawaii. This sport is now engaged in worldwide.

Polynesian canoes varied in construction, and some were elaborately carved or decorated. In Hawaii canoes featured a very basic, extremely seaworthy design. Fragile decoration would not stand up in pounding surf. The canoes varied in size according to use: small canoes were made for women and children, larger ones for fishing, and even larger ones for travel between the islands, exploration, or war. The biggest could be up to 108' in length and carry many men. There were also long, narrow canoes for racing.

Each canoe was made from a single log, usually cut from the massive koa tree. The canoe was roughed out, with stone adzes, high in the forest, and then dragged down to the beach. There a shed was built in which work on the canoe was completed. The hulls were shaved to just 1½" thick, or even less, making the finished canoes lightweight. It is a mark of very fine craftsmanship that this work was accomplished using only stone tools. The canoe was sanded smooth by a succession of abrasive stones, lava, and coral, graded from coarse to fine, and then preserved and waterproofed with a mixture of plant juices and charcoal.

Having been carved from tree trunks, the canoes were round-bottomed and very unstable. To stabilize them, the outrigger (float) was invented, probably by the ancient Austronesians. In Hawaii the outrigger was made of a curved branch of very buoyant wili-wili wood and connected by two booms to the canoe. These were lashed on with cordage made of coconut husk fibers. The outrigger was traditionally placed on the port, or left, side.

Gunwales were lashed to the canoe to raise the sides and keep water from entering. End pieces at the bow and stern served the same purpose. Seats were placed on cleats in the canoe, and a bow cover was created. Pandanus leaf mats were stitched together to create triangular sails that were rigged to the mast (positioned at the bow outrigger boom) with the sharpest angle at the bottom. One side of the sail was lashed to the mast and the other to a slender sprit boom that rose at a curved angle. The tip of this boom was tied to the tip of the mast. A rope ran down the mast and could be used to adjust the sail to catch the wind. Paddles were made of one piece of wood.

Every step of making a canoe—from cutting huge trees, maneuvering the heavy log down to the shore, and carving the canoes with sharp tools—was dangerous, and the people held ceremonies and feasts at each stage, seeking help from their gods. A final ceremony celebrated the successful completion of the canoe.

Fig. 6-3 shows a Hawaiian outrigger sailing canoe that was drawn by John Webber, the artist who traveled with Captain James Cook in 1778–79. At this time, Cook estimated that his ships were greeted by as many as two thousand canoes, paddled with great skill by men, women, and children.

But his arrival marked the beginning of the end for many traditions, and soon few native canoes were built in the old way. However, in 1875, the Hawaiian King Kalakaua I promoted boat-racing events including canoes. Outrigger canoe racing continues to be very popular today. Though most of today's canoes are made of fiberglass, a few are built of koa wood but worked with modern tools in place of the stone adzes. (See Fig. 6-4.)

Fig. 6-4. A Healani Canoe Club crew competes using their outrigger canoe made from koa wood, in the 1981 Kualoa-to-Hawaii race. Photo taken in Kaneohe Bay, Oahu, Hawaii. Photo: © Carl Shaneff.

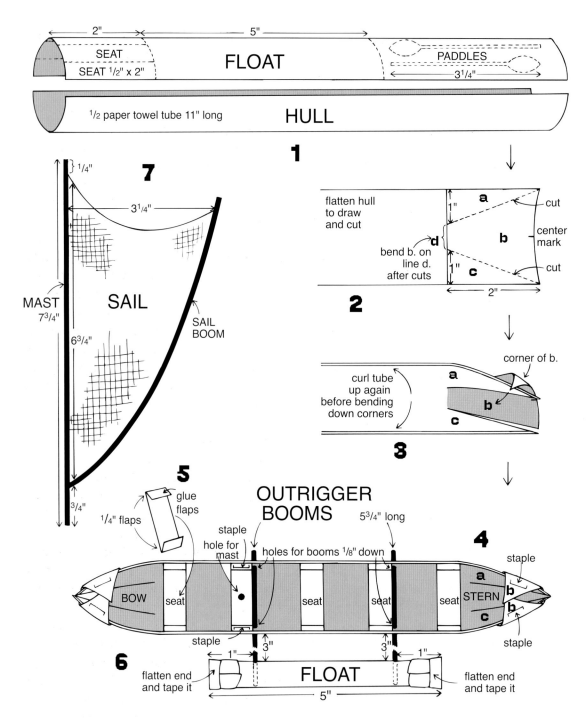

2"   5"
SEAT
SEAT ¹/₂" x 2"
FLOAT
PADDLES
3¹/₄"

¹/₂ paper towel tube 11" long
HULL

1

flatten hull to draw and cut
1"
a
cut
center mark
b
bend b. on line d. after cuts
1"
d
c
cut
2"

2

curl tube up again before bending down corners
corner of b.
a
b
c

3

7
¹/₄"
3¹/₄"
MAST
7³/₄"
SAIL
6³/₄"
SAIL BOOM
³/₄"

5
glue flaps
¹/₄" flaps
OUTRIGGER BOOMS
5³/₄" long
staple hole for mast
holes for booms ¹/₈" down

4
staple
BOW
seat
seat
seat
seat
STERN
a
b
b
c
staple
staple

6
flatten end and tape it
FLOAT
1"
3"
3"
1"
flatten end and tape it
5"

Fig. 6-5. Making an outrigger sailing canoe model. Start at the top and follow the numbers 1–7 (more or less clockwise). Supplementary directions are in the text.

152   The Arts of Oceania

Making Outrigger Sailing Canoe Models

Children in old Hawaii probably made model canoes from materials at hand—coconut bloom sheaths and folded ti leaves.[1] Today's children can make models from found materials also, as shown in Fig. 6-5. This plan is for a very simple model of an outrigger sailing canoe, but it illustrates dramatically the stabilizing effect of the outrigger. It is suggested that the teacher make a model first for the children to see (but don't float it—let that part be a surprise). Follow the numbers, clockwise, in the diagram.

Fig. 6-6. Gina, nine, has folded her canoe ends and is stapling them together.

The Hull

1. Cut a paper towel tube in half lengthwise.
2. Flatten one half of the tube and draw lines, as in the diagram, on the inner side of one end. Make two cuts on the dotted lines. Mark the center of the edge of *b*. Bend *b* up on line *d* and lay it back again. Repeat step 2 on the other end of the tube.
3. Curl hull up again if it has flattened out. Bend point *a* in on top of *b* and bring up *b* until the tip of *a* touches the mark on the center edge of *b*. (It will extend a bit beyond it.) Hold it there with thumb and forefinger. With the other hand, fold corner of piece *b* up and down over point *a*. Bend *c* into the center in the same way and fold the other corner of *b* up and down over point *c*.

4. Staple folds. Fold the other end of the canoe in the same manner, and staple it.

The Seats

5. Cut 2" from the end of the remaining half of the tube (see #1 in the diagram). From this piece cut five strips, ½ x 2". Fold up the ends to make ¼" flaps as in #5. Be sure the canoe hull is rounded up and not flattened out. Put glue on the outside of the flaps of two seats and insert them at each end, just before the ends curve in. Glue and place one seat in the middle; the remaining two go between the middle and the end seats. The second seat from the bow holds the mast. Before putting it in the canoe, place the cardboard on a piece of wood and make a hole in the center with a hammer and nail (the same diameter as the mast). After gluing this seat in, reinforce it with a staple in each flap. The seats should be about 1" apart in the hull. Set aside to dry.

The Outrigger

6. To make the outrigger, or float, cut off 5" from the remaining half of the tube (see #1 in the diagram). Roll this up as tightly as possible. (Rolling and re-rolling will get it tighter.) Pinch the ends flat and bind them with masking tape. Seen sideways, this gives a slight upward curve to the tips of the float. If you wish, paint the tape brown to blend with the float when, later, wax has turned all the cardboard brown. If the paint doesn't stick to the tape, add a drop of detergent. Turn the float on edge and poke a nail into the float 1" from each end. (Do not go all the way through the float.) This is best done if the students help each other: one holds the float on its edge, while the other gently hammers the nail into the float. The float is connected to the canoe with two booms. Put glue

[1]Mitchell, Donald D. Kilolani, *Resource Units in Hawaiian Culture.* Honolulu: The Kamehamena Schools Press, 1992.

Fig. 6-7. Olena, a parent volunteer, applies hot wax to a canoe. Wax should always be heated in a pot that sits in another pot of water. When it is hot enough it will sink into the cardboard and turn it dark brown. This wax shows some white, so is not quite hot enough.

on the ends of two 5¾" pieces of bamboo and insert them into the float. Make sure they are in line and parallel, and let dry. Do not insert them into the canoe yet.

The Sail

7. Cut a piece of burlap in the shape of a sharp triangle with one straight side 6¾" long, an incurved top 3¼" across, and another long side that curves down to the bottom. The Hawaiian sails have the sharpest point at the bottom—the opposite of Western sails, so it will look upside down. This is an unusual shape, and the teacher might make a cardboard pattern for the children to trace around with white chalk.

Cut a piece 7¾" long from a bamboo skewer (this is most easily done with metal snips). *A note of caution: Bamboo skewers have very sharp points, and these should be cut off by the teacher before the students work with the bamboo.* Glue this mast along the straight edge of the burlap. Leave ¼" free above the sail tip, which will leave ¾" free at the bottom. Then, for the sail boom, gently bend another piece of bamboo repeatedly until it retains a slight curve. It will be less likely to break while being bent if it is first soaked in water overnight. Or, instead, use a

flexible #5 or #6 reed for this purpose. Glue this sail boom to the other, upward curved edge, and cut off the top ¼" beyond the sail tip. Put glue along the top edge of the sail to keep it from fraying. Set aside to dry on wax paper.

Waxing

Melt wax in a can that is set in a pan of hot water. *Never heat wax directly over a heat source.* A parent or assistant teacher should always be beside the waxing pot. Brush melted wax over the entire canoe, inside and out, and over the float. Pay special attention to filling all cracks. The wax should be hot enough to penetrate the cardboard and turn it brown. If it is not, the wax will turn the surface white and crack off easily.

When cool, float the canoes (without sail or outrigger) in pans of water—disposable aluminum roasting pans are fine. Then try adding the sail. Place a piece of non-drying modeling clay underneath the hole in the second seat and poke the mast through the seat into the clay. Set the canoe in water again—it will tip over immediately! The students will see the need to solve this problem.

Remove the sail. Then punch four holes in the hull ⅛" down from the gunwales (the top edge of the hull). (See #6 in the diagram.) To do

Fig. 6-8. Emma uses modeling clay to make figures for her outrigger sailing canoe.

this, place the hull on its side on a block of wood and, using a nail and hammer, punch from the inside, making a hole the same size as the bamboo booms. The first two holes should be at the back edge of the second seat, one on each side of the canoe; the second two holes are placed where the second boom falls along the hull after the first boom has been inserted a short way into the first hole. Insert the booms through both holes. The Hawaiian outrigger is always situated on the left of the hull.

Fig. 6-9. Demyan's outrigger sailing canoe navigates a roasting pan with two paddlers and one passenger.

Insert the sail again and try sailing the canoe. Eureka! Children can blow on the sails to make the outrigger canoe zip across the water. They can model people from clay and make canoe paddles for them out of the remaining cardboard. (See #1 for paddle shapes.) The paddles should be waxed also.

This project can be simplified for younger children if the teacher cuts the tube in half first, and draws the lines they are to cut, or makes a form to place at the end of the tube which they can trace to get the lines to cut and bend. Older children can use rulers and follow the diagram to draw the lines. (You may photocopy the diagram and enlarge it.) This basic idea can also be expanded according to the age and interest of the students. Since real outriggers are lashed to the gunwales, not poked through holes, older children can sew the booms on to the gunwales with heavy thread. The booms may even be curved on the ends by soaking the skewers and pinning them

into a curve on cardboard and letting them dry overnight. Then the booms can enter the float from the top (as in Fig. 6-2). Rigging can be added using thick thread. A double voyaging canoe can be made by connecting two canoes with booms and constructing a little platform with a hut on top of the booms. Such canoes do not need outrigger floats since the second canoe acts as the stabilizer.

TAPA

The art of making and decorating barkcloth, or tapa, was widespread throughout the South Pacific. Each island had its own name for the cloth, but in the nineteenth century the name

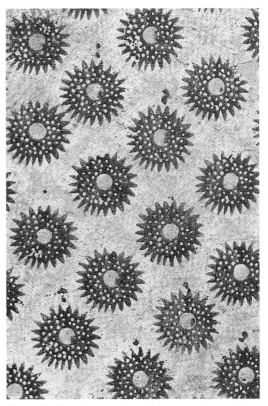

Fig. 6-10. Hawaiian tapa cloth with stamped sea urchin design, 19th century. Collected prior to 1938. © Peabody Essex Museum/Photograph by Mark Sexton.

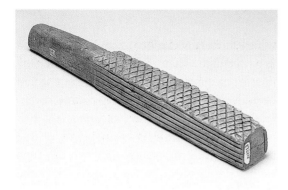

Fig. 6-11. Wooden beater for making tapa cloth from the Cook Islands, collected between 1928 and 1932. The beater shows two different surfaces—one with lines, one with cross-hatching. © Peabody Essex Museum/Photograph by Mark Sexton.

"tapa" came to be used by Europeans for all barkcloth. It is derived from the name used for the undecorated margin of Samoan barkcloth, *tapa*, and the Hawaiian name, *kapa*.

Tapa was an integral part of community life—it provided clothing, bed covers, and mosquito barriers in houses. On many islands

it was used for religious ceremonies. Special cloths were made for royalty and people in high positions, and other types of tapa were produced for common use. Tapa was made in great quantities for gifts and used in rituals and ceremonies, such as marriages, births, or funerals. Large bales of tapa were exchanged and stored in the houses of chiefs as evidence of wealth.

The details of making tapa varied somewhat among the different island societies, but the basic process was the same. The paper mulberry tree was brought to the South Pacific for this purpose by the ancient Austronesians. Cuttings of the tree were carried in their double canoes, carefully packed in damp leaves, and then planted in rows on the newly settled islands and skillfully nurtured. Other trees were also used on some islands, especially the breadfruit tree, but the paper mulberry made the best cloth.

The trees were cut when about finger sized in diameter. The bark, split at the bottom, was peeled off in one piece and flattened. The softer inner bark was separated from the darker outside layer in a stream, or with constant application of water, and scraped very carefully with a shell to remove impurities.

On some islands the process of beating the cloth could then begin; on others, the bark was softened by soaking it in

Fig. 6-12. A woman making tapa in Houma village, Tongatapu, Tonga. The narrow strips will become very wide as they are beaten. The anvil is raised off the ground which increases the resonance of the beater hitting the wood. Photograph courtesy of Auckland Museum.

Fig. 6-13. Sample piece of tapa cloth with stamped patterns on a dyed background. Hawaiian Islands, 19th century. © 2002 The Field Museum. Photo by Ron Testa, A108251c.

messages from village to village in this manner. Tapa cloth is fragile and did not last long, so the air was filled with the almost constant melodious sound of beater on anvil as the cloth was being manufactured. Individual homes had roofed sheds for making tapa, but sometimes it was done on a larger scale by a great number of women working together in special, very large houses.

There were two methods for joining tapa strips to create large pieces. In Hawaii and some other islands the cloth was felted together—overlaid and beaten so that the fibers interlocked with no visible seam. On other islands, very large sheets were made by overlapping tapa pieces and gluing the edges together, usually with cassava paste. These pieces could be extraordinarily long, sometimes up to several hundred yards in length,

seawater. In Hawaii it was soaked as long as two weeks and fermented to create a pulp that could be beaten to a veil-like thinness.

The bark strips, sometimes two or three together, were laid on an anvil of hard resilient wood, and pounded with wooden beaters to spread and soften the fibers. The beaters were sometimes round, but usually square sided, with a rounded handle. Each side was patterned or grooved. Initial beating to spread the fibers was with deep, widely spaced grooves, and as the beating progressed, finer, closer spaced grooves were used. A smooth surface was used for the final beating. The bark became thin and spread to many times its original width.

The anvils, set on stones, were hollowed out underneath, which enhanced the sound of the beating. It is said that these sounds carried long distances and women could even send

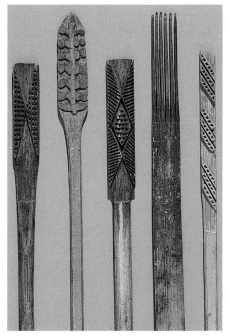

Fig. 6-14. Hawaiian bamboo stamps for decorating tapa cloth. All were collected in the mid nineteenth century, except the liner (second from right), which was collected prior to 1938. © Peabody Essex Museum/Photograph by Mark Sexton.

and were created as gifts for chiefs or to use in ceremonies.

When the tapa was finished it was spread to dry in the sun and weighted down with stones.

Making Paper Tapa Cloth

The process of making tapa cloth is not easily replicated in the classroom. Instead, light brown paper can be altered to give the appearance of a handmade product. Cut Kraft paper or paper bags to the desired size, crumple the paper, unfold it, crumple it again, and repeat this process many times, until the paper has a fine texture and is quite soft. Then spread it out, and iron it. It is now ready for decoration.

Some of the projects call for yellow tapa cloth. Crumple the brown paper and soak it in diluted yellow tempera paint. Very gently squeeze the paper in the tinted water repeatedly until it is softened, and then spread it out on newspaper. While it is still damp, iron it between sheets of newspaper until dry.

The methods of decorating tapa were much more varied among the Pacific islands than the process of making the cloth. Islands in relative isolation developed unique designs and techniques. Some of these are described below.

HAWAIIAN STAMPED TAPA DESIGNS

Hawaiians shared many of the same methods of decorating tapa cloth used by other islanders—painting, immersing the whole cloth in dye,

Fig. 6-15. Some traditional bamboo stamps and the designs they create. The white areas have been carved away, leaving the design raised so that it will take the ink for printing. Different patterns can result from the same stamp, depending on whether the stamp is printed in a vertical, horizontal, or diagonal line.

overlaying one color over another. But only on Hawaii was tapa decorated with wooden or bamboo stamps. Although some large stamps were made of wood (see Fig. 6-10), most were carved on the inner surface of narrow strips of bamboo with a tool made of a shark's tooth (see Fig. 6-14). The designs were linear and geometric. To print the cloth, the stamp was dipped in dye, tapped against the dye bowl to remove excess dye, and then carefully pressed against the cloth. Although the stamps were small, they were applied over and over to create large and effective decorations. A bamboo tool with parallel prongs was used for printing lines. The varied resources in Hawaii produced many dye colors, including red, brown, pink, yellow, black, green, and pale blue, all made from native plant materials; and lavender from sea urchins. Ochres were combined with oil to make red and yellow, and kukui nuts and shells were burned and the soot collected and combined with oil to create black. Pleasant scents were often added to the finished tapa by incorporating sweet-smelling flowers or plant material to the dye, or by sprinkling stored tapa with sandalwood dust or herbs. Although tapa making in Hawaii ceased soon after the arrival of Europeans, researchers are now investigating the old methods, and tapa making is being renewed.

Fig. 6-17. Kate prints her design on prepared paper tapa.

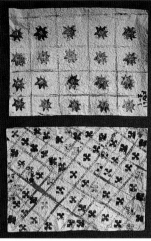

Fig. 6-18. A sea urchin design by Karl (top), and a geometric design by Jennifer, fourth-grade students.

Making Stamped Tapa Designs

This project is very similar to the project on adinkra cloth (see page 9) in that the cloth is decorated with stamps made of plastic or pieces of potato. However, the Hawaiian tapa cloth provides a good lesson in how very small stamps that are printed close together can create continuous elaborate patterns.

Prepare brown or yellow paper as described above.

Cut 3" squares of Styrofoam for larger stamps, and cut strips of Styrofoam ¾ x 5" for the smaller ones. The students should each have one square if they want to make a large figure (such as the sea urchin design) and one or two strips for small stamps. Draw the larger figure on the Styrofoam with a permanent black marker and cut it out. Other appropriate designs include such natural forms as starfish, leaves, sun designs, or flowers. Make spots by poking the Styrofoam with a pencil.

The narrow designs, like those of the bamboo stamps, are also drawn with a black marker, on one end of the strip. The entire form that is to be printed should be black (not an outline). Leave at least 2" at one end for a handle. The white area surround-

Fig. 6-16. Rachel, nine, brushes paint on her Styrofoam stamp and practices printing on newsprint.

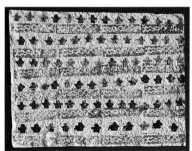

Fig. 6-19. Paper tapa design by Kate, ten.

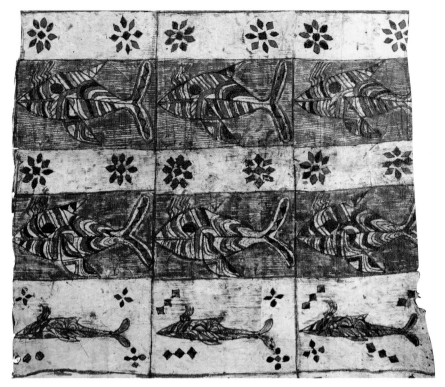

Fig. 6-20. Detail of Tongan tapa cloth (*ngatu*). The fish were rubbed from three *kupesi* tablets and variations were created with overpainting. Collected by Reverend Robert Gordon-Kingan, between 1927-1932. Detail. Photograph courtesy of Auckland Museum.

Have the students practice printing on newsprint. The small stamps must be lined up carefully to create complex designs. The most frequently used colors in Hawaii were red-brown, brown, yellow, and black.

The lines in Hawaiian designs were created with a bamboo liner (see Fig. 6-14). This tool is hard to replicate. It is best to use a strip of corrugated cardboard for a line with a pattern; or mat board for a plain line. (See Fig. 6-18.) Apply paint to the edge and press it on the paper. A precise design is difficult to do freehand. Rather, use a ruler and mark along the edges where the lines are to go, lining up the cardboard with these marks when printing.

ing the design is not to be printed. Push it down firmly with a dowel end, very dull pencil, or end of a paintbrush. This leaves the design raised.

Alternatively, these stamps may be made from potatoes. (See the adinkra cloth project.) To make the small stamps, cut strips that measure ¾ x ¾ x 3". Dry the surface of the potato slice on a piece of newsprint, and draw the design on one end of the potato strip with a black marker, as above. Using plastic knives or table knives, cut the potato away from the black design. Go down about ¼", leaving design raised.

To print, brush the Styrofoam or potato with tempera paint and press on the paper.

THE DESIGN TABLETS OF TONGA

In Tonga, tapa cloth decorations were often made with design tablets called *kupesi*, which were made of sewn-together pandanus leaves. A raised design was created by sewing pieces of coconut leaf mid-rib, bamboo strips, or sennit (twine made of coconut fibers) onto the tablet in geometric designs or flower or animal forms. (See Fig. 6-21.) The tablet was secured to a

Fig. 6-21. Tongan design tablets (*kupesi*), used in decorating tapa cloth, 19th century. A flying fish, and a fish, made of leaf strips and coconut leaflet midribs. Peabody Museum of Archaeology and Ethnology, Harvard University. © 2002 President and Fellows of Harvard College. All rights reserved. Photo by Hillel Burger.

Making Tapa with Design Tablets

Most of the tapa designs of Tonga are based on a grid of squares or rectangles. With a pencil and ruler, work out a grid design on a piece of paper about 9 x 12", creating seven to nine square or rectangular spaces. The design should be smaller than the previously prepared tapa paper so that a margin will be left.

Next, transfer the grid tablet design to a piece of poster board. Apply glue along the lines, either with the glue bottle tip or a brush. (Plumbers' brushes called acid swab brushes work well. Available in hardware stores, they are very strong, easily cleaned, and inexpensive.) Lay string down over the lines, pushing it down and guiding it with a pencil or scissors tip. String should be cut at the intersections, not crossed over. It is important

Fig. 6-22. A few of the traditional designs used in Tonga for decorating tapa cloth.

curved wooden base, the tapa cloth laid over it, and then the cloth was rubbed with a pad of pigmented tapa. This brought out the image of the *kupesi* on the cloth. The natural dyes used were various shades of brown and red-brown made from the bark of koka trees. Sometimes the tablet was entirely wrapped with cords and a small design tablet was fixed over the cords. Both were rubbed at the same time, creating an image with a striped background. After the rubbing was completed, parts of the design were emphasized by over-painting in brown or black. In making large pieces, arrowroot paste was rubbed on as well as dye, so that pieces were joined and decorated at the same time. Design tablets were used quite extensively in Western Polynesia and are still being employed in Tonga on a fairly large scale, where the tapa is used for ceremonies, gifts, and the tourist trade. Very large pieces are made by many women working together. Some of the tapa have even reached a mile in length.

Fig. 6-23. A tablet with a large grid design, three tablets with figures that will be rubbed in the spaces of the grid, and a tablet wound with twine that will be rubbed to make a background behind some of the figures.

Fig. 6-24. Fifth-grade students Ben (left) and Alex use rulers to draw grid designs on their tablets.

Fig. 6-25. Inga has placed a tablet under her paper tapa and is rubbing over it with a brown crayon. She holds the tablet firmly with her left hand so it won't slip under the paper while being rubbed.

Fig. 6-26. Caitlin emphasizes a few parts of her rubbed design with black paint.

to keep the top of the string as free of glue as possible. String with glue on the surface does not give a good rubbing. The best string is quite thin, like old cotton wrapping string. It is hard to make details with thicker string, and it tends to unravel. Set the grid tablet aside to dry.

Create smaller tablets by cutting two or three pieces of poster board that fit the spaces within the grid. On each piece draw a figure. Tongan designs are quite varied and include flowers, trees, sun, moon, animals, fish, and birds. The Tongan figures are not completely naturalistic but incorporate stripes, diamonds, and other embellishments. Purely geometric designs of triangles, diamonds, squares within squares, and stripes are also common. (See Fig. 6-22.) The designs will be repeated in the grid, so a student needs to make only two or three tablets. Paint the penciled figures with glue and apply string to them.

Finally, create another tablet, which will make a striped background, by simply winding string around a piece of cardboard that has been covered with glue. The cardboard should be as wide as the largest space in the grid. (See Fig. 6-23.) Use thicker string to make the work go more quickly. All the tablets should dry for several hours.

To decorate the prepared tapa paper, first place the grid design under it, leaving equal margins. Holding the paper with one hand, rub a brown crayon over the string lines to transfer the grid design to the surface of the paper. Next, place one of the design tablets under one of the spaces and rub. It is easy to place it correctly if the paper and tablet are held up to the light and positioned before putting them down on the table. Fill all the spaces

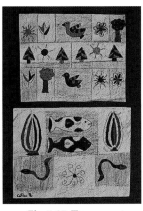

Fig. 6-27. Two paper tapa designs inspired by the tapa of Tonga. The top piece is by Inga, ten, and below is a design by Caitlin, ten.

Fig. 6-28. A paper tapa design by Ali, ten. Notice how much the use of a wrapped tablet, for background texture, adds to the design of all three of these student pieces.

THE FERN DESIGNS OF TAHITI

The Tahitians developed a unique method of decorating tapa by carefully laying ferns and other leaves and blossoms on the surface of a pot of red dye and then placing them on tapa cloth and pressing them down. The cloth was very fine and soft, usually either white or dyed yellow from turmeric roots.

Beautiful tapa with the sacred red and yellow color combination were worn by chiefs, or other dignitaries, and their wives. Fig. 6-29 shows a fine example of this. The detail is from a large tapa cloth, measuring about $8\frac{1}{2}$ x $6\frac{1}{2}'$ that was probably printed with a bright red dye on yellow but has faded with time. It was said to have been made by the Queen of Tahiti, and was collected by Captain Benjamin

with the rubbed designs. Although the students should be free to make figures of their own invention, if the art is to be made in the spirit of the Tongan tapa, the colors used should be restricted to brown, red-brown, and black, the colors of the dyes made in Tonga from island plants.

To further decorate some of the spaces, place the tablet wound with string under an already rubbed design. Position it so the strings are horizontal, and rub carefully *around* the figure, creating a striped background. Some spaces can be left with a plain background.

After completing the rubbing, the Tongan artists use black and red-brown paint to fill in small details—beaks, eyes, leaves, stripes, or triangles. Use a fine, pointed brush, which gives a few crisp details to the soft colors of the rubbed designs.

Fig. 6-29. A detail of tapa cloth from Tahiti with fern and other leaf prints. © Peabody Essex Museum. Photograph by Jeffrey Dykes.

Fig. 6-30. Teffaaora, chief of Borabora, Society Islands, wearing a tiputa, or poncho, made of soft tapa cloth. The tapa was dyed yellow and printed with fern fronds dipped in red dye. 1820s. Drawn by L. I. Duperrey, *Voyage Autour du Monde* (1826).

Vanderford on one of his voyages. He gave the tapa to the Peabody Essex Museum in 1823.

Tahiti is one of the Society Islands, and neighboring islands in this grouping also made tapa with leaf prints. Fig. 6-30 shows Teffaaora, chief of Borabora, Society Islands, wearing a *tiputa* printed with fern designs. Notice how the fern frond circle echoes the tattoo on his arm. Contemporary Tahitian artists are researching old methods of tapa making and there is a revival of interest in this art.

Making Fern and Leaf Designs

This project should be done using the royal colors—make paper tapa cloth dyed with yellow paint (see Making Paper Tapa Cloth, page 158), and print with red paint.

Collect some fern fronds. Most florists use leather leaf fern in some arrangements and are very willing to allow a search through their discard barrels for cast-off pieces. This fern is strong and will hold up well. The Tahitians also used other leaves and mosses. Evergreens, such as cedar, are strong and will give good prints. Experiment with what you find in your community. Leaves may be placed between newspapers and weighted down overnight so that they do not curl as they dry.

Mix red tempera with a little brown to make it more like a natural dye color. The Tahitians made perfect prints by dipping the leaves or laying them on the surface of the dye. Their artistry was exquisite—for the untrained, this method usually creates nothing but blobs. An easier solution is to place a fern frond on newspaper, and paint it with a brush, spreading the color out well so that it is not too wet and drippy. The paint may adhere better if a drop of liquid soap is added. Place the fern, painted side down, on the prepared paper tapa (which should be on a pad of newspaper), and put a clean paper towel or newspaper over

Fig. 6-31. Teddy gently kneads brown paper in a yellow paint solution to make yellow paper tapa.

it. Hold the fern down with one hand and rub hard with the other, using the side of the thumb, heel of the hand, and even hitting it with the fist. Remove the towel and pick up the fern carefully. It can be re-inked and used over

Fig. 6-32. Emma has painted a fern frond with red paint and is printing it for the fourth time to make a design on her paper tapa.

Fig. 6-33. Fifth-grade paper tapa designs inspired by the tapa cloth of Tahiti. Top, a fern design by Emma, and below, a design using several different kinds of leaves by Joshua.

THE STENCILED DESIGNS OF FIJI

The artists of Fiji used a wide variety of decorative methods, but they also developed a unique process of stenciling designs onto white tapa. Designs were cut into flat banana or pandanus leaves and pigment was rubbed into the opening with a wad of tapa dipped in dye. In another technique, a leaf was cut into a positive shape, placed on the cloth, and the dye was passed over it, creating a white design, masked from the dye by the leaf.

The tapa designs are often extremely fine and intricate and sometimes combine different methods. In Fig. 6-34 the bold pattern was probably painted on the tapa (though such designs were also made with stencils), but the very fine crosshatching of the border was done with stencils. Geometric designs predominate, but figures of leaves, flowers, stars, turtles, and other natural forms and manufactured items

and over. In some Tahitian designs, ferns and leaves are placed randomly; in others, they form circles or other geometric shapes, or are used in borders. It is wise to have the students practice printing on newsprint before using the prepared paper.

The best prints can be made by using a brayer and water-based printing inks. Again, mix red and brown inks together first, using a spatula on the inking plate. Put the fern on newspaper and roll on the ink, quite wet, always going in one direction, from the stem up, and roll right off onto the newspaper. Then place the fern on the prepared paper and print as above. If the printing ink gets too dry and sticky, it will tear the fern.

Fig. 6-34. Stenciled and painted tapa cloth from Fiji. This design is typical of the Cakaudrove district. © Peabody Essex Museum. Photograph by Mark Sexton.

Fig. 6-35. Detail of *masi kesa* (white tapa with black and brown designs), Fiji. A central stenciled leaf pattern is surrounded by more complex stenciled borders. Edge-Partington Collection/Leys Memorial, Auckland Museum. Photograph courtesy of Auckland Museum.

were also stenciled on the tapa, and geometric borders were stenciled around them. Lines were often first drawn on the cloth as a guide for the geometric stencils.

Stenciled tapa cloth is still being made in Fiji, although now old X-ray film is used for stencils as it is strong and long lasting. The tapa is used in traditional ways, for gifts and ceremonies, and for tourist markets.

Making Stenciled Designs

Although commercial stencil paper may work best, other papers can be used. Even construction paper works if the design is very simple and the stencil is not going to be used many times. If the teacher brushes a paper stencil with varnish, either before or after the design is cut, it will be made more durable. With this

in mind, even typing paper can be used—it is easy to cut designs in the thin paper before it is varnished.

If possible, show the children a real example of tapa cloth from Fiji, or show them the fine examples in the books listed in the bibliography. Appropriate designs are geometric patterns—lines, triangles, diamonds, zigzags, circles, stars, and also natural forms such as flowers, leaves, trees, and animals. Draw the design in black marker on the stencil paper. Be sure to leave sufficient margins around the design so that paint, when applied, will only go

Fig. 6-36. Stenciling a *masi kesa*, 1995, Suva Fiji. This Fijian woman uses an old X-ray plate to stencil a design. Both positive designs (black) and negative designs (white, lower left corner) can be seen. The zigzag designs are made by stenciling two rows of attached triangles, with a space between. © Federico Busonero.

Fig. 6-37. Some of the traditional stencil designs for borders and figures used in decorating tapa cloth in Fiji. The black represents the stencil; the white is the cutout design through which color will be brushed. (The black surrounding the design would be wider in actual stencils.)

through the opening and not over the edge of the stencil onto the paper tapa cloth. With a hole puncher, make a hole in the black shape to gain access for scissors, and cut out the design. Or fold the paper and cut a shape, such as a flower petal or triangle, from the fold, and then flatten out the paper again. The students may want to make at least two stencils—a small one for making a border, and a larger one for the space inside the border.

Make the border first. Hold the stencil down firmly with one hand, and using a brush that is quite dry, apply paint gently, in short *vertical* strokes. (If the paint is too runny it will seep under the edges of the stencil.) It will be more in keeping with the tapa of Fiji if the colors are limited to black and a red-brown earth color. Lift the stencil, turn it over on a piece of newspaper, and wipe the back clean. Position the stencil adjacent to the first stenciled design

Fig. 6-38. Zhenya, eight, lifts the stencil from the paper tapa, revealing a neatly stenciled tree design. He has also started a border of diamond shapes.

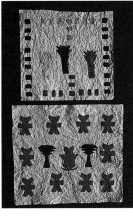

Fig. 6-39. Paper tapa designs, inspired by the stenciled designs of Fiji, by third-grade students Ben (top) and Mia (below).

and repeat. Continue this process to form the border. Then, larger forms can be stenciled into the center of the piece. It is a good idea for the students to practice stenciling first on a piece of newsprint to learn both the correct amount of paint to put on the brush and the positioning of adjacent stencil designs.

Figures can also be stenciled in white by laying a positive design, such as a flower shape, on the paper tapa and painting over it. After lifting the stencil, the painted area around the negative image may need additional painting to make the outer edges even. This technique was sometimes used in Fiji to make a black border that incorporated a white design that was repeated throughout its length.

Fig. 6-40. Shell inlaid bowl given to Captain Henry Wilson in 1783 by the king of Belau. It contained gifts of a fresh drink, coconut sweetmeats, and oranges. © The British Museum.

THE GIFT-GIVING BOWLS OF MICRONESIA

Several island societies in the Caroline Island archipelago (part of the Oceanic area called Micronesia) created beautifully designed bowls to be used in giving gifts. When the English captain Henry Wilson was shipwrecked in 1783 off Belau (now called Palau), the king presented him with drinks, oranges, and coconut sweetmeats in wooden bowls that were stained, incised, and inlaid with elaborate shell designs. (See Figs. 6-40 and 6-41.)

There are 20,203 islands in Micronesia, and 343 of them comprise Palau. The custom of giving gifts was established there and on other islands as a way of promoting good relations between autonomous regions. The bowls were also used for gifts of food among top-ranking people and within families to reinforce bonds. There were many other exchanges of gifts as well, which included textiles, necklaces, and pottery. Women presented finely crafted turtle shell plaques to each other to mark births, deaths, and marriages.

Within the Caroline Islands, the art of making inlaid bowls was unique to Belau. Pieces of shell were cut into triangles, diamonds, and other shapes and inlaid into carved wooden bowls, making intricate, beautifully realized patterns. Since the Micronesians were fine navigators and traveled long distances, the Belau bowls may have been influenced by the shell inlay work of the Solomon Islands in Melanesia, where the art is used to decorate canoe prows and many other items.

One of the bowls given to Captain Wilson was in the shape of a bird. Birds and fish are frequently represented in Micronesian art. Bird bowls for gift giving are also found in several other Caroline Islands, such as Puluwat and Yap, where they are carved from wood, without inlaid designs, and are often painted white to represent gulls. Some are made to present food, and others hold paint for canoes. These beautifully designed bowls lend grace to daily life and are valued family heirlooms.

Because of the elaborate shell work, we have chosen the Belau bowls for this project—but the bowls in the shape of gulls could also be the inspiration for a good project. Simply papier-mâché balloons (use oval balloons if possible) as directed in the following project. Cut each in half to make two bowls. Then tape on cardboard tails and heads and use papier-mâché to round out the forms and secure them to the bowl. Wings can also be taped on and papier-mâchéd, or simply painted on the sides. Paint the bowls white or brown. (See Fig. 6-42.)

Fig. 6-42. Puluwat bird bowl, used as a palette for paint. The bowl could be hung up or carried by the stick. Catalogue No. 398176. Courtesy of the Department of Anthropology, Smithsonian Institution.

Making Bowls Inspired by the Shell Inlaid Bowls of Belau

Actual inlay work would be too difficult for young students, but a very effective bowl can be made of papier-mâché and decorated with cut paper shapes. It is a good lesson in how complex designs can be created from the repetition of a few simple forms.

Blow up large round balloons to about 8" in diameter. Tie them very tightly so that no air escapes. To keep them from rolling around the table, either tape the knot to the table, or tape them onto empty cottage cheese or other containers for stability. After papier-mâchéing

Fig. 6-41. Shell inlaid container given to Captain Henry Wilson in 1783 by the king of Belau. © The British Museum, London.

Fig. 6-43. Jennifer, ten, has taped a balloon to a yogurt container for stability while applying papier-mâché.

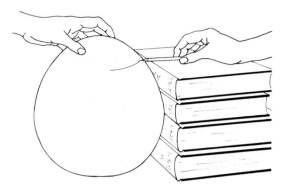

Fig. 6-44. Turning the bowl against a pencil held on top of a stack of books will create a horizontal line for the lid.

Fig. 6-45. To attach the lid, punch two holes in the top piece, and two directly under them. Thread string through and tie. Do the same on the opposite side.

the top portion, reverse ends in the container and finish the other end.

Since slow leaks sometimes occur, it is best to do all the papier-mâché in one session if possible. To do this, use a strong heavy paper, such as Kraft paper, alternating with newspaper or, better, use Kraft paper alone. Tear the paper into small pieces—no larger than 2 x 2". The smaller the pieces are, the stronger and smoother the bowl will be. Use two colors of paper and alternate layers to be sure that each layer completely covers the surface. There should be a total of at least four layers. Set the piece to dry on a sheet of plastic wrap; the part touching the plastic will not dry as quickly as the rest. When the piece is sturdy enough to maintain its shape, but before the bottom dries out, pop the balloon and pull it out by the knot. Gently press the bottom of the balloon shape down against the table. It will still be damp enough to flatten out and make a stable bottom. If the bottom has dried too much, place it in a saucer of papier-mâché glue until

it softens enough to flatten. Fill the hole where the balloon was knotted with four layers of papier-mâché.

To open the bowl and make a top, draw a level line about 2" down from the top. Hold a pencil on a block of wood or stack of books at the level you wish to cut. The pencil should project out from the block enough to reach the bowl. Turn the bowl against the pencil in a clockwise motion. This will make a level line to cut on. (See Fig. 6-44.) Before cutting off the top, draw a vertical pencil line from the top down to the middle. This will help you align the top correctly to its former position after cutting it off. Cut off the top, put it back in its original position on the bowl, and with a hole puncher make two sets of holes, two in the top directly above the two in the bowl. (See Fig. 6-45.) Do the same on the opposite side. These will be used to tie the top on. If you have used newspaper for the first layer of papier-mâché, apply a layer of Kraft paper to the inside of the

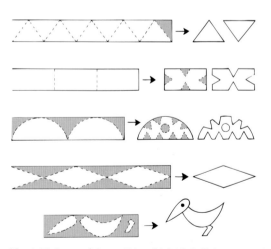

Fig. 6-46. Some of the traditional inlaid shell designs used on the gift-giving bowls of Belau. Use a ½–¾" strip of paper and cut on the dotted lines. The gray areas are discarded, except in the case of the diamonds, where the resulting triangles can also be used.

Fig. 6-47. Sarah, left, and Jade have painted their bowls and are now gluing on paper designs. A rubber band stretched around the middle of the bowl helps keep the lines straight.

Fig. 6-48. Karl threads string through the holes on the cover of his bowl before tying it on.

bowl and top. Set the top and bottom aside to dry further if necessary. (See photo page 267.)

When the bowl is dry, paint it with dark brown tempera paint, or with school-grade brown acrylic paint. Tempera paint should be waterproofed with an acrylic finish, or the acrylic can be mixed right in with the tempera. This is necessary to prevent staining when the paper designs are glued on.

To create paper shapes that resemble the shell inlay shapes of the Belau bowls, cut strips of paper on a paper cutter. For more interest,

cut two widths: some ½–¾" wide, and some ⅜" wide. From these strips the students can cut a number of different designs. To make triangles, cut one piece off the strip at an angle, and discard. Then cut the remaining strip into triangles. (See Fig. 6-46.) The broad X shapes in Fig. 6-41 can be created by cutting 1" rectangles from a strip and then notching the four sides. In a similar manner, cut half rounds from the strips and notch those. Students can devise their own geometric shapes as well.

The beautiful pelican-like bird shapes on the Belau bowls are made from a crescent shape combined with a teardrop shape and a leg shape. To be created in shell, a complex form like a bird had to be broken down into simple forms. In this project, once the student has drawn a bird that is pleasing, it should be cut out (into two or three pieces) and used as a pattern to make more identical birds. (After tracing the forms with a pencil and cutting them out, be sure to erase the pencil marks.) In some Belau bowls the birds have eyes inset in the teardrop shape. This can be done with a pen.

The students will need many identical shapes to create the patterns. A bowl that is about 8" high has a circumference of about 24" at its widest point! This means that they will need twenty-four 1" design pieces to go around the bowl. Even higher up where it becomes narrower, they will need twenty-four ½" triangles. One way to keep the cut pieces separated by shape is to give each student an egg carton. The triangles can go in one compartment, the rectangles in another, and so on.

It is very difficult to arrange the pieces in an accurate horizontal line on a round shape. Placing a large rubber band around the middle of the bowl is a helpful guide. Glue the shapes on with a white glue. It is easy to pick up a little piece of paper by touching it with the tip of a gluey brush. The artists who made the Belau bowls had a beautiful sense of design. Rows of plain cut triangles alternate with rectangular shapes with fancy edges. Horizontal lines of shell work around the top and bottom are relieved with vertical lines of designs in the middle. It should be pointed out that if the patterns were all horizontal or all vertical, the design would lose some of its energy.

After the glue has dried, add a final coat of clear acrylic medium to bring a shell-like gloss to the paper. Apply with a very light touch to avoid staining the designs. A heavy jute string can then be tied through the holes to hold the top on.

This is one project that should end in a party for the students' families or for another class. The beautiful bowls of Belau were filled with delicious treats to honor guests. Offering oranges, bananas, little containers of fruit juice, and pieces of coconut or coconut candy would be in keeping with this Micronesian custom.

Fig. 6-49. Three gift-giving bowls by fifth-grade students Karl, Vera, and Alex.

Fig. 6-50. A group of students share fruit punch and coconut candy using their gift-giving bowls. From left: Vera, Roberta, Franziska, Alex, Madeleine, and Jennifer.

Fig. 7-1. Two contemporary
didgeridoos courtesy of
Hawk Henries.

7 THE ABORIGINAL ARTS OF AUSTRALIA

There are several different belief systems concerning the origins of the Aboriginal people of Australia. Current scientific thought is that about 40,000 years ago, people crossed the ocean in small boats from Southeast Asia to Australia and New Guinea, which then shared a single continental landmass.

Fig. 7-2. Bluey Roberts holds his carved emu egg with emu designs. 1987. Photographer unknown. Courtesy of Bluey Roberts.

is described more fully below.

The Aboriginal people spread over the continent. Ancient rock engravings and paintings have been found throughout the land, and there has been no cessation of art making over the millennia. This prolific creativity has included body painting, and painting on bark, rocks, paper, and, since the early 1970s, canvas; sculpture in wood; decorated shields and tools; carved emu eggs; a trumpet-like instrument called the didgeridoo; coiled basket weaving; and earth constructions.

Permanent European settlement in Australia began in 1788, starting a tragic time for the Aboriginal people. Many died of disease or in battle or were driven off their land and into settlements. Today over half the Aboriginal population lives in cities and towns. Still the Aboriginal people have held onto their identity, and the culture has retained its uniqueness. There has been a great renewal of art, bringing an awareness of their rich culture to the world.

There is still controversy over exactly where these people came from. Probably many migrations took place over time from different areas.

However, the Aboriginal people themselves have other beliefs about their origins. The tradition, for some, is that they arrived from the sea near the Northwest corner of Australia; but many Aboriginal people believe they are a distinct people, created by Spirit Ancestors who also formed the earth and everything on it. This belief is maintained through stories of the Dreaming, and

Contemporary Aboriginal artists in the cities as well as some of those in the bush employ modern materials, and some use art to explore their heritage, to express outrage at past treatment, or to put forward current political points of view. The more traditional paintings continue to be made in rural Aboriginal communities. Sometimes art is used to educate the outside world about their culture.

Australian Aboriginal art is represented in this book by the bark paintings of Arnhem Land; by the musical instrument called the didgeridoo; and by emu eggshell decorating.

ABORIGINAL BARK PAINTINGS OF ARNHEM LAND

The Aboriginal people, traditionally hunters and gatherers, lived in small kinship groups, as many still do. There are more than 270 Aboriginal languages and 600 dialects. Many different beliefs about the creation of life are held—but most involve Spirit Ancestors who have roamed the land since the beginning of time. These spirits created the features of the land, such as rivers, waterholes, and rock formations as well as all the animals, fish, plants, and people that live on the earth. They also could change form and become animals, rocks, or bodies of water. The presence and activities of these Spirit Ancestors, both in the past and the present, are referred to as the Dreaming, which is potentially misleading because the concept has little to do with the English definition of the word. The Dreaming is at the heart of Aboriginal life. The Spirit Ancestors were, and still are, integral to the landscape and to all the life in it. Their presence informs the life of the people, their traditions, and how they live their lives. Most of the Aboriginal arts of Australia were, and often still are, expressions of this all-pervading religious concept.

A clan is usually associated with the Spirit Ancestor that created parts of the local landscape. Ceremonies incorporating paintings, dance, and music recount the adventures and history of these spirits. Artists often have rights to certain images connected to their clan—they learn these images from their elders—and no one else can use them. Both men and women make paintings and carvings, although subject matter and purpose are sometimes designated as men's business or women's business. They illustrate stories of Spirit Ancestors from the Dreaming. Some of the paintings use the same figures that were used on rock walls in ancient times. These forms have been continually re-created almost unchanged, for more than 18,000 years.

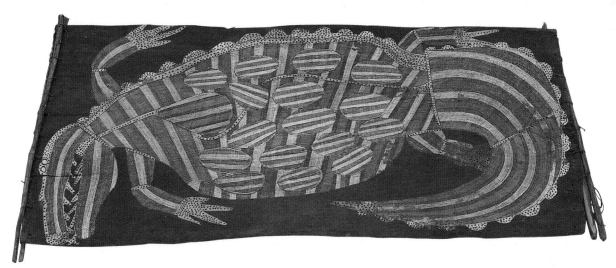

Fig. 7-3. Bark painting of crocodile. Arnhem Land, c. 1950s. An X-ray style painting showing stomach, intestines, and probably eggs inside the crocodile. It is very large, measuring 5' by 2' 2". © Peabody Essex Museum/Photograph by Mark Sexton.

There are many different Aboriginal painting traditions, each with its own style, in part because of the many diverse environments in Australia. The styles range from naturalistic to nonfigurative geometric forms and symbols. In Central Australia and the Western Desert, acrylic paintings are created with techniques derived from ground painting and body painting. The paintings are maps, created with dots, lines, and symbols of animal tracks; they are an aerial view of sacred or significant land areas and what happened there.

For this project we will examine the paintings of Arnhem Land, in the northernmost part of the Northern Territory. When Europeans first came to this area in the early 1800s they found that the Aboriginal people created paintings on the bark walls of their shelters. These paintings were collected first by anthropologists, but by the 1940s bark paintings began to be sought out by museums and private art collectors. Although the paintings have sacred religious meanings to the people that create them, they have come to be appreciated at a different level, as works of art, by the general public.

To make the paintings, the artists cut strips of bark from eucalyptus trees of the stringy bark variety. The outer layers are removed and the bark is flattened under weights. The colors are created with red and yellow ochre, white pipe clay or gypsum, and charcoal. These are ground on stones and mixed with water. Orchid juice, from both stem and bulb, is added as a fixative, although some-

Fig. 7-4. Aboriginal bark painting of echidna, or spiny anteater, by Nabadbara, Croker Island, Arnhem Land. The internal organs have largely been abstracted, but lines in the center symbolize spinal chord and ribs. © Peabody Essex Museum/Photograph by Mark Sexton.

Fig. 7-5. Johnny BulanBulan painting a design in yellow on his prepared piece of eucalyptus bark. Arnhem land, Northern Territories, late 1970s. Courtesy of Penny Tweedie/Panos Pictures. The figure at top right is a long necked turtle.

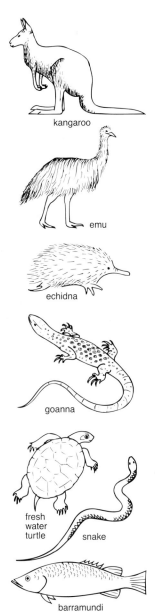

Fig. 7-6. Some of the Australian animals frequently depicted in Aboriginal art. (See also the crocodile shown in Fig. 7-3.)

times now a carpenters' glue is substituted. Brushes are made from frayed twigs or with human hair bound to sticks. Commercial brushes are now also employed. Dots are sometimes created with fingertips.

The bark is placed flat on the ground, inner side up, and a solid color—usually red ochre, but sometimes yellow ochre or black—is applied to its entire surface. Then a figure is outlined in a contrasting earth color—black, yellow, or white—and filled in. In some paintings the painted background is left bare to emphasize the figure; in others, the background is filled with crosshatching or dotting. This is not just a decorative device but is a sacred religious pattern imbued with meaning to the artist and community.

The clan paintings involve thin figures called Mimi spirits, hunters, human figures, and often animals, such as birds, snakes, monitor lizards, fish, echidnas, kangaroos, and turtles. Many of these images, now often referred to as X-ray paintings, show skeletal forms and internal organs: backbone, ribs, stomach, lungs, liver, and heart. This is a hunter's point of view, and shows the entire animal, not just the surface. In some paintings, these forms are less literal and the body is filled with geometric designs symbolic of body parts.

These figures from the Dreaming are embodiments of Spirit Ancestors and details in the painting often refer to stories of their activities. They are sacred paintings and used in combination with music and dancing in religious ceremonies.

Originally, paintings were created for ceremonies and therefore not intended to be permanent. Since the mid 1900s, when paintings began to be made for sale, sticks have often been bound to two opposite edges of the bark to keep it flat.

Making Paintings on Laminated Paper Boards

For this project we will make paintings inspired by the X-ray style of Western Arnhem Land. These paintings often show one animal on a plain background and are a little less complex than those from other regions.

The easiest way to simulate a slab of bark is to laminate several layers of heavy brown paper. A grocery bag works best, and will yield three pieces, approximately 12 x 16". Open up the bag, cut down along the glued seam, and then around the bottom of the bag. Then lay this long piece flat and cut it into three equal sized pieces. Turn any printing to the inside, apply papier-mâché paste to both sides of the pieces and layer them together. Smooth the paper firmly, moving from the center out to the edges to remove ridges and air pockets. Set this board aside to dry for a day or two. Kraft paper can also be used, but since it is thinner, four layers are needed.

The student should work out a design on newsprint cut to the same size as the board. It may be difficult to find an original Aboriginal bark painting to show the students, but there are many fine photographs in the books mentioned in the bibliography. Students should also have available resource books illustrating Australian animals and birds.

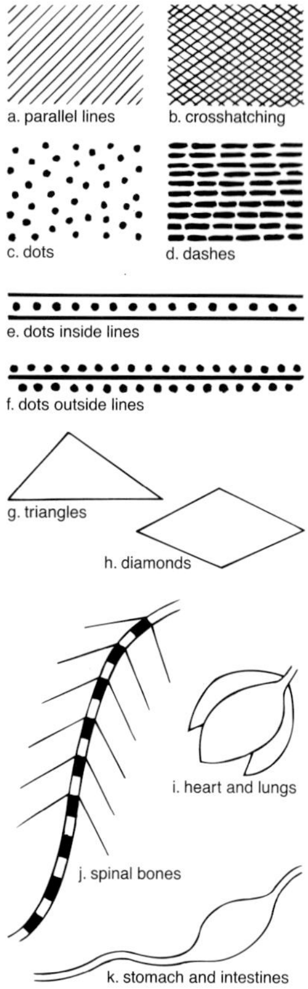

Fig. 7-7. Solomon paints *Mr. Armadillo Guy* a solid color before adding details.

Fig. 7-8. Nicole makes fine white lines on her kangaroo painting.

Fig. 7-9. Some design elements in Australian Aboriginal bark paintings. Elements a., b., c., and d. often have symbolic meanings and are used to fill in figures and sometimes backgrounds. Elements e. and f. are ways of decorating lines within figures. Elements g. and h. sometimes fill spaces within figures. Elements i., j., and k. are stylized bones and body organs used in X-ray paintings.

a. parallel lines
b. crosshatching
c. dots
d. dashes
e. dots inside lines
f. dots outside lines
g. triangles
h. diamonds
i. heart and lungs
j. spinal bones
k. stomach and intestines

Fig. 7-10. *A Crocodile Flanked by Two Snakes and Two Turtles*, by Colette, ten.

The most commonly used food animals—kangaroo, crocodile, and barramundi fish—are often painted and less the province of a particular clan and are therefore good subjects for the students. Draw the animal, fish, or bird in outline. Then draw the vertebrae, ribs, and some of the principal organs: stomach, intestine, lungs, heart, and body cavities. In Aboriginal paintings these are represented with traditional stylized shapes and sometimes only with completely abstract geometric shapes. (See crocodile, Fig. 7-3, and echidna, Fig. 7-4.)

When the laminated paper is dry, trim the edges to make them even. Paint the entire surface with a background color. A beautiful red-brown ochre is most common, though black has been used, especially in modern times, as well as yellow ochre. To mix red ochre, use almost equal parts of brown and red paint, adding a little extra brown. Yellow ochre can be made with a mixture of yellow, brown, red, and white. Mix a large quantity of these colors, so they don't run out and have to be matched.

When the background color has dried, transfer the outline of the drawing onto the board. To do this, turn the drawing over (placing it, if possible, against a window to make the lines visible), and apply white chalk to the back of the lines. Shake off excess chalk. Then position the drawing over the laminated board, and secure it well at the top with paper clips. With a pencil, trace only the *outline* of the form, and

then fold the drawing up without removing it. Paint the entire form with one of the other earth colors that contrasts with the background. When this color is dry, bring the drawing back down over the board and trace the inner organs and bones. These are then painted, or drawn with colored pencils, in contrasting earth colors including white. In the Aboriginal paintings some areas within the figure are left unpainted to represent body cavities, but much of the rest of the area within the figure is filled with thin parallel lines or crosshatching. (The lines in the crosshatching are at an oblique angle to each other, not at right angles.) These lines are typically so finely painted, and with such a steady hand, that the students will find it very difficult. For that reason it seems wisest to use colored pencils for this purpose. Frequently, when the figures are done, they are outlined in white, which sets them off from the background.

The finished painting should be bound on two sides with sticks. If the students can find straight sticks (½–⅝" diameter) in their community, that is fine. Otherwise, half-round molding or screen molding can be used. This new wood will look more natural if it is stained or painted with brown tempera paint.

Lay a stick on top of the

Fig. 7-11. Fifth-grade paintings inspired by Aboriginal bark paintings: *Goanna* by Laura and *Fish* by Andrés.

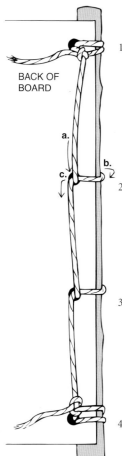

BACK OF BOARD

a.

b.

c.

1. Take a 3' piece of twine down through the hole and leave a 2" tail. Go around under the stick, bring the twine up, and go down through the hole again, up around the stick and tie the twine to the tail.

2. a. Bring the twine down and through the second hole.
   b. Take the twine around the stick and up.
   c. Take the twine across the board and under the twine that comes down from the first hole.

3. Go down to the third hole and repeat #2.

4. Finish by going twice around, as in #1, and tie to the twine that comes down.

Fig. 7-12. How to lash sticks to a painting.

painting, even with a side edge. Make four marks on the painting along the inside edge of the stick—one, down 1" from the top; one, up 1" from the bottom; and two spaced between. Use a large hole puncher to make holes at those points. With the stick in place, turn the painting over, and working from the back, thread a three foot piece of brown jute twine down through the top hole. Leave 2" of twine at the back. Proceed by following the directions in Fig. 7-12. Repeat this process on the opposite side of the painting with the other stick.

DIDGERIDOOS

The didgeridoo is a musical instrument that has been used since ancient times by the Aboriginal people of the Northern Territory and later, in the East Kimberley region in Western Australia. It is also called the *yidaki* in the Yolngu language. Called the world's oldest wind instrument, it is used to accompany dance and song as part of sacred ceremonies, called *corroborees,* that explain the Dreaming. The songs tell how the Spirit Ancestors made the land and all life, and guide the people in how to live their daily lives. Fig. 7-13 shows an old, somewhat faded didgeridoo, which was probably used in these ceremonies. The didgeridoo is now also used in contemporary Aboriginal bands along with other instruments.

The art of making didgeridoos has not changed much over the centuries. The artists seek out young eucalyp-

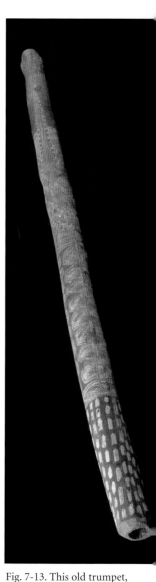

Fig. 7-13. This old trumpet, or didgeridoo, was collected by Lloyd Warner in 1929 from the Murngin tribe, northeast Arnhem Land. It is painted with the python design of the Wessel Island clan. Peabody Museum of Archaeology and Ethnology, Harvard University. © 2002 President and Fellows of Harvard College. All rights reserved. Photo by Hillel Burger.

tus trees that have been hollowed out by termites. This insect action creates a wooden tube that is anywhere from 3–6' long. The hollow core is then widened and flared out near the bottom, and the outside is pared down so that the tube becomes thinner. Modern tools are used now, but originally this was done with stone-tipped tools.

After the wood is smoothed, the didgeridoo is decorated. First an overall coat of red-brown ochre or black is applied. Modern paints are now often used. The designs painted on the background all relate in some way to the natural world and its origins in the Dreaming. (See Figs. 7-1 and 7-13.) Long, thin animals such as goannas or snakes are frequent motifs and there are often rings of color encircling the didgeridoo as well as painted footprints or handprints. Parallel lines, crosshatching, or dots symbolize water or other natural phenomena. Concentric circles of dots represent water holes, campfires, or gathering places. In Fig. 7-14, the didgeridoo on the right is painted in the style of the Western dot method. The U shapes flanking concentric circles may symbolize people sitting around a campfire. The didgeridoo on the left shows a crocodile, and is painted in the Northern manner, with crosshatching. It is painted entirely with colors made from earth pigments, and perhaps charcoal. After the didgeridoo is decorated, a mouthpiece is created with beeswax.

The resulting instrument is played by continuous blowing (a technique called circular breathing which is very difficult to master), and produces a mystical, expressive, droning sound. Birdcalls and animal noises are sometimes incorporated into the underlying drone, especially when these animals are being depicted in an accompanying dance. An

Fig. 7-14. Details of the two Australian Aboriginal didgeridoos shown on page 173. Courtesy of Hawk Henries.

extraordinary range of sounds and rhythms can be created with this simple instrument through the use of breathing techniques, tongue, and throat. The didgeridoo is often accompanied by clapping sticks, or click sticks, that keep the rhythm. Sometimes two boomerangs are used for this purpose also.

The didgeridoo is now found throughout the world and it is possible, in most big cities, to find someone who has learned to play one, though these instruments may be made of modern materials. Tapes and CDs of the music are available, and there are videos that show the instrument being made and played. (See the bibliography.)

Making Cardboard Didgeridoos

Although it would be extremely difficult for young children to learn the technique of producing a continuous drone, they can make a satisfactory "raspberry" sound (the basis of the drone) into a tube and also imitate animal and bird sounds—but the cardboard tube does not have the resonance of a wooden instrument. Therefore, the main focus of the project should be on the art of making and decorating their cardboard didgeridoos. Start saving paper towel tubes well in advance of this project! Each student will need four tubes. Place the tubes end to end, and tape them together well enough to make it possible to apply papier-mâché. Alternate layers of Kraft paper and newspaper so that you can see each time that

Fig. 7-15. Fifth-grade students, Tony, Mike, Peter, and Nevada, papier-mâché paper-towel tubes together, using at least four layers.

Fig. 7-16. Mike is painting a snake coiling around his didgeridoo.

the surface is completely covered. Small torn pieces of paper will give the smoothest finish. Four or five layers will give a strong tube.

When the tube is dry, apply an overall coat of red-brown or black paint as a base color. Each student should have a small block of scrap wood to place under one end of the tube to keep it off the table. Mix ample amounts of the earth colors (red and brown, for red ochre; yellow, red, brown, and white, for yellow ochre) so that there will be plenty of paint to correct splotches and errors without having to match the paint again. Painting on a tube is surprisingly messy.

Use fine detail brushes for crosshatching and parallel lines. (See Fig. 7-9 a, b, c, d.) Remind the students to put only the tip of the brush into the paint, and to just touch the surface of the tube if they want a fine line. In drawing wider lines that encircle the tube, a right-handed person draws the left side of the line straight, not worrying about the right side of the line. Then reverse the tube, end to end, and draw the other side of the line in the other direction. (Left-handed students will first draw the right side of the line.) This sounds complicated, but it isn't, and it works well. Crosshatching and round spots, which symbolize such natural phenomena as light glancing off water or shiny leaves, create a dazzling, shimmering effect. Uniform round dots can be made very easily by placing the end of a piece of dowel, or a pencil eraser, just onto the *surface* of the pot of paint, and then pressing this *lightly* onto the tube, making two dots before repeating the process. The Aboriginal artists sometimes use fingertips or cotton swabs or the bare end of a wooden swab stick. Placed close together, these dots create a wonderful background for a snake, goanna, or other figure.

When the tube has been painted and is completely dry, it may be a good idea to protect the surface, as it will be handled a lot. A flat varnish works well. Water-based acrylic polymer mediums tend to soften the tube and make the colors run. If you need to use one, be sure the colors are completely dry, and apply a satin medium with a very light touch.

It would be wonderful if a didgeridoo player can be found to demonstrate the art of playing the instrument, using circular breathing. Otherwise, have the students moisten their lips, and make a "raspberry"

Fig. 7-17. Six finished didgeridoos by fifth-grade students. From the left: a golden snake coils around Laura's; Nicole has a spotted design around her goanna; Noah's didgeridoo has a shark; Clara painted a spotted snake; Elisabeth chose a black goanna; and Joshua's features a gold goanna. All are embellished with dots, parallel lines, or V shapes.

sound into the tubes. If one half the class makes a sound and the other half takes it up when the first runs out of breath, it will be almost continuous! Their most successful sounds, though, will be imitations of birdcalls, dogs, and other animals.

CARVED EMU EGGS

Emus are flightless birds found only in Australia. (See Fig. 7-6.) They are 6' tall, feathered on the neck (ostriches, their near relatives in Africa, have bare necks), and can run as fast as 30 miles per hour over the open grasslands. Emus mate for life. Seven to ten eggs are laid in a loose nest of leaves and grass on the ground.

Fig. 7-18. Kangaroos gracefully circle this emu egg carved by Bluey Roberts in 2000. 5" high x 12" circumference. Lower Murray River region, South Australia. Photo by permission of the artist. Collection of the author.

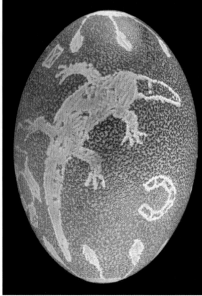

Fig. 7-19. Two sides of a carved emu egg, collected by E. Clement in 1922 in Northwest Australia, Kimberley Region. Peabody Museum of Archaeology and Ethnology, Harvard University. © 2002 President and Fellows of Harvard College. All rights reserved. Photos by Hillel Burger.

shows kangaroos gracefully encircling the egg. Bluey Roberts is from the Lower Murray River region, whose people are known as the Ngarrindjeri. He is well known, both in Australia and around the world for his paintings, carved and decorated boomerangs, and carved emu eggs. (See Fig. 7-2.) His work is in many museums and galleries.

Esther Kirby is another contemporary egg carver whose work is imbued with the traditions of Aboriginal life. She depicts hunters as well as animals, fish, snakes, and other Australian wildlife. Her work is much sought after.

The male is a devoted father—he incubates the eggs for sixty days, and then stays with the young for eighteen months. The birds are easily domesticated and were a prime food source for the Aboriginal people; they are often depicted in their art.

Emu eggs are extremely beautiful. They resemble a polished 5–6" oval piece of very dark blue-green stone, with a somewhat mottled or speckled surface. The shell has layers of color—the underlayer is a light blue-green—a characteristic that Aboriginal artists have capitalized on to make the eggs into works of art.

These carved eggs were used to illustrate stories of the Dreaming. The egg in Fig. 7-19 was collected in 1922, and the turtle, crocodile, and other designs have significance that is not known to the outsider. The original blue-green color has faded with age. The contemporary egg, in Fig. 7-18, by Bluey Roberts,

Making Eggs with a Scraped Design

Emu eggs are hard to come by. They can be purchased from farms in Australia, and there are a few emu farms in other countries, including the United States. It would be wonderful to obtain one to show the students. It might be possible to find duck or goose eggs, but chicken eggs are challenge enough for this project, which will enable the student to understand the principles of the art.

The eggs must first be blown. Using a very sharp point, such as the tip of fingernail scissors or a sharp paring knife, poke a tiny hole in

Fig. 7-20. Scraped-egg designs by fourth-grade students: *Snake* by Kathleen, *Fish* by Rebecca, and *Turtle* by Olivia.

one end with a short pecking motion. In the other end, make a slightly larger hole (⅛" diameter). With a very thin skewer, wire, or needle poke into the egg from both ends to break the inner membrane, and stir around a bit to break up the yolk. It is not wise to blow the eggs out with your mouth as raw eggs can transmit disease. However, it is easy to do this using an ear syringe bulb. Place it on the smaller hole, and holding the egg over a basin, squeeze the bulb. The contents of the shell will be blown out of the other hole. It takes a while, but after a little practice this goes rather quickly. Wash the egg well in detergent and dry.

Since chicken eggs do not have dramatic color layers in their shells, it is necessary to add a color to the eggshell first. The dark blue-green of an emu egg is very difficult to reproduce, but black is a good alternative. The shell can be colored in several ways: painted with permanent India ink or black tempera paint or colored with a black crayon. India ink gives a

very nice and permanent finish, but it is a little harder to scrape. Tempera paint is a bit easier, but will need to be protected with a coat of flat varnish after the design has been made. The easiest finish to scrape off is black crayon.

If using a painted finish, make an egg holder by pounding three nails into a piece of wood. They should be spaced about ¾" apart and flared out at an angle. (See Fig. 7-20.) Paint the bottom of an egg, place it in the holder, and then paint the top. Tempera paint may need to have a second coat after the first has dried. If the egg sticks to the holder when dried, especially after later varnishing, remove from the holder by bending the nails out, not by pulling on the egg.

To cover the egg with black crayon, hold the egg gently on a pad of soft cloth. The eggs are surprisingly strong, however, because their curved shape distributes the pressure. If an area is not thoroughly clean and will not take the crayon, sand the area with medium grade sandpaper and reapply the crayon.

When the egg is colored, draw a design on it with a pencil. (Unwanted pencil lines can be removed easily with a kneaded eraser.) Suitable subject matter would be animals, birds, fish, and plants, especially those native to Australia. (See Fig. 7-6.) Resource books should be available for the students. Aboriginal design motifs, such as crosshatching, dots, diamonds, and concentric circles, can also be used to decorate the eggs. This is a good project for teaching the concept of negative and positive areas. (If the figure itself is scraped away down to the white layer, it is called a negative design. If the figure is to remain largely black, with the background scraped away, it is a positive design. The negative design can have some features—eyes, stripes, etc.—that remain black; the positive design can have some features that will be scraped to become white.)

Place the egg on a thick pad of soft cloth. Use a flat-bladed linoleum cutting tool to scrape away the color. Be sure the students *scrape* in a sideways motion, and do not try to cut the design in. A cutting motion is not only ineffective but dangerous on a round object. Both crayon and paint can be reapplied to areas to correct mistakes and then rescraped if desired.

Eggs that were painted with tempera paints should be protected with flat varnish or a satin acrylic polymer medium. Apply the latter with a light touch. Crayon can be polished to a nice sheen with a soft cloth.

A stand can be made for displaying the finished egg by pounding three nails into a well-sanded square of wood, as was done to make the stand for drying the painted eggs.

Fig. 7-21. Yumeng scrapes a design on her painted egg using a flat blade.

Fig. 8-1. Eagle pendant, c. 900–1400 A.D. Panamanian. Gift of Mr. and Mrs. Theodore O. Yntema in memory of Eleanor Clay Ford and Robert H. Tannahill. Photograph © 2002, The Detroit Institute of Arts.

8 MEXICAN, CENTRAL AMERICAN & SOUTH AMERICAN ARTS

The Indians of the areas now known as Mexico, Central America, and South America developed architecture and many arts and crafts to a high degree of skill during the centuries preceding the Spanish Conquest. Enormous stone temples of sophisticated design and construction, with richly carved and painted decorations, were created by the Maya, Toltec, Aztec, Inca, and other Andean civilizations.

Much of the artwork of these cultures was destroyed at the time of conquest, and much more disappeared as monuments and tombs were plundered over the ensuing centuries. However, from what remains we can appreciate the skill of the artisans of those times and the works they produced in clay, gold, silver, wool, feathers, and other available materials. In the contemporary popular arts of these areas, we see a mixture of these original arts with Spanish influences. Arts and crafts in great variety have continued to be handed down in the traditional manner. Many arts are unique to particular villages, according to the degree of isolation of the village and its resistance to outside influences.

Many pre-Conquest structures, as well as some of the surviving examples of arts and crafts, were inspired by religious requirements and beliefs. This is true of many of today's folk arts as well; what to an outsider may be of purely aesthetic and decorative value may have religious or magical significance. However, many arts have lost their original purpose and are now created for the market.

Fig. 8-2. Huichol Indian yarn paintings. State of Nayarit, Mexico. Collection of the author.

MEXICAN ARTS

Mexican popular arts abound in such variety that it is difficult to choose only a few that are representative. Mexican arts are usually exuberant in their use of bright color and imaginative design. There is artwork in an endless variety of materials: bark, clay, wood, wool, metals, wax, and many other natural materials. Examples of these arts are available in import shops.

Huichol Indian Yarn Paintings

The Huichol Indians, who live high in the Nayarit mountains of western Mexico and are

direct descendants of the Aztecs, create brilliantly colored yarn paintings. The paintings are created both as religious tablets to be used as votive offerings to local deities and to sell. This distinction is traditional, and certain rules are followed in the design of the pictures depending on their intended use, but the animals, birds, plants, and people depicted are common to both types. The deer is a particularly important symbol and is seen frequently in the yarn paintings. Some of the pictures record legends or tell stories of village life. Although the designs are usually based on natural subjects, they are always highly stylized and sometimes quite abstract. Edged with a border of several colors, the paintings range in size from quite small to several square feet in area.

To make the paintings (traditionally men's work), beeswax is first warmed in the sun and then spread on thin boards. The picture is created by pressing yarn into the wax with the thumbnail. The border is made first in three or more colors, each color several strands wide. Next, the figures are outlined with one or two strands of one or two colors. This outline is then filled in with contrasting colors; rarely is a figure filled in with only one color. The background is done last and is usually a solid color. (See Fig. 8-2.) The yarn is not applied back and forth; instead it follows the contours of the figures that define each space, reducing that space to a smaller and smaller area with one continuous strand until it is filled in, creating a pleasing pattern.

The Huichol also decorate gourds and maracas with yarn paintings in the same manner; and in a related art practiced by women, beads are pressed into wax to form designs on boards and inside gourd containers.

Making Yarn Pictures

Making a small yarn painting takes patience, and it is wise to start out on a small scale. The beauty of the art lies in part in completely covering the board. A board 6 x 8" is ample for a fifth- or sixth-grade student. Use ¼" plywood, hardboard, or chipboard. Corrugated cardboard is a less satisfactory choice because it is so flexible that sometimes the wax cracks off.

Although the Huichol work freehand or make a light sketch in the wax, it is better for students to work out a design first on paper the size of the board. In a piece this small, it is best to develop one central figure rather than many very small ones. Include a border. When you are satisfied with the penciled design, transfer it to the board with carbon paper. It will show

through the subsequent application of wax.

Beeswax, available at art supply stores, is costly and can be somewhat extended with paraffin—but more than one part paraffin to two parts beeswax will result in a medium that is too hard. Melt the wax in a pan set in another pan of water over a hot plate or electric stove burner. (*Never* melt wax directly over the flame. It is highly combustible.) Using a wide, flat brush, spread the wax evenly on the board. If it becomes too thick in some areas, scrape it

Fig. 8-3. Lee made a border of several colors first. Next he outlined his butterfly design. Now he is beginning to fill in the outline, following the inner contours of the butterfly wing. He uses the points of scissors to push the yarn into the wax.

Fig. 8-4. The wingtip has been filled in and the strand will be cut off flush with the rest of the yarn.

level again with a table knife. Be careful to get wax all the way to the edges of the board.

Although the Huichol use their thumbnails to push the yarn into the wax, it is easier for students to use a popsicle stick, tongue depressor, or scissors points for this purpose.

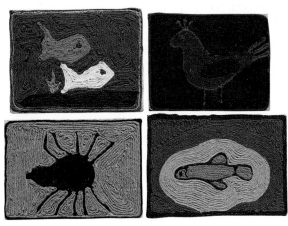

Fig. 8-5. Yarn paintings by fifth-grade students. Clockwise from upper left: *Two Fish*, by Nick; *Bird*, by Alex; *Fish*, by Slavik; *Spider*, by John.

have a stark and unusual beauty that seems to convey some of the magic for which they were created.

The paper from which they are cut is made from the bark of the amate tree. Strips of bark are boiled in a water and ash solution until they are soft. Then they are laid, crisscrossed and overlapping, on a smooth board and pounded with stones until the fibers mesh. The paper, which is strong and crisp, has a beautiful surface; the texture of the bark shows clearly. Both brown and white papers are made. This is an ancient art stemming from pre-Conquest times, when the paper was used for clothing and later for keeping records. Amate paper is now used to make symmetrical

Follow the Huichol method of making the border first. Try not to round the corners but to get the yarn to turn sharply with the edges of the corner. After the border is done, outline the figures with one or two colors and then fill them in with bright contrasting colors. (See Figs. 8-3 and 8-4.) The background is filled in last. The yarn is applied to an area in one long continuous strand until that area is filled up, starting around the outer edges of that space and filling in toward the center, not from the center out. Be sure that the strands of yarn are as close together as possible. When an area is filled in, cut off the yarn close to the board, tuck the end into the wax, and fill in another area. One strand should not cross over an adjacent strand to get to another area.

If wax is not available, white glue may be used as a substitute. Paint the glue on one small area at a time and press the yarn into it, keeping the top of the yarn soft and free of glue.

Amate Paper Cutouts

The amate paper cutouts made by the Otomí Indians of San Pablito in the Sierra de Puebla

Fig. 8-6. Amate paper cutout made by Otomí Indians of San Pablito, Sierra de Puebla, Mexico. Collection of the author.

Fig. 8-7. *Pajaro del Monte*, "Bird-of-the-mountain" cutouts. Otomí Indian, San Pablito, Sierra de Puebla, Mexico. These cutouts are kept in the home as protection against evil. They are made both in the two-headed and in the more powerful four-headed forms. Collection of the author.

cutouts for magical purposes—to protect crops, to rid a place of evil, to guard the home, or to bring health or illness (as a punishment or to harm an adversary).

The designs frequently use human forms (which sometimes represent spirits) and also reflect elements of nature that are important in the lives of the Otomí people: agricultural plants, domestic and wild animals, and birds. The figures, however, are not realistic but have added fanciful or symbolic ornamentation. A common design is a standing man combined with animal or plant forms (see Fig. 8-6). Other traditional motifs include the two-headed or four-headed bird-of-the-mountain (see Fig. 8-7), which protects the home, and the lion spirit, which is buried with the dead and is believed to lead the spirit of the deceased to fresh water and fruit. Bark cutouts are also used as tokens of gratitude to the earth for a good crop.

Making Symmetrical Cutouts

In planning their designs, students may want to refer to *Design Motifs of Ancient Mexico* by Jorge Encisco (see the bibliography). This book contains many design ideas, some geometric and others derived from natural forms. Students should be encouraged to use their imaginations. The emphasis should be on fanciful decorative designs rather than realism.

To simulate the heavy, textured amate paper, begin with a 9 x 12" piece of brown wrapping paper, brown Kraft paper, or a brown paper bag. Fold the paper in half. Using

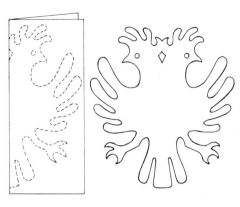

Fig. 8-8. To make a symmetrical cutout, draw half a figure on a folded piece of brown wrapping paper. Cut it out while still folded, and then open it to reveal a symmetrical figure.

Fig. 8-9. Alice, age ten, cuts out a lion design from the folded brown paper.

Fig. 8-10. Alfred crumples his design.

Fig. 8-11. After crumpling her design, Eileen spreads it open and irons it between sheets of wax paper.

Fig. 8-12. A sun design by a fifth-grade student. A hole puncher was used to create a lacy effect.

Fig. 8-13. A four-headed bird-of-the mountain by Helen, age nine.

the fold as a center line, chalk in half the form of a bird, animal, person, or other pleasing shape. Cut it out while the paper is still folded, as shown in Figs. 8-8 and 8-9. Open up the design (it will be symmetrical) and crumple it thoroughly several times to form irregular patterns in the paper. Carefully spread it open again, place it between two sheets of wax paper, and iron it.

Ironing should be done under adult supervision. First, protect the table with a pad of newspaper. Use medium heat. As the wax melts,

it stiffens the paper and adds some of the amate paper's color, texture, and feel. A second application of wax paper may be needed to deepen the color and bring out the pattern.

The cutout is greatly enhanced by careful mounting. Apply white glue very sparingly to the chalky side of the cutout and mount it on white paper, which should then be centered on a larger mat of brown construction paper.

The textured paper lends beauty to even the simplest designs. This is one project that allows all students to achieve satisfying results.

Amate Paper Paintings

The amate paper made by the Otomí Indians is purchased by the people of Amexaltepec, Xalitla, and other villages and used for making highly decorative paintings. These paintings, which are often available in import shops in the United States, usually show flowers, birds, animals, or scenes of village life and are painted with brilliant, sometimes fluorescent, paints. The paintings are very fanciful—flowers of many colors bloom from the same stalk, leaves may be blue or orange as well as green, fancy birds sport plumage never seen in the real world, horses may be turquoise, and spots of color leave the figures and trail in lines over the bark. Sometimes the painting is surrounded with a border of geometric designs. The background is never painted—the colorful figures stand out against the rich brown, beautifully textured handmade paper. (See Fig. 8-14.)

Making Paintings on Prepared Brown Paper

To make these paintings, prepare the paper first. Cut a rectangle approximately 7 x 10" with rounded corners from brown wrapping paper or a paper bag. Crumple it thoroughly several times and then iron it out between wax paper. Iron again with fresh wax paper if necessary to achieve a deep color and stiff texture.

Before they plan their designs, students should see some bark paintings if possible or

Fig. 8-14. Amate paper paintings, Mexico. Collection of the author.

Fig. 8-15. Third-grade students working on their "bark" paintings. Angela draws the lines with black ink. Thea fills in the designs with bright tempera paint and fluorescent colors. The background is not painted.

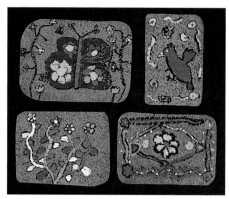

Fig. 8-17. Four "bark" paintings by third- and fourth-grade students. Clockwise from top left: *Butterfly*, by Lisa; *Bird*, by Sarah; *Flower with Border Design*, by Laura; and *Flowers*, unsigned.

Fig. 8-16. This "bark" painting by David captures the spirit of imaginative design.

a pencil. Then begin the painting by outlining the design with a fine brush and black paint or India ink. Next, when the outline is dry, fill in the figures with color, *leaving some of the black outline showing*. Use tempera paint in the brightest colors available: magenta, turquoise, yellow-green, pink, orange, purple, and white. The tempera paint may be supplemented with small amounts of water-based fluorescent paints (found in art supply stores). The background is not painted—the textured brown paper provides a beautiful contrast to the brilliant paint. If you have trouble getting the paint or ink to stick to the waxy surface, stir in a drop or two of liquid soap or detergent.

study examples in books. They should note the highly fanciful, decorative quality of the designs. The design may be drawn lightly on the prepared brown paper with

Fig. 8-18. Clay figures from Tonala, state of Jalisco, Mexico. The animals and birds are decorated with fine brushwork. (The little owl's back is decorated with flowers and a butterfly.) Collection of the author.

Clay Figures from Tonala and Metapec

The art of making clay vessels and figures has played an important part in Mexican life from earliest times. It is the most widely practiced art in Mexico. The style of work is as varied as the many villages and towns that specialize in works of clay, and pieces are so distinctive that their place of origin can be easily identified. Many different techniques are used, but usually the items are made entirely by hand. The clay pieces are fired in brick or adobe kilns constructed in the artisan's yard and fueled with wood or oil.

Tonala, in the state of Jalisco, is an important pottery center that produces plates, jugs, tiles, and figures decorated in a unique style. Particularly appealing are small animal figures: horses, cats, fish, turtles, and birds of many kinds—owls, ducks, toucans, and pigeons. They are painted in subtle grays and earth colors with overall free-flowing designs of leaves and flowers, butterflies, dots, swirls, and lines that seem to combine all that is joyous in nature. (See Fig. 8-18.)

Metapec, in the state of Mexico, has long been famous for its pottery that ranges from functional pieces for domestic use to very ornate "trees of life," which are fanciful interpretations of the Garden of Eden. There are statues of saints and of skeletons, animals, toys of all kinds, candlesticks, and masks. Most of the pottery is unglazed. After being fired, it is either left in its natural state or painted in brilliant colors.

The clay suns of Metapec are especially delightful. In many varia-tions they seem to express benevolent and life-giving energy. Timoteo Gonzales of Metapec claims to have been the first potter to make the now-famous suns, which range in size from 7" to 2' across. The rounded form is made by pressing a slab of clay over a mold. Facial features are created from additional pieces of clay, and rays, shaped from balls of clay, are attached around the edge of the sun. Slits are cut for the mouth and over the eyebrows. In some suns decorative perforations are also made around the rim, just inside the rays. Sometimes the sun is left undecorated after firing, and sometimes a base coat of white is brushed with floral designs in bright colors and touches of gold paint. (See Fig. 8-22.)

Making Clay Animals and Birds

Students can form simple animal shapes of clay (the Tonala figures are streamlined with only a suggestion of features, legs, or feet). After drying for two weeks, fire the pieces in a kiln, and then decorate them with tempera paints. First apply a base coat of color, and

Fig. 8-19. Lise, eleven, paints flowers and vines on a cat.

Fig. 8-20. Lucy and Ellen apply polymer medium as a protective finish to their decorated whale and mouse figures.

Fig. 8-21. Five sculptures inspired by Tonala clay pieces, by sixth-grade students. From left: *Whale*, by Ellen; *Bird*, by Lanette; *Cat*, by Lise; *Duck*, unsigned; and *Mouse*, by Lucy.

after this dries, add features and designs using a very fine pointed brush. After the paint has dried thoroughly, it can be protected with a coat of shellac or polymer medium, applied with a very light, flowing touch. Scrubbing with the brush will make the colors mix and run. Be sure to wash the brush immediately after use.

Making Clay Suns

Children of all ages enjoy making sun designs. Young children may form their suns freely from a fist-sized piece of clay. They can start by making a ball of clay and flattening it with their fists. The rays can be pinched out around the circumference of the disk (pinching works better than trying to attach pieces) or indicated by pressing fingers or thumb all around the edge. A face may be incised with a pencil point, poked in with fingertips, painted in later, or not indicated at all. After drying for two weeks, the pieces can be fired in a kiln and then painted with tempera paints. Each of the first-grade sun designs in Fig. 8-23 is unique and radiates an energy all its own.

Older children may want to study the Metapec designs, but they should also be encouraged to use their imagination in making a design of their own. The largest of the Metapec

Fig. 8-22. Clay sun design from Metapec, State of Mexico, Mexico. 19". Collection of the author.

suns requires a great deal of clay. For fifth- or sixth-grade students, suns approximately 9" across are probably about the right size.

First roll the clay into an even slab with a rolling pin and two sticks about ½" thick. Place the sticks 1' apart and put a baseball-sized lump of clay between them. Roll out the clay to form the basic slab. Next, to create a raised form, cut the lip off a paper bowl and invert it on a piece of newspaper. Then lift the clay slab

Fig. 8-23. A group of first-grade sun designs.

Fig. 8-24. A sixth-grade sun design.

Fig. 8-25. Christine painted her sun with a base coat of white tempera and now adds decorations with gold paint.

and press it down gently over the bowl. If the clay extends an inch or so beyond the bowl, you can cut rays in the edge with a table knife. If not, form and add on rays, taking great care that the clay is well joined. Place the ray somewhat up on the rounded form, not just butting the edge. The joining should be as thick as the main body, or cracks may form and the rays may break off during drying.

Now that the basic shape is formed, let imagination guide the students in creating their own sun designs. If the sun is to have features, these may be added with additional clay, eyes and mouth may be cut out, or a combination of these methods may be used. Two holes may be pierced in the top of the sun (not in a ray) and later, after the sun is fired, a string can be pulled through and tied to be used as a hanger.

Fig. 8-26. Heidi applies a protective coat of polymer medium to her design.

Fig. 8-27. Three sixth-grade sun designs after having been fired in the kiln. They can be left this natural clay color or decorated with tempera paints.

The suns should be dried for two weeks and then fired in a kiln. They can then be left in their natural clay color or painted with tempera paint. It is best to paint a base coat of one solid color (in Metapec it's usually white) and to add further designs when this has dried. A protective layer of shellac or polymer medium should be applied when the paint is thoroughly dry. Be sure to apply it with a light touch. Scrubbing with a brush will make the colors mix and run.

ARTS OF CENTRAL AMERICA AND SOUTH AMERICA

CUNA INDIAN MOLAS

The Cuna Indian women of the San Blas Islands off the coast of Panama decorate their blouses with beautifully designed and sewn cotton panels called molas. (Although *mola* technically means "blouse" in their language, it has come to mean the panel itself.) This tradition has been carried on for over 100 years. Girls begin to learn this skill from their mothers or grandmothers when they are seven or eight years old.

When making a mola, a Cuna woman first bastes together several layers of brightly colored cotton cloth. She creates the design by cutting away pieces of cloth to expose the layers beneath. The edges of the cuts are skillfully turned under and sewn with almost invisible stitches. In some areas of the design, material may be appliqued to sections that have previously been exposed, and small areas may be underlaid with a piece of cloth that does not extend under the entire work. The cloth surface is therefore cut into and built up in a

Fig. 8-28. Cuna Indian mola, *sikwi* (bird) design, from the San Blas Islands, Panama. Collection of the author.

sculptural way. A really fine mola may take many weeks to complete.

There is a great variety of subjects in the designs. The molas most frequently have stylized designs based on the natural world—birds, animals, fish, leaves, and flowers—but some are based on Cuna mythology or religious beliefs. Others may be inspired by dreams or fantasies, and a few are purely geometric in design. Whatever the subject, the design forms an elaborate labyrinth of color. Characteristic rounded slot shapes surround and are internal to the main figures. Although red, orange, or black frequently dominates a color scheme, the whole range of colors is used

in making molas. A predominately red mola may also have flashes of bright green, blue, or yellow. Fig. 8-28 shows a bird and a tree or plant design with leaf and flower forms made of three main layers of cloth: red, green, and then red again. The pink has been appliqued on the bottom red layer, and then red has been appliqued on top of the pink. Small pieces of yellow, blue, and purple underlay the top red layer in many areas. This fine example is typical of the very complex Cuna molas that are executed with great skill and are unique in conception and design to this tiny part of the world.

Making Paper Molas

Junior high students may wish to create a mola in the same manner as the Cuna Indians. The sewing required is too intricate for most elementary school children. However, molas made by using successive layers of colored paper are very satisfying and challenge enough. Whether they are made of paper or cloth, the design is created in the same way, with layers of color.

It is not possible to work with all the colored papers together at once. Cut into the piece that is to be on top first, working either with pointed scissors, a flat linoleum cutting tool, or X-acto knife. In the latter cases, place the paper to be cut on a thick pad of newspaper. The first shape cut out should be larger and less defined than those in succeeding layers. Place the second piece of colored paper under the first cutout, lining up the outside edges, and clip them together. Then, with a pencil, define the shapes more accurately ¼" or so in from the edges of the first cutout, and cut them out. The third piece of paper may be another color or repeat the first color.

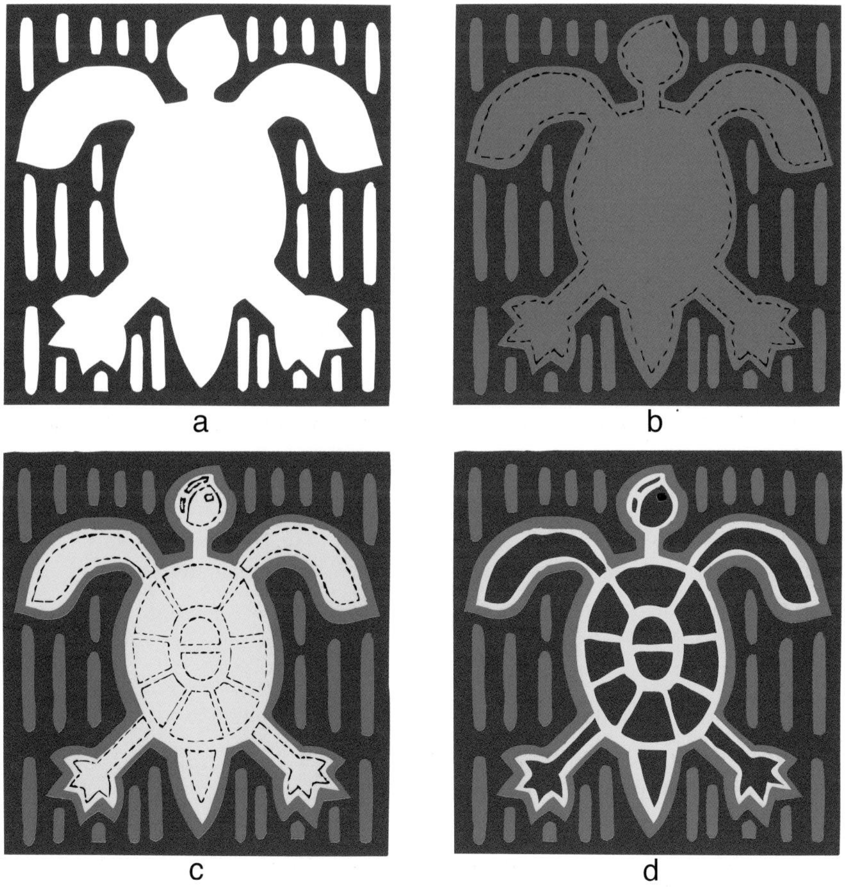

Fig. 8-29 shows the steps in making a four-layer mola. In *a*, the turtle shape and slot designs have been cut out of a red piece of paper. In *b*, a second piece of paper of a contrasting color, blue, has been slipped underneath and a dotted line drawn where it will be cut out. In *c*, the blue layer of paper has been cut out and a third layer, yellow, put underneath. Lines have been drawn on the third layer where it will be cut out. In *d*, the lines in the third layer are cut out and the fourth piece of paper,

Fig. 8-29 a, b, c, d. Diagram of four steps in making a paper mola design. This is a *yauk* (sea turtle) design, adapted from a mola in the collection of Captain Kit S. Kapp.

Fig. 8-30. Geometric paper mola design by Sarah, nine.

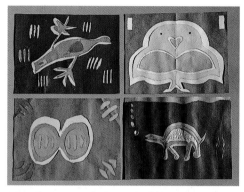

Fig. 8-31. Paper mola designs by fifth-grade students. From top left, *Bird on branch*, by Rachel; *Bird*, unsigned; *Turtle*, by Debbie; *Geometric Design*, unsigned.

red again, has been slipped underneath.

This is one project that is easier to understand as one begins to work, and it may be a good idea to experiment with scraps of paper first, cutting simple shapes to see how successive layers are exposed.

The sandwich of layers should usually total at least three colors. Additional colors can be added by slipping small pieces of paper under particular areas for emphasis. Some very effective molas, however, use only two colors with a small bit of embroidery to create an eye on a figure; in a paper mola, the eye

would be glued on. When all the cutting is complete the layers are attached to each other with white glue.

GOLD AND SILVER SCULPTURE OF PRE-CONQUEST PERU, COLOMBIA, ECUADOR, PANAMA, AND COSTA RICA

The art of making jewelry and sculpture in gold and silver reached extremely high levels in Central and South America before the Spanish Conquest. Few of these pieces survive—countless treasures were melted down and sent back to Spain as bullion—but enough have remained for us to catch a glimpse of this beautiful work. We can only guess at what was made that we can never see.

Fig. 8-32. Panamanian frog, excavated in Costa Rica. c. 500–1500. Gold-surfaced copper. Bequest of Robert H. Tannahill. Courtesy of The Detroit Institute of Arts.

Fig. 8-33. Silver, long haired alpaca. Peru. 9½ x 8". Neg. no. 132578. Courtesy of The Library, American Museum of Natural History.

In the area now known as Colombia, artisans cast very heavy sculptures that required great skill and knowledge of metallurgy. Equally awe-inspiring are the delicate, tiny sculptures that have been uncovered in Ecuador. The priceless gold and silver work of Peru is perhaps the best known, because it was the first discovered in the New World. Large quantities of gold sculpture were also cast in Panama and Costa Rica, and pieces are still being found in excavations there.

Several methods were used in making gold and silver sculpture. Much work, such as the double-headed eagle pendant from Panama in Fig. 8-1, was cast using the lost-wax method. The little Panamanian frog in Fig. 8-32 was made of cast copper and surfaced with gold. It

was excavated in Costa Rica. Little balls in the eyes make them ring like bells. Sculpture was also created of gold or silver hammered into paper-thin sheets and decorated with repoussé designs. In repoussé work, the thin metal is pushed up from the back, raising the designs on the front. (See the lines that create the woolly coat on the alpaca from Peru, Fig. 8-33.) Sometimes fine wires of gold or silver were braided, twisted, or coiled and added to the sculpture to form hair, ornaments, or designs.

Using these methods, artists made a great variety of gold objects. Many sculptures were created in honor of the Sun God or for other religious purposes. Gold jewelry and household items for the wealthy—pendants; ear and nose ornaments; figures of people, birds, fish, and animals; cups and other utensils—were made. Masks of sheet metal were attached to mummy bundles. They were usually almost flat, with only a gentle curve. The stylized repoussé eyes sometimes had turquoise or shell centers attached with wire. Some masks were encircled with radiating snake designs symbolizing the sun's rays.

Making Gold and Silver Cardboard Sculpture

Although working in precious metals is obviously impossible, students enjoy making designs in light cardboard or tagboard. Brushed with gold or silver paint, this resembles the work made of thin sheets of metal.

To make cardboard sculpture, students should cut out a basic shape first. They can make raised designs by gluing more pieces of cardboard to the base. Cotton string can also be used: braided, twisted, or coiled, it can be glued to the cardboard to form designs like

Fig. 8-34. Sculpture and pendant designs of gilded cardboard by fifth-grade students.

Fig. 8-35. Butterfly pendant by Ruth, ten. The butterfly body and wing designs were made by braiding and coiling string.

those made of gold wire in the pre-Conquest sculptures.

Students can design pendants, masks, or sculptures of people or animals. The animal shapes may be cut out and folded into standing figures. Experiment first with heavyweight scrap paper until you have a pattern you like, and then trace around it on the cardboard and cut it out. (See the birds and cat in Fig. 8-34.) Feathers, scales, fur, eyes, whiskers, and so forth are cut out of cardboard or formed from a piece of string and glued on. Remind students that any feature or design on the cardboard sculpture must be *raised* for it to show after it's been painted.

When the sculpture is finished, it should be painted with gold or silver tempera paint or polymer. The added layers of cardboard and string give an effect very much like that of repoussé work.

PERUVIAN EMBROIDERY

The ancient Peruvians excelled in textile arts. Because of the arid climate, many examples of pre-Columbian weaving and embroidery have been preserved and can be found in museums today. The cloth was often woven with intricate designs that required great skill, and the tradition of fine weaving continues today.

Fig. 8-36. A textile fragment from Lake Tiahuanaco, Peru, of a seabird c. 800–1200. Private collection, Zurich. Photo © Ferdinand Anton.

Fig. 8-37. *People Dancing to the Music of a Flute*, embroidery on homespun cloth by a Qolla Indian child of Chijnaya, Peru. c. 1965. Courtesy of Phyllis Swonk.

Fig. 8-38. *Spring Plowing*, embroidery by a Qolla Indian child, Chijnaya, Peru c. 1965. Photograph courtesy of *Woman's Day*.

Cloth was also embroidered with colorful stylized birds, snakes, pumas, and human figures. Many centuries later, descendants of those early artisans also made embroideries on handwoven cloth. The artists were the children in the Qolla Indian village of Chijnaya, in the Peruvian Andes. For them, it was a very recent art. Although the chain stitch that they used resembled the cross-knot loop stitch used in ancient times, the modern stitchery in their village had not come down by tradition over the centuries.

Before 1962 the Qolla Indians occupied lands on the banks of Lake Titicaca. Heavy rains caused a great flood which forced them to flee to higher land. They lost their homes and most of their possessions. Some of these destitute families accepted relocation by the government in a new village called Chijnaya. New artisan activities were introduced in an attempt to increase the community income. These included the production of handspun alpaca yarn and related weaving projects. The

Qolla Indian adults were already proficient at weaving, knitting, and making colorful embroidered clothing. However, as a part of this program a Peace Corps volunteer introduced the children of the village to the art of embroidered cloth, not for clothing but to create a piece of art to sell. The children were taught the chain stitch, but no attempt was made to influence the designs they created.

The children soon mastered the technique. In a very short time their imaginative embroideries were selling in the markets. Exhibitions were arranged in the United States, where they were received with great enthusiasm. The children, from six to sixteen years of age, worked after school during their free time, usually in groups, enjoying the work as a social time together. With the money from their embroideries they bought school supplies, clothing, and other necessities. After awhile, adults also joined in making embroideries. It became a village effort, and ultimately some very large 8 x 6' panels were created.

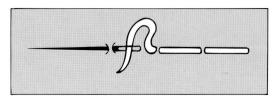

Fig. 8-39. The running stitch.

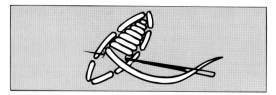

Fig. 8-40. The satin stitch, used for filling in areas.

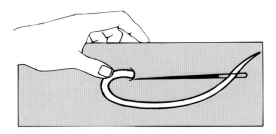

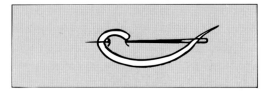

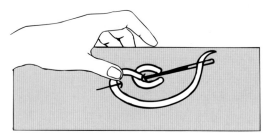

Fig. 8-41. The chain stitch. Bring the yarn up from the back of the cloth. Hold a loop of yarn with the thumb, insert the needle right beside the place where the yarn emerged, and bring the needle up just inside the loop.

Fig. 8-42. First-grade students Chris and Debbie working on their embroidery designs.

The embroideries were made on a cream-colored cloth made from handspun sheep's wool. It was woven by the men of the village, on upright looms. Some of the designs used only natural colored alpaca yarns—black, brown and grays. Others used brightly colored commercial yarns. The designs depicted scenes of village life in the Andes Mountains—domestic animals, such as alpacas, pigs, ducks, and oxen; land being plowed; fiesta days; or religious themes. Sometimes the images were quite realistic, and sometimes they were fanciful (an ox may be striped with rainbow colors), but they were all made with a fresh directness of spirit and skillful mastery of needlework.

Making Embroidered Designs

Young children from first to third grade can make simple embroideries on a square of burlap. At this early age a running stitch to outline their figures and a

Fig. 8-43. *Puppy*, by Daniel, first grade. Daniel used the running stitch.

satin stitch to fill in some areas are all they need to learn. (See Figs. 8-39 and 8-40.)

Natural color burlap most closely resembles the homespun cloth background used by the Qolla Indian children. Its loose weave also makes the stitching easier. A piece 7 x 7" is large enough for a beginner. The students should use a blunt yarn needle. First, frame the square with an embroidered border. This should be at least ½" from the edge, as burlap unravels easily. After completing the frame, lightly sketch the outline of a simple design on the burlap with chalk, and follow these lines with a needle and yarn. Show the children how to keep the burlap flat by pulling the yarn gently as they sew and caution them not to pull their yarn too tight. Knots are not necessary. A 2" "tail" can be left at the back of the material when starting a new piece of yarn. Some areas, such as the flower petals in Fig. 8-44, can be filled in with the satin stitch.

Older students, from fourth grade on, can learn the chain stitch used by the children of Chijnaya (Fig. 8-41). The students may want to draw on some aspect of their own life in planning their embroidery. The background of their design may be skyscrapers instead of mountains, or they may want to embroider a portrait of a pet rather than an alpaca.

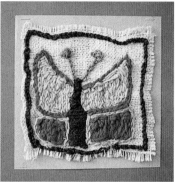

Fig. 8-45. Fifth grade chain-stitched embroidery designs: *Horse and Rider*, by Jason; *Butterfly*, by Theresa; *Sun, Mountain, and Flower* design by Angie.

Fig. 9-1. Haitian steel design with pig, bird, and plant forms, signed "Charles." Collection of the author.

9 ARTS OF THE CARIBBEAN ISLANDS

The projects chosen for this chapter illustrate several different characteristics of the arts and crafts of the Caribbean Islands. Necklaces created from the seeds of island trees and shrubs are made on many of the islands including Puerto Rico, and symbolize the natural beauty common to them all.

Maracas—rhythm instruments first made by the Indians who were the original inhabitants of the islands—represent the all-pervading musical traditions that have been enriched over the centuries with contributions from many different cultures.

The steel designs of Haiti illustrate a modern rather than traditional art. These designs make ingenious use of scrap metal, not a naturally found material, and often explore concepts concerning humanity's relation to nature and to the spiritual world.

PUERTO RICAN ARTS

Puerto Rico is the smallest, easternmost island of the Greater Antilles, situated in the Caribbean Sea. Before Columbus, the Taino Indians living on the island called it Borinquén (boh-ree-KEN). It was a green and fertile island with mountains in the center and coastal lowlands. The Tainos, a peaceful, agricultural people, lived in villages and raised corn and sweet potatoes and gathered the island fruits. Tragically, few of them survived the arrival of the Spanish, but much Taino culture endured: their cultivated vegetables, the arts of hammock and basket weaving, such musical instruments as maracas (round gourds filled with seeds) and guiros (a bottle-shaped gourd played with a wire fork), their foods and ways of cooking them, and a feeling of love for the land that is shared by Puerto Ricans today.

When the Taino population declined, slaves were brought from Africa to work for the Spaniards, and eventually the culture of Puerto Rico became a mixture of African, Indian, and Spanish influences. In 1898, after the Spanish-American War, Spain ceded Puerto Rico to the United States, and once again a new, dominant culture was brought to bear on the island. Since 1952 Puerto Rico has been a commonwealth; it elects its own governor but has ties to the United States. Puerto Ricans are United States citizens at birth.

Puerto Ricans are proud of their island and their roots in Taino culture. Ancient ruins on the island have monuments of incised stones from pre-Columbian times. They depict the Taino gods, called cemies. Smaller figures of clay and wood have been found in excavations. Craftspeople today make replicas of the stone and clay sculptures, and the Taino designs are used in modern fabrics.

Perhaps the best-known Puerto Rican folk art is that of the carved wooden santos (SAN-tohs), meaning saints. Santos have been made for more than 300 years, and until recently, most families had santos that were handed down for generations. A santo might be the village or family patron saint or one that brought special healing powers. Originally they were decorated with natural pigments. By the nineteenth century, santos were painted in many colors and sometimes included metal as well as wood. The sculptures are recognized for their unique beauty, and many are now in museum collections.

The African heritage in Puerto Rico is perhaps most clear in its many contributions to the music of the island and in the annual Fiesta de Santiago Apostol (Festival of St. James the Apostle) held in the village of Loíza Aldea. Historically, the village population was predominantly of African descent. The festival is famous for its feathered and horned masks, carved from coconuts and made only in this area. Singing satirical ballads and dancing the African bomba, the villagers depict the story of the conqueror and the conquered with a mixture of love and hostility, fun and solemnity that represents many aspects of the Indian, African, and Spanish heritage of Puerto Rico.

SEED NECKLACES OF PUERTO RICO

Several of the trees and plants found on the island are known only in Puerto Rico. There are also many beautiful flowering trees, such as the flamboyan with large red blossoms, and the jacaranda with its violet-blue flowers. One variety or another blooms throughout the year. Children in the country are familiar with many trees and plants and use them in their games. The seed of the mango is made into dolls. It is large and flat and oval, and some varieties have a covering of long fibers. The children polish the fibers off the front and draw faces on them, combing the rest of the fibers into hair around the face. There are canna lilies, which are called maraca plants because the fine, hard seeds are gathered and put into gourds to make maracas (see next project). And there are games played with the *algarrobo* seeds. These 1" seeds are oblong, dark red, and very hard. They grow in long pods on tall trees. A hole is made in the seed, and a heavy string is put through it and tied. Then children take turns swinging their *algarrobo* seed against their opponent's until one of the seeds breaks.

Along the rivers in marshy ground grow the *camándula* plants. They have shiny, pearly gray seeds (also called Job's tears) with a natural hole just right for stringing, and children make necklaces of them. *Camándula* means "rosary beads," and they have also been used for rosaries for many years.

Necklaces made from native seeds and beans are sold in the tourist shops in San Juan. The two most commonly used seeds are the camándulas (both in natural colors and dyed) and the small, brown tamarind, or *zarcilla*, seeds. There are the smooth, brown, striped oval seeds from the earpod tree and shiny, bright red *granate* (or red sandalwood) seeds. The

Fig. 9-2. Seed necklaces from Puerto Rico, containing (from left) seeds from the earpod tree, alternating with red *granate* (red sandalwood); *camándula* (Job's tears); *flamboyan* (datelike), with red granate, earpod, and *matos gris* (gray *niker* seeds); and tamarind (*zarcilla* seeds).

flamboyan has a datelike seed frequently used in necklaces. Beads are also sometimes made of coffee beans. From vines growing near the beaches come the softly striped and satiny gray *niker* seeds, or *matos gris* (Fig. 9-2).

The beads made from all these seeds speak of the land most tourists never see.

Making Seed Necklaces

We can learn from Puerto Rico to see and use what is in our environment. Look both indoors and outside for seeds that can be used for necklaces. Perhaps you have never noticed before how many seeds are thrown away or passed by and how beautiful some of them are on close inspection. Save apple seeds—shiny, brown, and much like the Puerto Rican *zarcilla* seeds. Squash, watermelon, and pumpkin seeds make fine necklaces. Sometimes a grocer has spoiled produce that you can check for seeds. Separate the seeds from the pulp, wash them, and spread them out to dry on wax paper (they will stick to other papers). You can buy sunflower seeds with subtle gray stripes, round

Fig. 9-4. A sampling of some seeds suitable for necklaces. Clockwise from top: acorn squash, watermelon, corn, apple, pumpkin, coffee beans, cantaloupe, and allspice. Gray-striped sunflower seeds fill the center.

brown allspice seeds, and coffee beans (perhaps from Puerto Rico). Frozen corn and peas can be used for beads; they will dry to half their original size, so in stringing them you must make the necklace twice as long as the final length you wish.

Outdoors, look for seeds on ornamental shrubs or seeds that have fallen from trees. Acorn cups or husks, from oak trees, are beautifully shaped, smooth and brown inside, rough and patterned on the outside. *Some berries and seeds from plants and shrubbery may be poisonous. The castor bean is quite commonly planted and is highly poisonous and should never be used. If you do not know a plant, check with a botanist or poison control center before using it.* For proper identification you will need leaves as well as berries or seeds.

If the seeds are too hard to push a needle through (such as coffee beans and allspice), they should be soaked for several hours in warm water before you make the necklace. Use a heavy carpet thread. Think of a pattern for stringing your beads—alternate size and shape or colors. However, sometimes especially beautiful seeds are more noticeable if only that one kind is used.

Fig. 9-3. Necklaces made by fourth-grade students. From left: Jenny's is made of allspice and acorn squash seeds, Bill's alternates yellow corn with coffee beans, and Amy's uses corn and coffee beans in a different arrangement.

ISLAND MARACAS

Music plays an important part in the lives of the people of the Caribbean Islands. The area is a rich mixture of many cultures, including Indian, Spanish, African, French, British, and American. From the Indians came two instruments that were developed in pre-Columbian times and are still in use today: the *guiro* and the maraca. The guiro *(gwee-roh)* is made from a hollow bottle gourd with lines incised on it. When the tines of a metal fork are scraped over the ridges, it makes a rasping sound. Maracas were used by Indians throughout the islands and in Mexico and South America as well. They are made of hollow gourds or the large, hard-shelled fruit of the calabash tree. Small seeds are put in the gourds and a handle is attached. Sometimes island scenes are painted on contemporary maracas, and sometimes designs are cut into the surface of the gourd while it is still green. Maracas are usually used in pairs and are shaken to the rhythm of a dance or to accompany a song.

Several kinds of guitar-like stringed instruments are made on the islands, often by hand in the villages. One of the most popular is the *cuatro*, which is a four or five double-stringed instrument. Perhaps the most widely known instrument from the area originated in recent years in Trinidad. During World War II percussion instruments were made of steel oil drums cut down into finely tuned pans. Notes are played by hitting different areas of the pan. Steel bands, which play with great skill, are now popular on many Caribbean islands.

Each island has its own particular musical heritage and styles, but much of the music played and sung is strongly African in origin with Spanish overtones. Under Spanish rule, slaves were not allowed to talk while they were working, but they could sing. They developed songs to record history and keep it alive, to pass information, and to comment on current events. Today Caribbean songs include religious songs, love songs, and work songs, but perhaps one thing they all share is that they frequently recall memorable events of the past or comment on present political or social conditions.

After making maracas, students may want to learn the song we have included here and emphasize the beat with

Fig. 9-5. Island maracas. From left: two carved maracas from St. Thomas, collection of Irene Tejada; a carved and painted maraca from Cuba, collection of Mrs. Juanita Lopez; one painted and two carved maracas from Puerto Rico, collections of Yolanda Marino and Irene Tejada.

¡Temporal!
(Hurricane!)

Spanish and English
Text by Ruth Gomez

Puerto Rican Folk Song
Arranged by Elsa Adamson

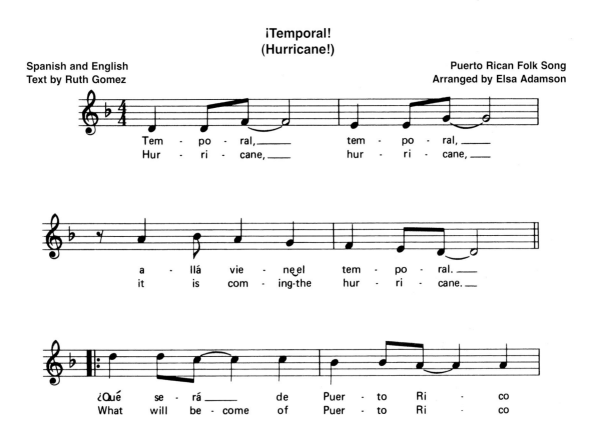

Tem - po - ral, _____ tem - po - ral, _____
Hur - ri - cane, ____ hur - ri - cane, ____

a - llá vie - ne el tem - po - ral. _____
it is com - ing the hur - ri - cane. __

¿Qué se - rá _____ de Puer - to Ri - co
What will be - come of Puer - to Ri - co

cuan - do lle - que el tem - po - ral?
when the hur - ri - cane ar - rives?

Fig. 9-6.

their maracas. This folk song is very popular in Puerto Rico and probably came into being to memorialize one of the terribly devastating hurricanes that periodically do great damage to the islands. This type of song is called a *plena* and is of African origin (see Fig. 9-6).

Making Maracas

Maracas can be made quite successfully from papier-mâché. Blow up a round balloon to about 5" in diameter. Tie the end. Apply at least four layers of torn newspaper dipped in papier-mâché glue. (See appendix for general papier-mâché instructions.) The pieces should be no larger than 2" square if there is to be a smooth surface. Do not cover the knot.

After several days, when the papier-mâché is thoroughly dry, pop the balloon at the place where it is tied. (This is fun—the balloon will pull away from the inside of the globe, making

Arts of the Caribbean Islands **211**

Fig. 9-7. Applying newspaper dipped in paste to a balloon. Smaller pieces than are shown here would result in a smoother surface.

Fig. 9-8. Michael listens to his balloon "talk" inside the papier-mâché shell. (When the balloon is popped, it pulls away from the dry shell, making crackling sounds.)

Fig. 9-9. Maracas made by third-grade students Roy and Chris.

Fig. 9-10. Second and third graders sing ¡Temporal!, accenting the rhythm with their maracas.

mysterious crackling noises that go on for some time.) Remove the broken balloon.

Put a teaspoonful of dried split peas, rice, other smaller seeds, or very tiny pebbles into the hole. Insert an 11" piece of ½" dowel into the hole and all the way through to the top of the globe.

Place the maraca upright on its handle, and hammer a large-headed tack through the papier mâché into the dowel at the top. Now add three layers of newspaper dipped in papier-mâché glue to the area where the globe joins the handle, applying narrow strips vertically and lapping the paper well down over the dowel. One more layer to the whole maraca will cover the tack and give added strength.

When the maraca is dry, it can be painted with tempera paints. A good method is to give one base coat of a solid color, and let it dry before painting on a design with a fine detail brush. Students may want to try a typical island scene with palm trees and ocean or some design of their own. After the paint is

thoroughly dry, it should be protected with a coat of shellac.

HAITIAN DESIGNS IN STEEL

Haiti, "land of mountains" in the Arawak Indian language, has had a long and often tragic history resulting in a mixture of Indian, Spanish, African, and French cultures. An uprising against colonial rule in 1791 began a long struggle toward self-rule by the largely black population that was brought to Haiti from West Africa as slaves during both Spanish and French rule. In 1804 Haiti won complete independence, but the next century brought internal struggles and occupation by the United States from 1915 to 1934.

Although there had been continuous artistic activity dating back to pre-Columbian times, the unrest and extreme poverty did not allow for much formal artistic development. But when the Centre d'Art opened in Port-au-Prince in 1944, art blossomed. Supported by

Fig. 9-11. The Haitian steel designs often merge human and animal forms. This design by Louis Bruno appears to be part human, part rooster, and part fish. Collection of the author.

designed iron crosses for cemeteries. When it was suggested by people from the Centre d'Art that he make iron sculptures, he began to create mostly flat metal figures that are now prized in museums worldwide. He has become one of Haiti's most famous artists. The figures portray a mixture of Catholicism and voodoo (a folk religion of African origin) that is unique to Haiti and often expressed in Haitian art. They represent spirits that embody fears and joys and sometimes a fine sense of humor.

The sculptures are usually made from steel oil drums that are opened and flattened to a 3' x 6' piece of metal. Precise drawings are trans-

the combined efforts of American and Haitian authorities, it had been suggested by DeWitt Peters, who had come to Haiti from America as a teacher. The Centre d'Art provided support for the artists and a market for their work. Many people came forward or were discovered who had been working privately at art for many years. They were intuitive painters who earned their living by working at other trades but were devoted to painting whenever they could find time and afford materials. The Centre d'Art brought fame to these painters, and other young people found in art a means of expressing the unique beauty and spirit of Haiti. Many Haitian artists have since become internationally recognized.

One man who was affected by this new respect for art was Georges Liautaud. When he was discovered in the early 1950s, he was a blacksmith who made tools and uniquely

Fig. 9-12. Steel sculpture by Seresier Louisjuste. From the collection of Frances Crowe. Photograph by Nathaniel D. Smith.

ferred to the metal and the shape is cut out with chisels, a large hammer, and shears. The sculptures emphasize the contours, or silhouettes, of forms. Sometimes designs are pierced through the metal. It is an art of many meanings. Animal and human forms are often combined in one sculpture. One of Liautaud's favorite spirits is Maîtresse La Sirène. He portrays her as part woman, part fish, sometimes part bird or goat. She is a goddess of love and symbolizes universal woman.

Many other artists in metal followed. Murat Brierre became the first to make designs from the round ends of the steel oil drums. Three brothers, Janvier, Joseph, and Seresier Louisjuste, became well known in the 1970s. Their work is almost lacy, an intricate combination of men, birds, animals, and gods that is usually contained within the boundaries of the original square, rectangular, or round piece of metal (see Figs. 9-1 and 9-12). In some sculptures, surface designs are worked into the metal with a chisel, but in general the great dramatic effect is from the silhouette cut in the strong, hard steel.

Fig. 9-14. Sandra rubs brown shoe polish on her cardboard design to darken the cut edges and add warm tones.

pencil and paper. The elements most frequently seen in the Haitian designs are people and all forms of nature. These are sometimes a religious expression, a merging of human and animal forms characteristic of voodoo spirits. In some designs it is more an integration of plant, animal, and human forms that seems to express a joyful closeness to nature. Students choosing similar themes for their designs might think of them as symbolic of the interdependence of all forms of life.

Students may want to consider a design that is enhanced because it conforms to a particular shape: round, square, or rectangular. Although the edge may be cut into, enough should be retained to suggest the original form.

It is helpful to crosshatch areas that are to be cut out later. This helps students see that the design must be connected and that connecting parts must be thick enough so that they do not break in cutting. The cutting is difficult, and it is better not to try a design that is too delicate or lacy—cardboard does not have the strength of steel!

When the penciled design is ready, place carbon paper under it and clip both the design

Silhouette Designs

The students should first work out their designs with

Fig. 9-13. Peter cuts his design out of cardboard with an X-acto knife.

Fig. 9-15. Seventh- and eighth-grade silhouette designs inspired by Haitian steel sculpture. Clockwise from top left: by Randall, Susan H., Susan G., Sandra, Kelly, and Laura.

and the carbon paper to a piece of black railroad board or other lightweight cardboard. Draw over the design with a pencil to transfer it to the cardboard. Include the cross-hatching as a guide for what is to be cut away.

With an X-acto knife (or flat linoleum cutting blade), start cutting out the design in the center and work toward the edges. Work on an old magazine or thick pad of newspaper.

Sometimes the Haitian steel designs also have surface lines cut in with a hammer and chisel. Names are usually signed on the steel in this way, and some interior lines are added to the design as well. You can do this on the cardboard by placing a screwdriver (or the head of a large nail) on the cardboard and tapping it with a hammer.

The cardboard will have white edges where it is cut. It will look more like steel if it is rubbed with dark brown shoe polish. This will stain the edges and also add the warmer tones seen in the metal sculptures.

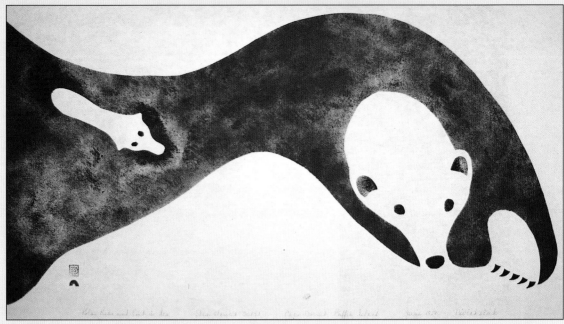

Fig. 10-1. *Polar Bear and Cub in Ice,* by Niviaksiak, Cape Dorset, Baffin Island, June 1959. A print made from a sealskin stencil. It is unusual in that the bears are created in negative space—the ink is applied only to the water and small details on the bears. From the collection of Eugene B. Power. Copyright 1969. Reproduced by permission of the West Baffin Eskimo Co-operative Limited, Cape Dorset, Canada.

10 ARTS OF THE UNITED STATES & CANADA

Before the coming of European settlers to North America, Native American arts, products of the various cultures and the different materials in each area, were already firmly established. When European traders came, some of these arts developed in new ways. For instance, when glass beads became available they replaced porcupine quills for decorative work. In some areas artwork also came to be produced for economic reasons instead of for personal use.

This is the case with Inuit prints and sculpture and with much of the Navajo weaving and Pueblo pottery.

Early American and Canadian arts were derived from several sources. Some, such as the making of applehead dolls, were adapted from Native American arts. In other cases, ideas brought from Europe were developed further. A few arts, such as scrimshaw carving, came about because new materials became available.

NATIVE AMERICAN ARTS

Archaeologists believe that in about 25,000 BC, when the floor of the Bering Strait was dry land, people crossed from Asia to North America. These early inhabitants of North America formed cultural groups that depended on local resources for food and shelter and therefore developed different ways of life. These cultures were not completely isolated, however, and some arts were learned from other tribal groups. Materials not available in one area were sometimes acquired through trade. For example, the Plains Indians traveled to the woodlands to get porcupine quills for decorative arts.

All these groups lived in harmony with the natural world, using what their environment provided resourcefully and respectfully. The arts of early Native Americans reflected their ways of living and traditions. Above all, they expressed a feeling of spiritual interdependence with all the forces of nature.

With the coming of Europeans to this continent the Native peoples suffered greatly. There was much loss of life through wars and illness, and most American Indians were moved from their land and forced to live on reservations. This is a tragic part of American history. Contemporary Native Americans take great pride in their heritage. Many treasure and are preserving as much as they can from their past, and are engaged in maintaining their cultural and artistic heritage.

Art from four major areas will be discussed: the Southwest, the Central Plains, the Woodlands, and the Arctic.

Pueblo Indian Pottery and Outdoor Kilns

The Pueblo Indian culture is the oldest in the Southwest. The word *pueblo* means "village" in Spanish. Long ago, they lived in remarkable cliff houses, constructed in such a way that they seem part of the mountains. These dwellings are still there after many hundreds of years. Current Pueblo tribes, who are settled farmers and live in flat-roofed houses built of stone or adobe, feel a continuity with their past that has never been broken in spite of foreign domination. The early Pueblo artisans did much fine work in pottery, basketry, weaving, and painting, and Pueblos still engage in these arts today.

Pottery making began as early as 300 BC. Early clay pots were made for household and ceremonial vessels. Most were entirely utilitarian, but the people who lived in the Mimbres Valley of New Mexico painted black and white designs on their pottery. Rabbits, turtles, lizards, and other lively drawings still bring to life the clay fragments that have been found in the area.

Pottery making has continued ever since those early times. When, in 1880, the railroad

Fig. 10-2. Polished black bowl with matte black design by Maria Martinez. San Ildefonso, New Mexico. Collection of Gilbert and Jean Davis. © Davis Art Slides.

motif. At Taos cooking vessels are made of a clay that contains mica. When they are fired, the undecorated pots have a golden sheen. Hopi pottery is traditionally a creamy orange clay with black and red decorations. In 1919 Maria and Julian Martinez of San Ildefonso invented a new style of pottery with designs of matte black painted over a polished black background. San Ildefonso and nearby Santa Clara are now famous for this ware.

In the early 1930s, another style of pottery was created by Rose Gonzales of San Ildefonso. Her husband, while hunting, found a small piece of ancient carved pottery. Inspired by this, Rose developed carved pottery, which has become as famous as the black-on-black pottery. The pottery is usually decorated with traditional designs such as bird feathers, cloud symbols, and Awanyu, the plumed serpent (a Pueblo design since prehistoric times). The design is drawn on the pot and then clay is scraped away from around it, leaving the design raised. The carved-out portion is usually matte, in contrast to the high polish of the pot and raised design. Both red pottery and reduction-fired black pottery (see below) are made in this way at San Ildefonso and nearby pueblos.

made commercial pots available and created a market for their handmade wares, some of the Indians stopped making pottery for their own use and began creating it as art for non-Indians. Although fewer Pueblos make pottery now, there has been a steady increase in artistic achievement among some of them.

Different Pueblo tribes have developed distinctive styles of pottery because they use differing natural materials and because they are isolated by distance and language barriers. However, neighboring Pueblos often borrow ideas from each other. Zuni pots of red clay are decorated with black designs painted on a white background. The intricate geometric designs have reduced bird shapes to lines and circles so abstract most people would never recognize them as such. Deer are also a frequent

In all pueblos the basic pots are made in much the same way they were in prehistoric times. Clay is dug from the ground, pulverized to a powder, and mixed with sand. It is then soaked in water and kneaded to the right consistency. A round cake is patted out to make the base of the pot. Thick coils of wet clay are rolled out and curled on top of each other to form the pot, which is then scraped and smoothed with pieces of gourd and set aside to dry. Earlier potters knew a glaze technique that is now lost. Potters now achieve a high-gloss surface by applying several layers of slip (a liquid mixture of water and pure clay) and rubbing the surface with a smooth stone while it is still damp. A stone is selected that fits the curvature of the pot. These stones have often been passed down within a family for generations; some are believed to be dinosaur gizzard stones, found in fossilized skeletons.

Fig. 10-3. Jar with deep carved kiva step design by Tony Roller, Santa Clara Pueblo, 1990. Bequest of Rick Dillingham to Museum of Indian Arts and Culture/Laboratory of Anthropology, Museum of New Mexico. 54311/12. Photo by Blair Clark.

Painted designs are applied with brushes made of yucca leaves. The leaves are chewed until soft and the fibers have separated, and then they are trimmed to shape. The design is painted with slip or with natural pigments. There is no presketching; the designs are applied directly with the brush. They are usually based on symbols from nature, stylized or abstracted: rain, lightning, animal tracks, water, mountains.

A shallow pit is dug in the ground. A metal grate is laid in this, sometimes raised on tin cans to allow air circulation. The pots are stacked carefully, upside down, on the grate. A metal sheet on top protects them from direct contact with the fire. Then a fire of wood or cattle chips is built up in a mound over the pots and kept burning for several hours. At this point, if black ware is desired, finely powdered horse manure is thrown on the fire. This smothers the flame and creates a reduction firing; the lack of oxygen turns the pots black. When the firing is completed the pots are removed and rubbed clean with a dry cloth.

The finished pots are semiporous. In the pueblos this was desirable, because seepage kept stored water cool through evaporation. Most of the pots produced now are sold as decorative nonfunctional pieces only.

Making Clay Pots

Moist clay of any color may be used. First pat out a round cake about ½" thick to form the base of the pot. Using fingers and palms make

Fig. 10-4. Amy presses a coil of clay down on the base of her pot.

a roll of clay about ½–¾" thick. Press the first roll down on the edge of the base, coiling it around. Add more coils on top of the first, pressing them together as you go. This is easier if the bottom of the pot is placed on two small pieces of newspaper: the pot will then turn easily on the table. Smooth the coils together on the inside and outside of the pot as you work. To make the walls of the pot go out, place the coil so that it protrudes slightly beyond the outer edge of the coil beneath. To make the walls go in, place the coil toward the inside edge. After building to the desired height and shape, smooth the outside of the pot carefully with the fingers while supporting it on the inside with the other hand.

If the pot is to have an incised design, it should first dry to the leather-hard stage, hard enough to hold its shape but not too hard to cut into easily. Use linoleum-cutting tools to make the design. It is easier for young children to cut in a simple line design (Fig. 10-6) than to try a more complicated raised design (with background cut away as in Fig. 10-3).

While the clay is still leather-hard, apply a coat of slip evenly with a brush. Slip can be purchased at art supply stores. If the clay is too dry, the slip will flake off. Adding slip is not absolutely necessary, but if you polish the clay body directly, the sand that has been added to the clay may cause some scratches.

Fig. 10-5. Jill has smoothed the coils in her pot together with her fingers. Sometimes using a tool like a spoon helps. She supports the inside of the pot with her other hand.

Fig. 10-6. Danny carves a design in his pot with a linoleum-cutting tool. This must be done before the pot is dry, at the "leather-hard" stage.

Fig. 10-7. Jenny polishes her pot by rubbing hard with a spoon before the clay is completely dry.

While the slip is still damp it can be polished with a smooth stone or with the back of a spoon. You can keep unfinished pots at the leather-hard stage by storing them in tightly closed plastic bags.

Firing in an Outdoor Reduction Kiln

If there is a supply of wood and a proper place, the pottery can be fired outdoors in the Pueblo manner described above. However, you can obtain good results with materials more easily found in modern city environments. Firing should take place on a windless, dry day. *Keep plenty of water and a fire extinguisher handy.*

For a class of about thirty, with pots measuring approximately 4" high, you will need seventy-two bricks and a heavy metal top measuring 19 x 19". Place eight bricks in the

outline of a square (two bricks and the end of a third brick on each side) directly on the ground or asphalt. Place eight more on top of these, shifting them to cover the cracks of the first layer. Build nine rows. (See a finished kiln in Fig. 10-9.)

Fig. 10-8. Third-grade students have built an outdoor kiln, using bricks. It is filled with layers of sawdust alternating with layers of pots. A final 3" layer of sawdust will cover these pots.

Fill the bottom of the kiln with 3" of dry sawdust. Put in a layer of pots, spaced 1" apart. It is best to place them upside down. Cover with 1" of sawdust and proceed with the next layer of pots. Repeat until all the pots are covered and finish with a 3" layer of sawdust on the top.

Fig. 10-9. The cracks between the bricks are filled with wet clay and then the fire is started in the kiln. The metal top is put on, and the long wait begins.

Now fill the cracks between the bricks with wet clay. Light the sawdust from the top so that it burns evenly. Crumpled newspapers will help it get started. Put the metal lid on top and weigh it down if it doesn't lie flat. Leave the kiln burning until all smoking stops—this may take all day. *Do not leave the area unattended.*

At the exciting moment when the kiln is opened the pots will be found all together in the bottom of the kiln if the firing has gone correctly and all the sawdust has burned. They are not high fired, and they will be porous and break if they are dropped, but they should all

Fig. 10-10. Four clay pots fired in an outdoor kiln by third-grade students Danny, Erik, Jenny, and Charlie.

have become quite hard, turned black, and have retained a fine polish. Dust them off well with a cloth.

Navajo Weaving

Navajo Indians, now the largest tribal group in America, live in parts of Arizona, New Mexico, and Utah. Originally from the north, the Navajo were late arrivals in the Southwest. They learned sheep herding from the Spaniards and weaving from the Pueblos in the early eighteenth century, eventually becoming among the finest of all Indian weavers.

Fig. 10-12. Navajo rug woven with a mixture of natural fleece colors (white, black, brown, and gray), a yellow dye from plants found on the reservation, and a commercial red dye. Collection of Mr. and Mrs. Richard I. Ford.

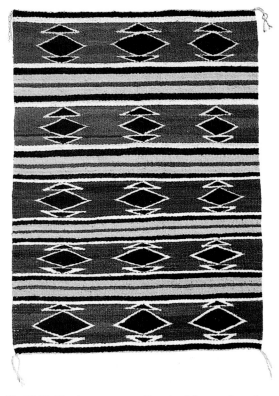

Fig. 10-11. Navajo rug woven with natural fleece colors of white, black, and brown, with stripes of yellow made with dye from the chamiso plant. Collection of Mr. and Mrs. Richard I. Ford.

Early Navajo weavings were made into clothing in the form of blankets worn around the shoulders. Later, the Indians began to wear manufactured blankets, and weaving began to die out. However, the trading posts realized the commercial value of the fine work, and the Navajos began to weave saddle blankets and rugs to sell.

The early blankets were designed with edge-to-edge stripes. The weaving made to sell became heavier so that it could be used for rugs. With this change came changes in design: new geometric shapes and borders. Over the past 200 years, the Navajo have

Fig. 10-13. Navajo Indian weaver in Monument Valley, Navajo Indian Reservation, Arizona. The loom is constructed of logs under a shelter that gives shade from the summer sun. The weaver is beating down the weft with a wooden comb. Photograph by Josef Muench.

sheep are raised and the wool is sheared, carded, spun, dyed, and rolled into balls. The loom is usually set up outdoors with the vertical warp strung between heavy logs suspended from trees or a wooden frame. The rug is woven by passing the weft over and under the warp threads and beating it down securely with a wooden comb. Heddles attached to every other thread open a shed to pass the weft through. A rug may take many weeks or months to weave, depending on its size. The design, no matter how intricate, is kept in the head of the weaver until it appears, wondrously, centered and perfect, row by row. (See Fig. 10-13.)

acquired skills through experimentation and handed them down through the generations; some designs have become very complex. There are now, in general, four categories of Navajo rugs: those using natural fleece colors—white, black, brown, and gray (made by carding white and black fibers together); those using bright commercial dyes in many colors; those using natural dyes made from plants, berries, and roots, creating mostly soft shades of brown, green, yellow, and pink; and those combining some of these elements in Yei designs, which are derived from designs used in sand paintings.

Different areas have become famous for distinct styles and designs, but all basically follow traditional methods. Although some wool is now purchased commercially, generally

Weaving on a Cardboard Loom

In order to weave, a loom must keep the vertical threads, or warp, taut. A simple but effective loom can be made from a piece of strong cardboard. At the third- or fourth-grade level a piece 7 x 10" is ample. Cut notches, ½" apart and ¼" deep, at the top and bottom edges. Wind strong cotton twine around the cardboard: starting at the bottom notch on the left and leaving a "tail"

Fig. 10-14. Colorful third-grade weavings on display. At this age, a striped design is challenge enough.

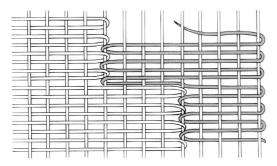

Fig. 10-15. Dovetailing two colors in a weaving. Where the colors meet, each color circles the same warp thread before turning back.

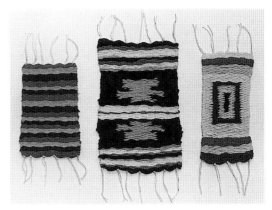

Fig. 10-17. Three weavings by Amy, nine; Laura, ten; and Rebecca, nine.

10" long, carry the twine up to the top left notch, down the back, and up through the second bottom notch from the left. Continue in this manner until the loom is completely wound, leaving a 10" tail at the top right notch. These two tails are then pulled to the back and tied together to hold the warp tight.

The weaver can then proceed by passing yarn over the first warp, under the second, over the third warp, under the fourth, etc. At the end of the row the yarn circles the last warp and comes back, this time going over every thread it went under on the previous row (and under every thread it went over). Children will soon see that this creates a strong fabric that holds together.

Fig. 10-16. When dovetailing one color with another, a needle helps to separate the weft in the parts already woven.

Since the weft must go up over and curl under every warp thread (instead of going in a straight line), it takes more than 7" of yarn to weave a 7" width. Students have a tendency to pull the weft straight across, but unless extra yarn is added the weaving will pull in as it progresses, and the sides will not remain straight. To counteract this, students should add yarn by putting a "hill" into the weft, after it has been passed through the warp and before it is pushed down against the weaving. (See Fig. 3-20 in Chapter 3, but use fingers instead of a fork to push the weft down.)

Before beginning to work, students should think about their design. If they want to make a striped pattern they should choose a few colors that go well together. These can alternate in sequence, or children can design a pattern that creates symmetry in some way—for instance, wide areas of color alternating with narrow areas, or a wide center color with several narrow stripes on either side.

When a piece of yarn has been woven in, start with a new piece at the place where the other ends. Yarn should never be tied; it creates unsightly lumps. If the yarn is packed down tightly with the fingers, the weaving will hold together. When it is completed, the weft ends are cut flush to the weaving and cannot be seen.

If a design is to be worked into the center, sketch a simple shape with a pencil on the cardboard behind the warp as a guide. When the weft reaches this outline it should turn and go back to the edge. Another color of yarn begins at the line and fills in the design, both yarns circling the same warp thread before turning. This is called dovetailing. (See Fig. 10-15.) Using a needle sometimes makes it easier to get between the weft threads (see Fig. 10-16).

When the weaving is completed, turn over the loom and cut the warp threads *in the middle* of the loom. Turn the loom face up again. Starting at the left bottom, release two warp threads and tie them with an overhand knot.

(See Fig. 3-21.) Push the knot up against the weaving before tightening it. Proceed two at a time to tie warp threads until the bottom is completed. Then do the same for the top. The fringe may need to be trimmed, but leave a good length as part of the design so that it doesn't look chopped off.

Navajo Sand Paintings

Until very recently, Navajo sand paintings were made only as part of a religious ceremony to heal the sick. Traditionally the Navajo believe that illness is caused by breaking taboos or in some other way being out of tune with the natural world. Tradition says the ceremony was taught to the Dineh (the Navajo word for themselves, which translated means "the

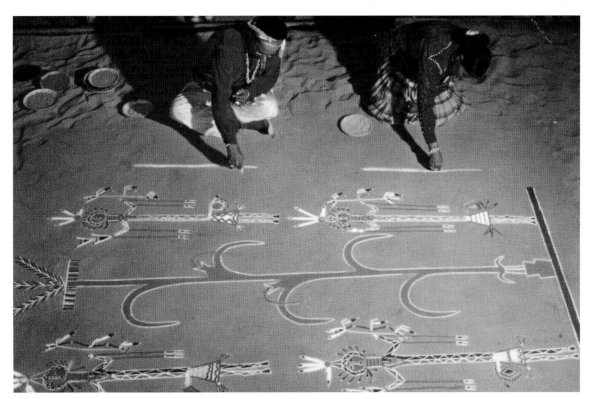

Fig. 10-18. Two Navajo artists creating a sand painting. Courtesy of the National Museum of the American Indian, Smithsonian Institution. P28161.

People") by the Holy People, or gods, as a method to restore health of body and soul.

To bring a person back in tune with the universe, a medicine man will draw designs on the floor of a hogan (Navajo home), using materials he has gathered from the environment: pollen, crushed flowers, charcoal, pulverized sandstone,

Fig. 10-19. *Holyman,* sand painting by E. Hunt. This is a permanent design, not made for a healing ceremony. Collection of the author.

and other minerals. First, he spreads clean sand (or occasionally a buckskin) evenly on the floor. Then, with a skill born of many years of practice, he lets these dry materials sift down from his fingers, creating designs that are traditional for each specific illness. He draws figures that represent the Holy People—elongated, straight-bodied figures. He represents the four directions, north, south, east, and west; and some of the sacred plants: corn, beans, squash, and tobacco. Many other symbols of his natural and spiritual world are used: the bluebird (symbol of happiness), sun, moon, rain, lightning, reptiles. A rainbow, which protects the painting from evil, often surrounds it on all sides except the east.

The paintings range from small to as large as twenty feet in diameter. The biggest require the work of many men and most of a day to complete and are made in a hogan erected especially for that purpose.

Chants are sung for each element of the design as it is being made. They ask for the help of the Holy People and recount long stories, which keep them in the minds of the people. The person to be cured, the family, and many friends gather to take part in the ceremony and gain strength from its performance. They believe that if the ceremony has been correctly performed, the patient will over-

sun & eagle feathers

snake

lightning

eagle

corn

bluebird

Fig. 10-20. Some symbols used in Navajo sand paintings.

come the evil that is causing the illness and will again, in the Navajo words, "walk in beauty." Since the sacred painting must never be desecrated, the medicine man scatters it to the four winds after the ceremony.

Modern medical treatments are sometimes combined with sand painting ceremonies. In this manner, tradition and science work together to overcome illness.

Non-Navajos, observing these ceremonies, used to marvel at the beauty of the sand paintings and wish that they could be preserved. At the urging of museums and for commercial reasons, the Navajos now make sand paintings on boards, using glue with the sand to make a permanent design. These are created as an art form quite separate from any religious ceremony.

Making Sand Paintings

Collect sand from the beach or at a sand pit, or purchase it at a building materials store. It can be colored by adding a small amount of tempera paint and mixing it well with your fingers. Spread the sand out on newspapers, and stir

occasionally with your hands as it dries to separate all the particles. If the sand paintings are to have the feeling of Navajo work, the colors should be subtle earth tones: the white of limestone, the yellow and brick red of sandstone, gray, black, and turquoise blue. (See Fig. 10-19.) After the colored sand is completely dry, rubbing it through a piece of screening will restore it to a fine texture. The sand should be separated by color into large, low containers.

Cut a piece of cardboard and paint the entire surface with white glue. Dip this into a container of uncolored sand, being sure to cover the entire piece. Tap it lightly, letting all unglued grains of sand fall back into the box.

While this sand is drying, work out a design. Students may want to use some of the symbols used by the Indians of the Southwest. The designs are highly stylized, not realistic.

When the prepared board is dry, sketch the design lightly on the sand with charcoal. With a fine brush, paint a small area with white glue, and holding the board over one of the containers, drop the appropriate color of sand over the

Fig. 10-21. Eric, eight, drew his design with charcoal on a prepared board. Now he is applying glue to a cloud symbol.

Fig. 10-22. Sean, nine, has applied glue to the tailfeathers of his eagle design and is sprinkling them with colored sand. After the sand is applied, he will tap the board gently against the box so that loose sand falls back in.

Fig. 10-23. Above, eagle design by Kim, age eight. Photo by David Wade. Below, snake design by Ellen, age eleven.

Fig. 10-24. Mato-tope's buffalo robe, Mandan, c. 1836. Horses, warriors, and a sunburst painted by a Mandan chief. Courtesy Bernisches Historisches Museum, Abteiling für Völkerkunde, Bern, Switzerland.

(commonly called buffalo) grazed peacefully or thundered on their northern and southern migrations. The earliest Indian tribes of the Great Plains area were seminomadic, living much of the year in mud and grass lodges on the edge of the prairie. They were farmers as well as hunters. Later, after the Spaniards introduced horses to the Indians, some became nomadic and followed the buffalo as they migrated. At least thirty different tribes lived on the Great Plains.

glued area. Tap the edge of the board lightly so that unglued grains fall back into the container. Then paint another small area and follow the same procedure, continuing until the painting is completed. Emphasize to the students that the Navajo paintings are mostly line drawings, beautiful against the natural sand background. They should not overwhelm the background with too much colored sand.

Plains Indian Buffalo Robes and Headdresses

It is hard to imagine the Great Plains of central North America as they were before Europeans came, when many millions of great bison

All of these tribes were dependent on the bison. The bulk of their diet was buffalo meat, both fresh and dried to last through the winter. Their tipis, a shelter that was beautifully adapted to a nomadic life, were covered with buffalo skins. Heavy winter skins with the fur left on became warm robes and blankets. Specially cured hides from younger animals became shirts and other clothing. Skins were also used as canvas, to record the history of the tribe and the exploits of war. These were painted with porous buffalo bone brushes and yellow paint from the buffalo gallstones (other

Fig. 10-25. Engraving of a buffalo by George Catlin.

pigments were made from minerals and plants). Buffalo ribs made sled runners, the horns became spoons, bones became hoes and hide scrapers, old tough hides became shields and moccasin soles, sinews became rope and thread. Scores of other products were made, too. They used every scrap of the buffalo, and every part of the Indians' lives, from birth through death, was affected by this huge animal. Even the buffalo dung was used for a hot, smokeless campfire in a mostly treeless prairie.

Religious ceremonies often centered around the buffalo. Animals, especially the sacred buffalo, were believed to have spirits that could be influenced through certain rites. There were ceremonies before the hunt to bring good hunting and ceremonies afterward for thanksgiving. Plentiful as they were, at times the buffalo did not wander close enough to be hunted safely. To bring the buffalo closer to the village, the Indians held dances. The nineteenth-century artist George Catlin traveled among the Indians and recorded their lives and ways in sketches and paintings. He described a buffalo dance in a Mandan village. Ten or fifteen men of the tribe would start the dance wearing their buffalo headdresses, which included the horns and completely covered their heads (see Fig. 10-27). To the accompaniment of drums and rattles, the dancers

Fig. 10-26. *Making the Buffalo Come.* Engraving of a Mandan dance by George Catlin.

Fig. 10-27. Mandan buffalo headdress. Courtesy of the National Museum of Natural History, Smithsonian Institution.

warrior on horseback

tipi

thunderbird

sunburst

bearpaw

buffalo

deer

turtle

Fig. 10-28. A few Plains Indian designs used in decorating buffalo robes, drums, tipis, shields, and other items.

Fig. 10-26, an engraving by Catlin, depicts this dance.

Painting was an important art to most of the Plains Indians, and buffalo skin was the usual canvas. Many tribes painted tipis with designs and historical events. Buffalo robes were decorated on the skin side. A man's robe was often designed with a sunburst or recorded his brave deeds in war. (See Fig. 10-24.) A woman's robe was usually decorated with a geometric design. Some hides, called "winter counts," recorded a history of the tribe. A symbol represented the most important event that had occurred each year: war, an eclipse of the sun, a smallpox epidemic, peace, or the coming of the white man. These symbols usually started in the center of the hide and spiraled out counterclockwise. Some of the hides record well over 100 years of history.

Because their lives were so entwined with the buffalo, the mass slaughter of these great animals by the white man—for hides and sometimes just for sport—spelled doom for the Plains Indians. Even had they not been mercilessly pushed onto reservations, the Indians' life as they had known it could not have existed without the buffalo. Now a unique lifestyle

stamped and pawed the ground, imitating buffalo sounds and movements. They continued, without food, until they were exhausted. When a dancer dropped, he was "shot" with a blunt arrow and pulled from the circle by onlookers, who pretended to cut him up for meat. While resting, he was replaced by a fresh dancer. The dance continued for days, if necessary, without interruption, until the buffalo were sighted.

is gone. What is left of the original culture consists of a few examples of beautifully decorated hides and clothing and finely crafted tools and household items that are now preserved in museums.

However, the young descendants of these tribes are showing a renewed interest in the traditions, songs, dances, arts, and legends of their people, and a new commitment to the Indian concept of reverence for the land. Perhaps now that so many are concerned about saving natural resources, we can at last learn from the original inhabitants of North America how to live in harmony with nature.

Designing a Buffalo Robe, or "Winter Count"

Leather can be simulated with heavy brown wrapping paper, brown Kraft paper, or paper grocery bags. Tear (do not cut) the shape of a buffalo hide from a large piece of this paper. Make designs with crayons. Indian robes frequently showed historic events, such as wars or buffalo hunts, or designs such as the sunburst of concentric feathered lines or geometric patterns. (See Figs. 10-24 and 10-28.) Or students can make a winter count of their own lives by drawing symbols to represent events that were important each year: birthplace, illness, vacations, siblings born, pets acquired, and so on. The crayon should be

Fig. 10-29. A brown paper "buffalo robe" by Rebecca, age six.

put on with heavy pressure. When the drawing is finished, crumple the paper and immerse it in a bucket of water to which a cup of brown tempera paint has been added. Knead the "hide" gently but thoroughly in the solution. Then remove it and spread it out to dry on newspapers. The crayon work resists the paint and will show well against the leatherlike surface. If it does not show, either the crayoning was too light, or there was too much paint in the solution. The paper can be rinsed, dried, and recrayoned if necessary.

Creating a Buffalo Headdress

A headdress can be made from a large grocery bag. Cut the bag at the open end at an angle, so that, when worn, the side that will be at the back of the neck will be longer than the front. Tape horns cut from corrugated cardboard to either side of the head. Apply at least three layers of newspaper dipped in papier-mâché glue to the entire surface of the paper and the horns. (See appendix for general papier-mâché instructions.) To round out the horns, make a mash of sawdust and glue and mold this to the cardboard horns. When the mask is

Fig. 10-30. A paper bag is used as a base for a buffalo headdress. On the right, Doug puts layers of newspaper dipped in papier-mâché glue (see appendix) on the bag to strengthen it. On the left, Jenny is giving her headdress a coat of brown paint.

Fig. 10-31. A mixture of sawdust and glue is applied to a cardboard base to make rounded horns.

Fig. 10-32. After painting, excelsior is added between the horns and under the chin. The headdresses, piled and ready for a dance, look like a buffalo stampede!

Fig. 10-33. Third-grade students Larkin, David, Amy, and Cynthia performing a buffalo dance.

dry, cut holes for eyes and nostrils. (The mask wearer will actually be looking through the nostril holes.) Paint the mask brown with tempera paint. To depict the long shaggy hair on top of a buffalo's head and under its chin, glue excelsior that has been dipped in brown paint and then dried to the area between the horns and to the chin.

Buffalo dances are described in several books. Students should accompany the dancers with a drumbeat. The Mandan dance described earlier can be used. The dance could end with great rejoicing when several buffalo (nondancers imitating buffalo with their headdresses) appear in the distance.

Plains Indian Shirts and Vests

The Plains Indians wore beautifully decorated shirts and dresses, originally made from the hides of animals they hunted, and later sometimes from cloth obtained through trading. The vest became popular after the Europeans came to the plains.

Buffalo hides were thick and heavy, so the shirts and dresses were usually made from other animal skins, most often from tanned and smoked deer hide, but skins from ante-lope, elk, and mountain sheep were also treated and softened in this way. The earliest decorations were made of dyed and flattened porcupine quills, and this method is still in use today. Shells were sometimes sewn on. Shirts were also painted with deep bright colors

Fig. 10-34. Cheyenne quilled shirt, Oklahoma. Courtesy National Museum of the American Indian, Smithsonian Institution. T03/2624. Collected by Mark R. Harrington. Photo by Katherine Fogden.

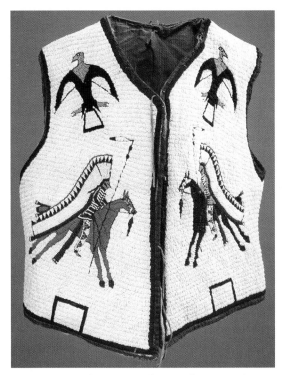

Fig. 10-35. Vest, about 1875, unknown Cheyenne artist. Beads, skin, cloth. A symmetrical design of warriors on horseback, and eagles. The back of the vest is similar, except that the eagles are replaced with buffaloes. Denver Art Museum Collection: Native Arts acquisition funds, 1948.95. © Denver Art Museum.

made from earth pigments and plants. Yellow was obtained from buffalo gallstones. Brushes were made from carved, porous buffalo bones. In the early 1800s, beads became available and were widely used in the traditional patterns. Long fringes often decorated the arms and the bottom edges of the clothes.

The most highly decorated shirts, created by women and worn by men, were symbols of bravery, earned through courageous acts. Hair was often incorporated into the decorations. Sometimes the hair of relatives was used, showing their support for the warrior. Power over an enemy was established by wearing a lock of his hair. Battles and horse raids were commemorated with symbols or pictures on the shirts.

Symbols of animals (such as bear footprints) gave the animal's power to the wearer.

Plains Indian shirts and vests are still being made today and can be seen at Native American powwows, which are increasingly held throughout America. A shirt is sometimes made for a young man in order to celebrate his accomplishments in sports, or for academic achievement. Women now also make highly decorated shirts and dresses for themselves. Men, women, and children wear these beautiful clothes with pride in their artistry and in the rich heritage they honor.

Making Paper Vests

A decorated paper vest can be made to look like leather in the same way as that described in the project for designing a paper buffalo robe.

Fold one piece of heavy brown wrapping paper, or natural brown Kraft paper, to make a rectangle 18 x 20". (Or use two paper bags, each of which will yield a piece 18 x 20".) Cut

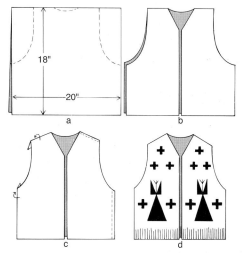

Fig. 10-36. Diagram for making a vest of heavy brown Kraft or wrapping paper. Design is adapted from a Sioux beaded vest.

Fig. 10-37. David pushes hard on his crayon so that the turtle design will resist the paint when his vest is immersed in a paint and water solution.

on dotted lines, as in the diagram. Cut up the front of the vest and open to a V-shaped neckline. Fold the shoulder over at an angle and staple to make for a better fit. (In Figs. 10-37, 10-38, and 10-39, this technique had not yet been used.) Fold sides over and staple and then fold them again and staple. The vest will be even stronger if it is sewn with large stitches on a sewing machine instead of being stapled. This is the inside of the vest. Turn right-side out. Cut fringe and decorate the vest with bright crayon work. (Crayon work can be done before stapling the sides. If so, turn the artwork inside before stapling.)

In decorating the vests, the children may be inspired by illustrations in the books mentioned in the bibliography. In addition to the Plains Indian designs pictured in Fig. 10-28, floral patterns were also used on vests. The crayon should be applied with heavy pressure to make it as thick and bright as possible. This is a good project for introducing the concept of symmetry, for vest designs were usually sym-

Fig. 10-38. Three paper vests, by David, Danny, and Sophia.

metrical, both on the front and on the back.

Crumple the vest and gently knead it in the paint solution described in the project on buffalo robes, and spread it out to dry on newspaper.

Fig. 10-39. First-grade students Danny, Aaron, Debbie, and Sophia wearing their vests.

Woodland Indian Quillwork

Just as the Pueblo Indians used the clay in their environment and the Plains Indians the buffalo, Woodland Indians knew and used their environment with wisdom, respect, and great skill.

There were about thirty major tribes in the area east of the Mississippi and north of what is now Tennessee. They fell into two major language groups, the Iroquois and the much larger Algonkian. Although there were variations in culture, they shared many things. Some tribes were primarily hunters and wild food gatherers. Deer and other game provided them much the same range of items as the buffalo provided the Plains Indians. Other tribes did a good deal of farming and raised corn, beans, squash, and pumpkins. Because the region was dominated by woods, the trees, especially the birch, were used for a great variety of products. From the birch came graceful canoes, covers for the wigwams, baskets, cooking pots, decorations for clothing, and cradles. Birchbark provided material for an unusual art form done just for fun: pieces of paper-

Fig. 10-40. Buckskin bag, decorated with porcupine quill-work in geometric and thunderbird designs. The lower part of the bag is decorated with a mallard duck pelt. Sauk and Fox, c. 1820. Courtesy of the Chandler-Pohrt Collection.

bowls, ladles, masks, clubs, and ritual objects.

A very fine art, known only in North America, was porcupine quill decoration. How inventive to take the quills of this spiky animal and use them so beautifully! This art, in use for about 200 years before Columbus, probably began in the east. Eventually it spread to the Great Lakes area, prairies, and throughout the Plains, where it was used extensively in decorating clothing. Although the quills are only 5" long and require great skill and patience to work with, large areas of clothing and other items were decorated with them.

A porcupine provided as many as 40,000 quills of varying thicknesses. These were plucked, sorted by size, washed, and the barb removed. The quills were softened in the mouth or soaked in water and then flattened by pulling them through the teeth or by using a bone tool. The Indians developed many dyes, by boiling plants, bark, and roots. These were mostly red, black, yellow, and blue. Undyed white quills were also used.

There were many techniques for applying the quills to leather or birchbark: wrapping, in which they were twisted around strips of leather or birchbark; sewing with sinews; plaiting; and weaving on

flower

deer

star

underwater panther

geometric

floral

thunderbird

Fig. 10-41. Woodland Indian quillwork designs.

thin bark were folded several times and bitten along the edges in such a way that when they were opened up, geometric designs and snowflake patterns appeared! Other trees with special properties were used for toboggans, snowshoes, medicines, and even sugar (from maple sap). The Woodland Indians excelled in wood carving, and they produced many fine a loom. One method, which used unflattened quills, was to apply designs to birchbark by inserting the quill ends into holes punched in the bark with an awl and bending the ends over on the back (see Fig. 10-42). Fig. 10-40 shows a buckskin bag in which many different quillwork techniques were used, including wrapping, zigzag bands, and sewing.

Two favorite motifs for quillwork designs—both spirit animals of great power—were the thunderbird and the underwater panther. The panther was lynxlike with a long tail and great knowledge of medicines. Many designs were based on native flowers and leaves or geometric shapes.

Quillwork decorated both men's and women's clothing, moccasins, birchbark boxes, medicine bags, and pouches. Cradle boards for infants were often elaborately decorated. The leather on which the designs were sewn was frequently dyed dark brown or black to emphasize the bright colors of the quills.

The women did the quillwork and took great pride in decorating clothing for their families. Quillwork was given as gifts during visits to other tribes. A woman gained recognition for her designs and was challenged to do even better. Thus the artists grew in skill, and the complexity of their work increased.

When beads were brought to this area by European explorers and traders, most quillwork was abandoned. However, some Native American artists still make birchbark and sweet-grass boxes decorated with quills. Quillwork on shirts and other clothing has been re-introduced, especially by Plains Indians, and can be seen at many Indian powwows.

Making Quill Designs

Porcupine quills are not readily available, but flat toothpicks dyed in various colors give a similar linear effect.

Food colors make fine dyes. Place the colors in shallow containers and soak flat toothpicks until they have absorbed the dye. They should be a shade darker than desired because they will lighten as they dry. Remove the toothpicks and spread them to dry on newspaper.

However, it might give students a greater understanding of Indian art to make dyes from their own environment. Many colors can be obtained from canned or fresh fruits and vegetables. If there is time to experiment, students should also gather leaves, berries, and flowers from their yards or vacant lots. (If wild plants are used, be sure they are not endangered, also caution students that many quite common plants are poisonous and must never be tasted or swallowed.) Wash hands after gathering.

Crush the material and boil in a small amount of water for about half an hour. Test

Fig. 10-42. Alison is holding a Woodland Indian sweet-grass basket. The birchbark cover is decorated with a white porcupine quill floral design.

Fig. 10-43. Reinder, eleven, places a glued toothpick in position on his headband.

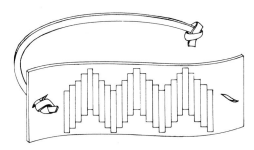

Fig. 10-44. Diagram of a wristband with toothpick quill design. Toothpicks must be perpendicular to the curve of the wristband, as here, or they may break. A leather thong knotted at the ends holds the wristband on.

Fig. 10-45. Topher, eight, with his "quilled" leather wristband.

Fig. 10-46. Reinder's head-band is a striking design of red, blue, yellow, and green geometric shapes.

on white paper to see if the dye is strong enough to give a good color. Many plants give no color at all or one other than expected.

Strain the liquid and simmer the tooth-picks in this solution until they have taken on a shade darker than the desired color. Here are some materials that work well:

Red: raspberries. Use only the juice drained from canned or cooked fresh or frozen berries.
Pink: cranberries. Cook and save. Use only the liquid.
Rose: beets. Cook and save. Use only the liquid.
Orange: onions. Use outside skins, which grocers throw away. Makes a very good dye.
Yellow: marigold flowers.
Green: grass. *Do not boil.* Rub *fresh grass* on toothpicks.
Blue: outer purple cabbage leaves boiled with a rusty nail or piece of iron.
Red-Purple: blueberry juice drained from canned or cooked fresh berries.
Blue-Purple: outer purple cabbage leaves.
Brown: black walnut husks. Permanent; be careful of clothes.

These colors may fade in time. The Indians knew various natural mordants that set the colors permanently. After simmering the toothpicks in the dye, spread them to dry on newspapers.

Many leather craft stores sell bags of scrap leather at a very reasonable price. From these scraps, cut small pendant shapes, wristbands, headbands, or chokers. Students should study examples of Indian designs—geometric, and animal, flower, and leaf shapes—and work out a design on paper. Then cut or break the dried toothpicks into the desired lengths (try to match them by width; they taper at one end) and glue them in place with white glue. A piece of leather that is to be curved while worn (such as a wristband, choker, or headband) must have the toothpicks glued in a position that is at a right angle to the direction of the curve, or they will break when the leather bends. Bands may be tied by cutting thin strips of leather into thongs. Make a

Fig. 10-47. Bright quills radiate from the center of Dawn's pendant.

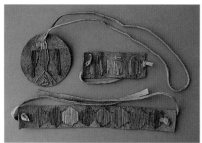

Fig. 10-48. A pendant with a thunderbird design, by John, age ten; a wristband with a thunderbird design, unsigned; and a headband by Reinder, with a geometric design.

small cut at an angle in each end of the band, insert the leather thongs, and knot them at the ends (see Fig. 10-44). Either leave two loose ends to tie, or make one thong the exact length needed with a knot at each end. Keep one end of the thong knotted in one end of the band, and "button" the other end into the other slot each time it is to be worn.

Woodland Indian Beadwork

For many centuries before the Europeans came to America, Woodland Indians made beads for personal adornment. The beads were made from natural materials: stone, fossils, bone, shell, copper, bear teeth, and pearls from freshwater clams. These materials were shaped and pierced as necessary.

The best known of the Indian beads is called *wampum*, made by shaping and drilling quahog clam shells. They were cylindrical in shape and were white and, less commonly, purple. They were considered very valuable and used for many purposes beside adornment: in burial rituals, for exchange at the making of treaties, as a document during the sale of property, and as history belts (with designs symbolic of important happenings worked into the beads).

Glass beads replaced most of the handmade beads when they became available

through trade with Europeans during the mid-seventeenth century. They were made into necklaces and used instead of porcupine quillwork in decorating clothing. Many of the same design motifs were used, but the beads allowed for both a wider range of colors and more intricate designs.

Beads were sewn onto clothing and also woven into colorful bands on three types of looms: a simple wooden frame, a bow that held the warp taut, and a belt loom. The women made belts, garters, headbands, chok-

Fig. 10-49. Woodland Indian beadwork. From left, beadwork sash, Chippewa, Wisconsin, c. 1890; heddle-woven bead sash, Potawatomi Reservation, Kansas, c. 1885; beadwork garter, Chippewa, Wisconsin-Minnesota, c. 1890. Courtesy of the Chandler-Pohrt Collection.

Fig. 10-50. Native American Joyce Tinkham demonstrating beadwork to a sixth-grade class. She is wearing wide beaded wristbands of floral design.

Fig. 10-51. Joyce explains the technique to Staci while Kathy watches.

Fig. 10-52. Cathy works on her cardboard bead loom. If the warp threads are wound on the left side of the loom, beads can be picked up to the right.

ers, and bands to be applied to clothing. See Fig. 10-49. They used thread and needles that were obtained from traders.

Beadwork came to be done by Indians throughout most of North America. Each tribe had characteristic designs, which used symbols meaningful to them, but there was also some borrowing of designs. The Woodland Indians were noted for fine naturalistic floral and leaf patterns. Today artists in many Indian communities are still producing items beautifully decorated with beadwork.

Making Indian Beadwork

A loom can be made from any box. An ideal shape is the cardboard container that is frequently used for holding fruit in the supermarket. It has two higher ends on which to wrap the warp, and lower longer sides, which

makes access to weaving easier. They measure approximately 6 x 8". If another box is used, cut the two longer sides lower than the others.

You will need nylon thread for a good strong warp. When wrapping the warp around the box, make an even number of warp threads—this enables you to have an odd number of beads and consequently a center line in your design. The warping thread is wrapped firmly around the box and spaced slightly farther apart than the width of the beads. Wrap the warp close to the left side of the loom and leave a space at the right. Beads can then be kept in the bottom of the loom and picked up to the right of the band being woven. Secure the two ends of the warp by tying them together on the back of the loom.

Before beginning, work out a design with crayons and graph paper ruled in ¼" squares. It will be much larger than the beadwork and

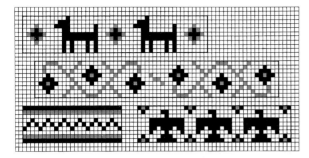

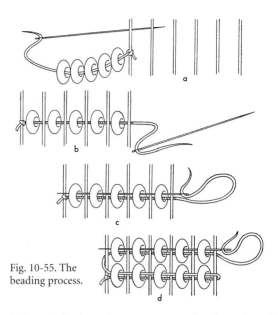

Fig. 10-53. Use graph paper to work out designs. These are deer, floral, geometric, and thunderbird designs based on modified Woodland Indian beadwork designs.

Fig. 10-55. The beading process.

easy to follow. For the beginner a design nine beads wide (ten warp threads) and fifty to sixty beads long is sufficient to make a small wristband. Simple geometric designs that repeat are easiest for beginners. (See Fig. 10-53.)

Beads are available in several sizes. Be sure to use ones of uniform size, to avoid bumps. Put the beads in a small shallow container or in the bottom of the loom itself.

After the loom is warped, thread a beading needle (available where beads are sold) and tie the end of the thread to the first warp thread on the left. (If you are left-handed, reverse this

Fig. 10-54. Adam holds the beads in place with a finger of his left hand, while his right hand pushes the needle through on *top* of the threads.

and work from the right.) Follow your pattern and pick up the first row of beads by putting the point of the needle into one and tipping it up to let the bead fall to the base of the needle. Continue until all the beads of the first row are on the needle. Check to see that they are in the right order. Push the beads on the thread down to where

it is attached to the warp, pass the thread and needle *under* the warp (Fig. 10-55a), and push the beads up in the spaces between each warp thread (Fig. 10-55b). Hold them there with the left forefinger. Bring the needle up to the top of the warp and pass it back through the beads (from right to left) *on top of the warp threads*, to the other side (Fig. 10-55c). Pick up new beads and follow the same process (Fig. 10-55d) until the pattern is completed. After finishing the last row, tie the thread to the outer warp thread and pass the end back through the beads in the row above.

Fig. 10-56. Sixth-grade beaded wristbands made by (top to bottom) Adam, Katya, Jenny, Nicola, Annette, and Kamala.

When the beading is finished, cut it from the loom, leaving at least 2" of warp threads. Take the threads of one end between the thumb and forefinger, twist them into a cord, and pull them to the back of the beadwork, securing them with a piece of masking tape. Do this on both ends, and tape the entire back of the beadwork to give it some firmness.

Leather scraps may be obtained from leatherworking shops. Be sure to pick some that are soft enough to pass a sewing needle through easily. Place the beadwork on a strip of leather, leaving ½" or more of leather at either end for attaching thongs. Sew the beadwork to the leather using an overcast stitch, bringing the needle up inside the outer warp thread and down around the leather edge. Sew all four sides of the beadwork. Felt can be used if leather cannot be obtained.

You can secure the wristbands in any number of ways, as Fig. 10-56 illustrates: by using thongs and slits, commercial snaps, or buttons and buttonholes.

Inuit Stone Sculpture and Printmaking

The last group of people to cross the Bering Strait and settle on the North American continent arrived about 4,000 years ago. They spread from the Aleutian Islands and Alaska in the west across the Arctic to eastern Greenland. By outsiders they are called Eskimos, an Indian name meaning "eats raw flesh." However, the people of the Canadian Eastern Arctic prefer to be called Inuit, which in their language means "the people." Living in small, isolated groups in that vast land of snow, ice, and tundra, they frequently spent their lives without seeing any other inhabitants of the continent.

Two thousand years ago there were two main cultural groups in the east, the Dorset and the Thule. These prehistoric tribes left evidence in the form of tools and artifacts that lead anthropologists to believe their culture was much like that of early historic times, although more primitive. They were seasonal hunters; in the summer they lived on the land, fishing and hunting caribou and musk ox. In the winter they lived on the sea ice, hunting seal and walrus. The Thule were also great whale hunters. Every man carved harpoons, knives, and other tools from ivory and stone. These were sometimes incised with lines that enhanced the shape. Saucers and lamp bowls were also carved from soft stone, and driftwood was made into dramatic masks probably used in religious ceremonies.

The Dorset people used stone tools to make very small, smooth carvings from narwhal and walrus tusks and from seal teeth. These tiny, highly polished, beautiful pieces were probably magical in purpose (for instance, to ensure good hunting). Worn as amulets, they depicted birds, walrus, bear, and other game.

Fig. 10-57. A tiny ivory carving of a polar bear, 2¼", artist unknown. Collected in 1954 by Shirley Paul. Although obtained in the Aleutian Islands, it is similar to those made by the early Dorset people. Collection of the author. Photo by David Wade.

Fig. 10-58. *Bird* by Isa Smilen, and *Seal* by Joe Adamie Tuki, both from Inoucdjouac Co-op, on the east bank of Hudson Bay. Courtesy of Denali Arts, Inc., Ann Arbor, Michigan.

Until recent times the Inuit lived in very small groups to increase their chances of successful hunting. Theirs was a barren and cold climate. Survival meant very hard work in the best of times, and when storms or other disasters made hunting unsuccessful, they faced starvation. And yet the Inuit seem to have had a warm and joyous spirit, enduring long stretches of deprivation but taking much pleasure in each other's company when bad times were over. They appreciated the stark beauty of their land. How much more joy the summer sun brings when it barely clears the horizon in the long dark

Fig. 10-59. *Polar Bear*, by Niviaksiak, Cape Dorset, Baffin Island. From the collection of Eugene B. Power.

winters! Animals were not merely adversaries or food— they were fellow inhabitants of the land. They were killed only when necessary and then given thanks; atonement was sometimes made in some symbolic way.

In the nineteenth century, as contact with the outside world grew more frequent, changes began to occur. Since the Inuit alone had the skills to survive successfully in the Arctic, they were not forced onto reservations, like the Indians to the south. Rather, their lives were changed by the gradual encroachment of different cultures (Russian, Danish, Canadian, and American); new diseases (the common cold caused thousands to die); and dwindling game. Some Inuit began living in larger settlements, often relying on government support to survive.

When different cultures come together, new lifestyles form. Inuit in some areas still hunt in the old ways, but they may use guns and gasoline-powered vehicles instead of harpoons and dogsleds. Some skills, such as carving, which were once developed only for their own use and pleasure, are now used to provide a new economic base to supplement hunting and trapping. Their carvings give great pleasure to countless numbers of people in other parts of the world.

The idea of producing sculpture to sell developed in 1948, when James Houston, traveling on the coast of Hudson Bay, noticed some Inuit carvings in stone and felt there could be a market for them. The Canadian Handicrafts Guild sent Houston to Cape

Fig. 10-60. *Seagulls and Geese*, by Louisa Quasalik. Povungnituk, 1980. The design was first cut into a slab of smoothed stone, and then ink was rolled on, and a print made from the inked surface. Collection of the author. Photo by David Wade.

Dorset on Baffin Island in 1951 to encourage the Inuit in this endeavor. This idea was new to them, since the Inuit had carved objects to be used as tools or as ornaments for clothing—items to be held in the hand, not to be put in one place and admired. Houston stayed at Cape Dorset for ten years, and over that period of time the sculptures became well known in the United States and Canada.

In the United States this was due in large part to Eugene Power, who in 1963 established a nonprofit organization, Eskimo Art Incorporated, which arranged with the Smithsonian to mount a traveling exhibition of sculpture to be sent to museums throughout the country. This exhibition promoted an interest in the carvings and helped create a demand for them.

Inuit sculpture is imbued with a strong feeling for animals, a remarkable portrayal of the spirit of the bear or seal or bird created. The sculptures of people show a deep affection for family life and relationships: for times of pleasure, times of backbreaking work, and times of incredible patience in hunting. The skillful carving is done with great sensitivity to form and respect for the solid quality of the stone. In the best of them, the forms seem less to be imposed on the stone than discovered and revealed in it. The Inuit do not have a preconceived idea of what they are going to carve; they let the grain and structure of each individual stone suggest what is to be brought out.

In 1957 a new technique, printmaking, was introduced at Cape Dorset, and again the Inuit used this medium to express their own feelings in art. Two methods are used. In the first, large slabs of stone are cut and polished to a flat surface. A design is transferred to the surface, and the surrounding stone is chiseled away, leaving the design raised in relief. Ink is rolled onto this surface, paper is laid on, rubbed with the hands or a sealskin baren, and then lifted off. In this way as many as fifty prints are made from one design. (See Fig. 10-60.)

The other method, adapted from the Inuit craft of cutting designs out of sealskin for appliqué work, is to make stencils. Originally, designs were cut in flat, stretched pieces of sealskin. Ink was then daubed through the holes cut in this stencil to make the designs on the paper placed underneath. (See Fig. 10-1.) Now the Inuit use paper prepared with wax for the stencils so that seals will not have to be killed for this purpose.

Frequently the prints are visual representations of spirit forms. In Inuit mythology, animal and human forms and activities fuse, and the prints often show these spirits that inhabit the sea and the land.

The prints are designed by both men and women, but men usually cut the stones and apply the inks for printing. The Inuit now sell the prints and sculpture made at Cape Dorset through their own cooperative. Several other Inuit communities, such as those at Holman Island, Baker Lake, Port Harrison, Povungnituk, Lake Harbour, and Pangnirtung, are also producing art.

Carving Artificial Sandstone

The Inuit use soapstone, whalebone, and other materials in their environment for their sculpture. In the urban setting, it is sometimes possible to find an artificial sandstone, which makes a fine medium for young students to carve. If there is a metal casting foundry in the area, it may use a process that makes molds out of a manmade sandstone. After the molten metal has been poured into these molds and cooled, the molds are broken away and discarded. Most foundries are only too glad to have them put to creative use. Non-toxic stonelike products can also be obtained from art supply stores.

The mold sand will be in many irregular chunks. If the chunks are too large, saw them into smaller pieces. Before starting, students should turn their pieces and view them carefully from every angle. The ancient Inuit believed there was a form already inside the piece of ivory they were to carve; it was only to be discovered and released. The success of the final piece may be in this initial process of looking at the form and being in tune with what it suggests. The mold sand can be carved easily with table knives, forks, or other tools. In fact, it can be carved too easily. It should be *gently* scraped to bring out the form. It is easy

Fig. 10-61. Jeannie uses sandpaper to smooth her sculpture of a bird.

Fig. 10-62. Some fourth-grade sand-stone sculptures. *Owl* by Laura; *Whale* by Masashi; *Bird* by Jeannie.

to take too much off at once—and there's no putting it back.

Place the mold sand on a pad of newspaper. As the sand accumulates, dump it into a wastebasket at regular intervals or it will soon be tracked around the workroom. Lines can be etched in the sculpture with a nail. The piece should be lightly smoothed with fine sandpaper. To prevent sand from coming off the surface of the finished sculpture, seal it with a coat of shellac or fixative spray.

Plaster Carving

Older children (from sixth to ninth grades) may find it more challenging to work in a harder medium. Plaster may be a better choice for them. To mix the plaster, follow the directions and note precautions given in the appendix. The plaster can then be poured into waxed cardboard milk containers or better yet, since it will produce more natural shapes, into plastic bags. If you pour the plaster into plastic bags, you can shape the form slightly as the

plaster sets. Let it harden overnight and remove the plaster from the containers.

Then turn the piece of plaster and look at it from all sides to see what forms its shape suggests. Plaster dust is not good to breathe. To prevent dust from getting into the air while carving, run the piece very *quickly* under water at frequent intervals to keep it damp. (It should not be soaking wet, which weakens the plaster.) Damp plaster is also easier to carve.

Carve on newspaper, and dump the scrapings frequently in some container. Many different tools can be used. A hammer and chisel can be used for cutting a rough form. The flat, oval-shaped linoleum-cutting tool works well but should be used in a scraping rather than a cutting motion. The tools with wire ends made for shaping clay can be used safely and effectively. After roughing out the form, work closer and closer to the final shape. Try to make the sculpture interesting from every angle, not just one side. Also, if the students study some examples of Inuit work, they will realize that the sculptures keep the solidity of the stone; the Inuit make no attempt to carve delicate, spindly shapes. Minor holes and mistakes may be corrected by mixing a small amount of plaster and applying it to the area, which should be dampened first.

Fig. 10-63. Plaster carvings by sixth-grade students: *Whale* by Mike; *Seal* by Jason; and *Kayak* by John.

Tools used in carving plaster should be thoroughly cleaned after use, because plaster is highly corrosive to metal.

When the carving is completed it should be smoothed by rubbing with a damp cloth. Then it can be given one or two coats of liquid black shoe polish, which will give it a smooth, slightly shiny black surface. Inuit soapstone sculpture is rubbed with oil to create the same effect. In the final step, carefully add a few details, such as eyes or flipper lines, by cutting through the black surface to the white plaster beneath with a nail or pin.

Printmaking

First, study Inuit prints and get a feeling for the subject matter. It ranges from superbly delineated birds and easily identified animals to supernatural animal spirits that often combine human and animal characteristics. Some are very humorous, some are quite frightening, and others radiate wild beauty.

Carving a stone block for printing is a long and tedious process. But students can create their design in relief by a different method.

Draw a design on paper and then transfer it to a smooth piece of rubber inner tubing (another item to be found in our urban environment). This can be done by thoroughly chalking the underside of the design, which turns it into a kind of white carbon paper. Place the design, chalky side down, on the rubber and trace over the design with a pencil, pressing firmly. Then cut out the shape with scissors. Some interior design lines may be made by cutting off a portion, such as a wing, and then placing it slightly away from the body so that a line or space will be formed when printing. (See the wings on the birds in Fig. 10-71.) Eyes may be made with a hole puncher.

After the piece has been cut out, glue it to cardboard with white glue to make a printing block. One side of the rubber may have ridges or texture; be sure this is glued down and the smooth surface is up.

After the block is thoroughly dry, cut away any extra cardboard, leaving only a small edge around the rubber. This will make it easier to keep all the ink on the rubber when you are inking the block.

Squeeze out some water-based printing ink onto a flat surface. A floor tile or piece of window glass is fine. With a brayer, roll the ink until it forms an even, slightly sticky surface that crackles as the brayer passes over it. With the inked brayer,

Fig. 10-64. Dawn, ten, applies ink with a brayer.

Fig. 10-65. She places the paper on the inked block and rubs it vigorously.

Fig. 10-66. Dawn checks to see if the block was well inked and the print is good.

Fig. 10-67. A helper peels back the paper so that more ink may be applied to the block.

Fig. 10-68. Dawn examines her finished print.

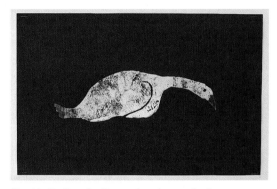

Fig. 10-69. *Goose* by Dana, nine. A second color was blended into the beak and tail before printing.

ink and then use the same up-and-down motion on the rubber (smearing back and forth will give a different surface texture than the rest of the block).

Place the paper to be printed on the inked block. Rub the paper carefully with the side of the hand (or the bowl of a spoon), feeling for every part of the block (see Fig. 10-65). Check to see if you have rubbed enough by holding the paper firmly at the bottom and peeling down only the top half (Fig. 10-66). Then replace the top and peel back the bottom. If you need more ink, add some while a helper peels back half the print at a time (see Fig. 10-67). It is better to work this way than to discard poorly made prints. Once the paper has been lifted completely, it will not be possible to replace it accurately.

Many prints may be taken from one block. You can create interesting colors by rolling a new color over the first one on the block. If an entirely new color is desired, the block should be cleaned with a damp cloth only (washing in water will disintegrate the cardboard). A more permanent block can be made using a water-proof glue and a wood base.

Some of the Inuit prints are a solid color. Others grade one color into another. This adds a texture and emphasis of form. Students can add an area of color by blending a second color into the edge of the first with the brayer or with

apply ink to the raised rubber design, being careful not to get any on the cardboard base (see Fig. 10-64). If the rubber is not completely flat, there may be areas that don't receive the ink. In that case, apply the ink with your index finger. First pat the finger up and down in the

their index fingers.

Sometimes it is effective to print the block several times on one piece of paper to form a group, such as a school of fish or a flock of birds (see Fig. 10-70).

Fig. 10-70. *Narwhals* by Mike, ten. One block was printed three times to make this group.

Fig. 10-71. *Birds*, a print by Sarah, ten.

EARLY AMERICAN FOLK ARTS

Applehead Dolls

Wherever there are children, there will be dolls. When the early settlers came to North America, they made dolls for their children from materials they found in their new environment: there were dolls made of twigs, corncobs, and cornhusks; dolls made of straw, of wood, and of nuts. These materials were supplemented with precious scraps of cloth and rags from old clothing.

The Native Americans already living on this continent also made dolls for their children, sometimes to instruct them in the names

Fig. 10-72. Applehead doll made by Mrs. Leah Rae Greenberg, Toronto, Ontario. Exhibited at the "In Praise of Hands" exhibition, Ontario Science Centre, Toronto, 1974. From the collection of Leah Rae Greenberg.

and attributes of spiritual figures and sometimes for play. Young Indian girls learned to make and decorate clothing by dressing their dolls. The Iroquois Indians, living in what is now the northeastern part of the United States and southeast Canada, made doll-like figures (thought to have been created for sacred rituals) that used dried apples for heads. The early settlers learned this craft from the Indians.

Although the bodies were made in many different ways, the significant part of this kind of doll was the head, which was made from a carved apple. As the apple dried, it softened and wrinkled into amazingly lifelike expressions, especially of old age. The applehead doll became a tradition with early settlers and was made in many parts of Canada and America, especially in New England and Appalachia. Applehead dolls have become popular again in recent years and are made by many craftspeople, less as dolls for children to play with than as fine figures made only for display. They are a reminder of the past, when dolls were not mass produced in factories and advertised on television but lovingly made by hand by a father or mother, an aunt or a grandmother, to fit the needs of a particular child.

Making Applehead Dolls

Choose a large apple and peel it, leaving some skin around the stem and blossom ends. Make as smooth a surface as possible. Carve a face into the apple, beginning with the nose: with the point of the knife make a triangular cut in the middle of the apple about ¼" deep. Cut a flat plane on either side of this to bring the nose out. Remove a piece underneath the nose also (see the apple on the left in Fig. 10-73). Gently soften the lines of the nose by scraping

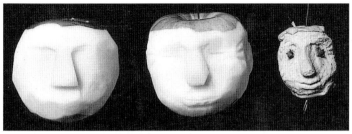

Fig. 10-73. Making an applehead. From left to right: first carve the nose by cutting a triangular shape and making flat planes on either side of it. In the center apple, the nose has been refined, eye area deepened, and slits cut in for eyes. Crow's-feet add a twinkle to the eye. A slit has been cut for the mouth, and ears have been carved on the side of the head. The third apple was dried for over three weeks.

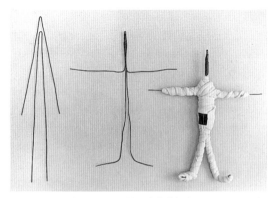

Fig. 10-74. Making the applehead doll body. Two pieces of wire, one 20" and one 13", are bent in half. They are taped together at the neck and the arms and legs bent out. Then the wire is wrapped with crepe paper or rags secured with tape.

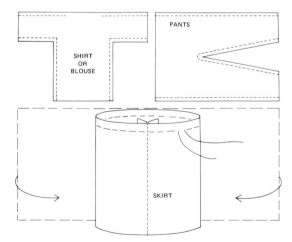

Fig. 10-75. Clothes patterns for applehead dolls. Gather pants and skirt at waist with a drawstring.

it with the knife. Deepen the eye cavities to create a brow, and make a slit for each eye. Scraping three lines that radiate out from the eyes will make laugh lines or crow's-feet. As with the eyes, cut just a slit for the mouth, about $\frac{1}{8}$" deep, either straight or curved in a smile. As it dries, it will open up. You can make a lower lip by scraping a shallow line parallel to and beneath the mouth. Ears may be carved in the side of the head, although this is unnecessary if hair is to cover that part of the apple. The middle apple in Fig. 10-73 shows one in which the carving has just been completed. The third apple has dried for over three weeks.

If you wish the apple to remain a light color, immerse it in lemon juice for a few minutes. Hang it up to dry by poking a wire through it from the bottom to the top. Bend over 1" of wire on the bottom so that the apple will not slip off, bend a hook in the top, and hang it over a line. Sprinkle it heavily with salt to hasten the drying and prevent the growth of mold. You will need to lay newspaper underneath to catch the drips.

It takes three to four weeks for the apple to dry, depending on the humidity in the air. Do not hang it in direct sun, but do hang the apple where you can see it, because it is fascinating to watch the slow changes taking place in the figure you have carved. After the first week or two, the apple will become somewhat pliable. Using your fingers, pinch the nose, cheeks, and chin into shapes a little more to your liking.

The hands should be cut from another apple that has been cut in $\frac{1}{2}$" slices. Cut mitten shapes at least twice as large as you want for the final size. Dip them in lemon juice and

Fig. 10-76. Lise's applehead doll, wearing a grand lacy collar, sits at a table made of scrap wood.

sprinkle them well with salt. Set them to dry by inserting toothpicks or short lengths of wire into the apple pieces and sticking the other ends into corrugated cardboard or Styrofoam. After they have dried for three or four days, they will become like soft leather, and fingers can be cut into the mitten shape with scissors.

While the head and hands are drying, the rest of the doll can be made. The body is made over an armature of wire. Take two lengths of 18-gauge wire, one 20" long and one 13" long, and bend them in half. (See Fig. 10-74.) Place these bent wires together. Pinch the bends with pliers to make them as sharp as possible, and then wrap them together with plastic electrical tape for 1½" to form a neck. Spread out the shorter wire to make arms, separate the

Fig. 10-77. Applehead dolls, left to right: *Gandalf the Wizard* by Hudson, age eleven; *Man* by Kreig, twelve; and *Lady* by Lisa, ten. Kreig cut the hat from scraps of leather. Lisa's lady wears a tiny yellow flower in her hair.

legs, and bend up the feet. Finally, wrap the arms and body with strips of crepe paper or rags to fill out the shape. Secure the ends of the wrapping with tape. Leave the neck and ends of the arms unwrapped. Wrap down one leg and out the foot almost to the end. Bend the last ¼" of wire and clamp it with pliers against the wrapping to keep it from slipping off the foot, and then wrap back up the leg to the body. Secure the end of the wrapping with tape, and complete the other leg in the same way.

To make clothing, use scraps of material appropriate to the character you have in mind. Fig. 10-75 shows how to make simple clothes. Shoes may be made from scraps of leather glued to the padded feet.

When the head has dried, it is ready to be put on the doll. First, remove the wire it was hung on and enlarge the hole in the apple, if necessary, with the point of a scissors or a nail. Put glue on the wire neck and push the apple onto it. Glue the ends of the arm wires also and insert them into the hands. Push in whole cloves for eyes. Hair may be made from cotton, untwisted yarn, or fleece. Eyeglasses can be shaped of thin wire and secured by poking the wire ends into the head under the hair. Such details as jewelry, hats, ties, and pipes add to the realism of the doll.

An applehead doll is especially interesting if it appears to be engaged in some activity, such as playing a musical instrument, knitting, or walking with a dog. Students can use all kinds of scrap materials to make miniature chairs, books, knitting needles, guitars, or other items.

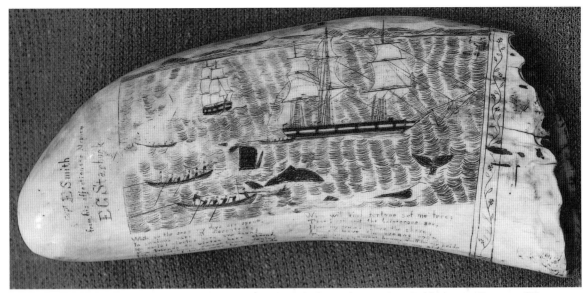

Fig. 10-78. Scrimshawed whale's tooth made by E. C. Starbuck for his uncle, Captain E. Smith, c. 1840. Courtesy of New Bedford Whaling Museum.

Scrimshaw

The art of scrimshaw, carving in whalebone and ivory, was practiced by most of the sailors who went on long sea voyages searching for whales. Carving in ivory had been done for centuries by people all over the world with the ivory of elephants, hippopotami, walrus, and whales. But scrimshaw is a nautical term, and it applies to the art as practiced by the whale-men in the eighteenth and nineteenth centuries.

The colonists first engaged in whaling in the mid-1600s. Whales were valued for their oil (for lamps) and for their meat. When a whale was sighted from the land, men put out in small boats to harpoon the animal and bring it ashore. These were baleen whales. Baleen is long strips of flexible material—not bone but more like the composition of finger-nails—that hang from the upper jaw, acting as food strainers and collecting small marine life from the ocean. Baleen, discarded at first, was later used for scrimshaw and also for many other articles, especially corset stays.

In the 1700s the search for sperm whales, which ranged much farther out to sea, brought about deep-sea whaling. Sperm whales were much sought after because they had more and better oil. They also had teeth, unlike baleen whales, and because it was not of commercial value, this ivory was used by the whalemen to make scrimshaw. By the late eighteenth century, great whaling ships from New England went out all over the world. They stayed out until all their barrels were full of oil—often several years. There were long boring stretches of time when the sailors' work was done and there were no whales in sight. This time was often filled with making items from the whale teeth and bones. Made captive on their ship by the sea, the artist-

Fig. 10-79. Ricky engraves his plaster pendant with a sharpened nail, while John R. collects soot from a candle flame by holding a ceramic tile over it. He will rub the soot into his engraving.

Fig. 10-80. Plaster scrimshaw pendants. From left to right: by Jack, John P., Lisa, and Alison, fifth-grade students.

prisoners whittled and carved and sawed beautiful items of great variety either to give to their loved ones when they returned or to use themselves. The smoothed teeth were incised with fine drawings. These designs perhaps most frequently depicted whaling scenes, but they also portrayed birds, fish, flowers, romantic recollections of home, and political events.

Scrimshaw also refers to more sculptural pieces made of ivory or whalebone: tools (pie crimpers, knitting needles, thimbles, handles for silverware), toys and games (such as chess pieces), letter openers, boxes, baskets, canes, and candlesticks. Some of the loveliest engraving was done on corset stays.

Whale teeth are deeply ridged. These ridges first had to be whittled, scraped, and sanded smooth by the scrimshander (one who makes scrimshaw). Sharkskin glued to a piece

of wood made a good sandpaper. When the tooth was smooth and polished to a fine finish, it was engraved. A design was worked out first on paper, the paper was placed on the tooth, and the design was transferred by lightly pricking along the lines with a pin. Sometimes it was drawn on freehand. Sailmakers' awls and needles, sharpened to a fine point, were used to engrave the lines. When done, the lines were emphasized by filling them with pigments—lampblack could be made aboard ship, and sometimes other pigments were used. Sculpted objects, such as pie crimpers and chess pieces, needed more equipment. The most-used tool was the jackknife, with which the sailors could do very delicate carving. Fine saws, small hammers and chisels, and even in some cases hand-powered lathes were also used. The sailing ships touched at ports all over the world, and fine woods were also used in combination with the whalebone and ivory. Beautiful writing desks and inlaid boxes were made of these materials.

So thorough were the whaling ships in their pursuit of oil that sperm whales became very scarce. The discovery of petroleum probably came just in time to save them from extinction. However, whales are still hunted by some countries and several species are endangered. International efforts are now being made to protect them.

The art of making scrimshaw, so much a part of the life on board the sailing ships, declined rapidly. But some artists today have revived the art using ivory substitutes. One such material is ivory nuts from the South American ivory palm tree which when baked, become hard and closely resemble ivory.

Making Plaster Scrimshaw

The engraving on scrimshaw is incredibly fine and takes a good deal of patience. Making a pendant-sized piece is a good introduction. Plaster can substitute for ivory. Mix the plaster as described in the appendix. Drop teaspoonfuls of plaster on waxed paper. The plaster pieces should dry for a day or two, being turned over occasionally after they are hard.

With a ¼" drill bit, drill a hole at the top. (A rotary hand drill can be used, but too much pressure may crack the plaster. A power drill, which should be operated by an adult, does a better job.) Smooth the plaster with a damp cloth, removing any bumps or irregularities.

Next, draw around the plaster on a piece of paper so that you can work out several designs to fill that particular shape. When the plaster is dry, give it two coats of acrylic varnish. Let the first dry well before applying the second. In the meantime, work on your designs. You may want to use a nautical theme, but scrimshanders used subject matter of all kinds. Remember that the lines are very fine and you will want lots of details—perhaps rows and rows of little waves or flower designs with delicate leafy vines.

After choosing a design, copy it onto the varnished and dried plaster with a pencil.

Mistakes can be erased and redrawn. Then, using a pin or a small nail with a sharpened point (sharpen by rubbing at an angle on a whetstone), engrave the design into the plaster. As the design is being engraved, clean off any plaster dust with a slightly damp cloth.

The whalemen most often used lampblack to darken the engraved lines, and that is easy to do. Light a candle and hold a ceramic tile or white ceramic saucer just above the tip of the flame. Soot will accumulate on it. *Place the candle in a secure holder, preferably on a large sheet of metal.* Keep papers away and don't leave the burning candle unattended. It is difficult to rub dry soot into the engraved lines, so rub your finger in the soot and then into a little dab of cooking oil, mix them together, and then rub this mixture into the engraved design. Make more lampblack as it is needed. Because the plaster has been varnished, the pigment will come off the surface with a clean cloth, staying only in the lines. Use a leather thong, ribbon, or piece of yarn to complete the pendant.

Weathervanes

Weathervanes have been made from early times. By indicating wind direction, they help both sailors and farmers predict the weather. Early American weathervanes are now recognized as an important American folk art; they often display original designs and excellent craftsmanship. Fine examples are sought after by museums and collectors.

A weathervane is constructed so that when the wind blows against it, the point turns in the direction from which the wind is blowing. It is mounted on a rod placed off center on the vane, nearest to the front, or

Fig. 10-81. Rooster weathervane made by Thomas Drowne in 1771 for the East Meetinghouse, Salem, Massachusetts. © Peabody Essex Museum/Photograph by Mark Sexton.

point. The larger, back area of the design collects greater wind pressure and is pushed away, moving the smaller, front area, or point, into the wind. Some weathervanes are made of flat pieces, and some are full-bodied and hollow.

American weathervanes derived from those of Europe. There were two main influences on their design. In the ninth century, the Pope ordered a rooster to be installed on the top of every church as a religious symbol. At some point, the rooster became converted to a weathervane. Although not carried on as a Catholic tradition, the rooster became common on Protestant churches, and it is still the most common form of weathervane in rural England. Perched on the spire of the local church, it can be seen by everyone in the village.

During the Middle Ages, the square heraldic banners of noblemen were used as designs for weathervanes on their castles, both to give wind direction and to inform strangers of the rank of those within. Pennants with single and double tails, called bannerets, signified people of lower rank.

The rooster and the heraldic banner designs were the most commonly seen in England and Europe, and such weathervanes were imported to America by early colonists. In this country banner designs were not restricted—there was no nobility—everyone was free to fly them and delighted in doing so.

Colonial New England soon had its own weathervane makers. Rural weathervanes were frequently made by the farmer himself or by the village blacksmith. They were usually constructed of wood or sheet iron. Not many survive, and we rarely know who the makers were. Besides the traditional rooster, barnyard weathervanes often took the form of animals the farmer specialized in: cows, pigs, and horses were among the most popular. Along the coast, weathervanes often took the form of fish, whales, and elaborate sailing ships.

The most famous early weathervane craftsman was Shem Drowne. In 1742 his golden grasshopper with green glass eyes was placed on Boston's Faneuil Hall; it is still there, turning in the wind. Although the weathervanes made for the tops of public buildings are dwarfed by the height of the buildings, they are really very large. Shem Drowne's copper rooster, made in 1721 for New Brick Church in Boston, was over 5' tall and weighed 172 pounds. The rooster in Fig. 10-81 made by

Shem Drowne's son, Thomas, is made of gilded copper and is 4' 4" long, with glass eyes. It was made for the spire of Salem's East Meetinghouse in 1771, where it could be seen by people in the village and also from ships at sea.

George Washington commissioned a weathervane portraying a dove with an olive branch—symbol of peace—for his home at Mount Vernon. (See Fig. 10-83.)

Fig. 10-82. Gilded galleon weathervane on top of the bell tower, City Hall, Portland, Maine. It is approximately 5' wide and weighs 100 pounds. Designed by Carrere, of Carrere and Hastings, an architectural firm, c. 1912. A replica of a 15th-century sailing ship, it is a fine symbol for this Atlantic coast port city.

Weathervanes were most commonly made of copper, but sheet iron, wood, zinc, tin, and brass were also used. The weathervane on Paul Revere's shop was in the form of a wooden fish, studded with nails to indicate scales. By the late eighteenth and early nineteenth centuries, weathervanes were a true American folk art involving original creative designs and very fine craftsmanship.

However, by the mid-nineteenth century, the majority were made near Boston or New York City by companies, often run by several generations of the same family. One of the popular designs was the American bald eagle, the designated emblem of the United States. The weathervanes of this period were frequently made by hammering sheets of copper into iron molds and then soldering the two halves together. Many could be made from the same mold, but they were all hammered out by hand and involved skilled workmanship. They were usually covered with gold leaf.

In the last half of the nineteenth century a great many weathervanes were produced in a wide variety of designs. Unique designs were also commissioned for special buildings. Weathervanes are still being manufactured and are easily available. Although rarely used as devices for weather prediction by the general public, they are decorative pieces of usually traditional design. However, there are artists today who, like earlier craftsmen, make fine unique weathervanes to grace buildings throughout the country.

Making Weathervanes

Depending on the age of the students, they may need an explanation of north, south, east, and west. Demonstrating with a globe and a compass will make this clear. Older students can learn to "box the compass," reciting eight points of the compass in a clockwise order. Eight points are not difficult: N, NE, E, SE, S, SW, W, NW. (Sixteen points are more of a challenge: N, NNE, NE, ENE, E, etc.)

The students may wish to make standard weathervane designs, such as horses or arrows. However, the project will have more meaning to them if they make a design that is relevant to their own lives. It can be a symbol, such as a dove of peace, or it can be a favorite animal or pet, a mythical creature, or a symbol of some family member's career or pastime (a musical instrument, sailboat, etc.). Encourage them to think this over carefully before beginning.

The vane itself is made from the flat side of a gallon or half-gallon plastic milk or juice bottle. Cut out the largest possible piece that is completely flat. There may be two large areas in one container. If there are labels that are difficult to remove, try using the citrus-based products on the market that have been developed to remove labels. Place the cut-out piece of plastic on newsprint and trace around it. This will indicate exactly how large the design can be. Encourage the students to use the full size of this area, and to spend all the time needed to make a careful design. This is the important part of the project—the rest is mostly assembly. Go over the design with a black marker.

When the design is finished, place the piece of plastic over it (the design will show through) and trace the design onto the plastic with a fine-point marker. Cut out the design. A hole puncher can be used for features such as eyes, to make designs, or to give the scissors access to an interior portion to be cut out.

With scissors, split the end of a straight plastic drinking straw, going down about 1". Insert the bottom of the cut-out design into this slot. Position the straw so that if a line were to be drawn straight up from it through the vane, there would be much more area at the back of the design; the portion of the design that you wish to point forward into the wind should have a smaller area. The wind blowing on the larger area will push it to the back and thereby head the smaller area toward the direction from which the wind is coming. (See Fig. 10-84.) Staple the straw to the vane, making sure that it is at right angles to the design. Staple it near the top, then turn it over and put in another staple below the first.

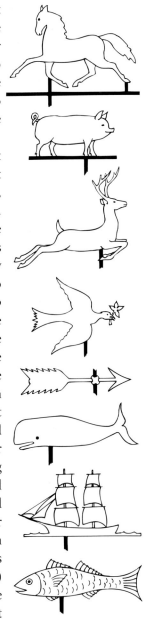

Fig. 10-83. Some traditional early American weathervane designs. The dove with an olive branch was commissioned by George Washington for his home at Mount Vernon.

You will need to have some clothes hangers—the kind that are made of wire with a cardboard tube along the bottom. Children can bring them from home, and frequently a dry-cleaning business has used hangers that they are very glad to donate. Be sure the tubes are straight. Two weathervane tubes can be made from each hanger. The teacher can cut the tube in half at the center using a paper cutter or a garden tool such as a lopper. (Leave the metal wire attached at both ends—it is not necessary to remove it.) Measure 6½" to the left and cut off the tube, about 1" from the end, and do the same on the other side, as in Fig. 10-84. You will not need the remaining parts of the hanger. After cutting the tubes they will be somewhat flattened on the ends—gently squeeze then back into a round shape.

Use a nail to punch a hole through the tube about 3" down from one end. The nail should be about the diameter of the bamboo skewers you will be using. This has to be done very carefully so that the entrance and exit holes are level with each other. The best way is to push or hammer the nail through the first, or entry, side and just up to the inside of the second, or exit, side. Then hold the tube vertically and be sure the nail is horizontal before pushing it all the way through.

A second pair of holes is then punched about ⅛" below the first pair and at a right angle to them—in other words, not directly below them, but halfway between them, a quarter-turn around the tube. (See Fig. 10-84.)

Cut about 1" off the pointed end of 8" long bamboo skewers. The teacher should do this, as the points are very sharp. Discard the points.

Make the N, S, E, and W wind directional letters (also called cardinal points). Draw

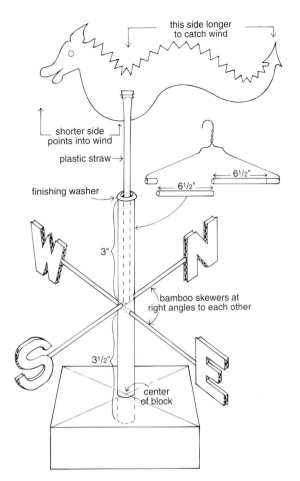

Fig. 10-84. Making a weathervane.

them on corrugated cardboard on pieces 1¼" square or larger. They should be made in thick block letters so that there is room to insert the skewers into them. Be sure that the lines of the cardboard are horizontal so that the finished letter will have holes in the sides in which to insert the skewers. Cutting the letters from corrugated cardboard is difficult and the students may need help. (If you are going to paint the weathervane with gold acrylic later, you could, instead, cut these symbols from thick foam trays. But if you are going to use a metallic spray paint, stick to corrugated cardboard because the ingredients in the spray will dissolve plastic.)

Push the skewers through the holes you have made in the cardboard tube. They will be at right angles to each other. Put a dab of glue on the end of one skewer. Enlarge one of the holes in the cardboard that falls halfway up the side of the letter. Push the end of the skewer into it. Repeat with the other letters. Be sure that N is opposite S on one skewer, and E is opposite W on the other. If you look down on the weathervane, with north at the top, east is always to the right, west to the left, and south at the bottom.

You can also make wind directionals if you can find some heavy wire that is easily bent. Push the wire through the holes and bend letters in its ends—an N and S on one wire, and

Fig. 10-85. Zhenya cuts his arrow design from a piece of plastic.

Fig. 10-86. Erin paints her fish weathervane with gold acrylic paint.

an E and W on another. The holes in the tube should be made with a smaller nail than that for a bamboo skewer. These cardinal points will be waterproof.

The weathervane is most attractive if it is painted with a bright metallic gold or brass color. Spray paint is volatile and toxic and should be used only by a teacher, outdoors or in a very well-ventilated area. Hold the vane by the end of the straw, spray it, and set aside to dry by sticking it in a piece of modeling clay. Then spray the tube and directional symbols in the same way. Alternatively, the students can paint the weathervanes with acrylic gold paint.

Finally, a base is made in which to stand the weathervane. If the school has a wood vise, the students can saw 4½" pieces from a length of 2 x 4" lumber using a handsaw. Any wood scraps can be used, but the 2 x 4" has enough weight that it will not be easily blown over. Otherwise a parent, teacher, or someone at the lumberyard should saw the pieces. The resulting blocks should have ½" holes drilled in their centers. An easy way to find the center is to draw diagonal lines from corner to corner—they intersect at the center. (See Fig. 10-84.) Again, if the school has a vise, the students can drill the holes with a brace and bit, which would be safe for them to use. Otherwise an adult should do this with a power drill. Use a ½" drill bit and drill to a depth of about ¾".

The student should sand this block carefully. Use coarse sandpaper to clean off the rough edges, and then finer grades to smooth the block down well. The block can then be stained and varnished (to make it look more early American) or painted flat black, which looks very elegant with the gold. Of course the students should be free to choose other colors if they wish.

Fig. 10-87. Four weathervanes heading north, by fifth-grade students: *Horse* by Rosemary; *Cat* by Kelley; *Dove* by Hannah; and *Fish* by Erin.

When the block is dry, push the tube and directional symbols into the hole in the block. Although not absolutely necessary, it is a good idea to place a #10 finishing washer on top of the tube. It will allow the weathervane to move more easily. A finishing washer has a groove on the underside that will fit snugly over the tube edge. A tiny dab of glue in this groove will keep the washer from getting lost, but be careful that extra glue does not block the hole. This washer keeps the straw away from the sides of the tube. Insert the weathervane into the tube.

Now test the weathervane outdoors, or with a fan. Use a compass and arrange the block so that the north directional is pointing in the correct direction. The prevailing wind will then shift the weathervane so that it will point in the direction the wind is coming from. If the point lies directly over the S, for example, the wind is coming from the south. If the vane does not respond correctly, there may not be enough area at the back of the vane. Pry off the staples and place the straw farther to the front of the vane, and staple again. Paint over any bare spots.

The weathervane can be used outdoors if you have used waterproof paints, though the cardboard tube and letters will still be vulnerable to heavy rain. A final coat of varnish over the paint may protect them. This is not necessary if the weathervane is primarily to be on display in the house—it will be a fine piece of sculpture to enjoy and to take outdoors on dry, windy days.

Making Paper Weathervane Designs

Younger children can make paper weathervane designs. Use the books listed in the bibliography to show them the great variety of weathervanes made by early American artists. They also may need an explanation of exactly what north, south, east, and west mean. This may be explained most easily with a globe and a compass.

The students should draw their designs on a piece of tag board approximately 5 x 8". Cut them out, and use a hole puncher for eyes, or to enable them to make interior cuts in their designs. Then the children should make their directional signs—N,S,E, and W—on square pieces of tag board, 1¼" or a little larger. Have

Fig. 10-88. Joei, seven, traces directional letters from patterns taped to the window.

Fig. 10-89. Joei is cutting letters out of gold paper for his cat weathervane.

Fig. 10-90. Two paper weathervane designs by second graders: *Fish* by Lily and *Turtle* by Leila. The west and south directionals are projected out and cast shadows on the paper.

them draw letters that fill the space, using wide black markers so that they will be sufficiently thick—otherwise they are likely to be too thin to cut out. Another way to do this is shown in Fig. 10-88. Large block letters are taped to the window so children can trace them. Lay the cut-out designs and letters on newspaper and spray-paint them with gold. (Spray paint is toxic and the teacher should do this outdoors or in a well-ventilated area away from the children.) Or have the children paint these designs with student-grade acrylic gold paint. Gold

paper can also be used, but it tends to flop when, later, the arms of the weathervane are extended.

Spray-paint a sheet of tag board gold, and from this cut poles for the weathervanes, about ¼" wide. Also cut black poster board strips ¼" wide. To assemble the weathervane design, paste the gold pole on blue paper (which represents sky). Paste the design over the top of the pole with more area to the back of the figure—explain that real weathervanes have more area to the back in order to catch the wind. Take two black strips of posterboard 6" long, and cross them in the middle to make a shallow X shape. Glue them together at the crossing point and then glue them at this point to the pole, about ⅔ of the way down. Reinforce this junction with a staple. A touch of black marker will make it less noticeable. Glue the gold N to the upper end of the left pole and the E to the upper end of the right one. Bend the two bottom arms up from where they cross. Bend a ¼" flap down at the end of each arm. Glue the W on the left (to the flap at the bottom of the E arm) and the S to the right at the bottom of the N arm. Having these project out will give a three-dimensional quality to the design.

Fig. 11-1. Looking down through a row of booths. In the foreground students demonstrate paintings inspired by Mexican amate paper paintings and explain Huichol Indian yarn painting techniques. Next to them students are making sand paintings using methods like those employed by Navajo Indians.

MULTICULTURAL ART FAIRS

A multicultural art fair can be a fine celebration that shares the children's creative work with the wider community, brings in people with special skills, and gathers everyone together to enjoy music, dance, art, and good food. The following are just suggestions, because each community will differ in its resources.

Fig. 11-2. Colorful banners made by second-, third-, and fourth-grade students inspired by Japanese fish banners, hang in the halls.

If the fair is held in the spring, you will be able to draw on the finished art projects of several months. These projects should be saved, and all the flat work put on display in the school's halls. Perhaps kites, inspired by those of Japan and Southeast Asia, can hang from the ceilings. In the gym, booths can be set up against the walls. Tie or tape long sticks to the legs of the tables. Secure brightly dyed old sheets to the tops of

Fig. 11-3. Art displays fill the halls. These sixth-grade paintings were created after students studied Persian miniatures.

Fig. 11-5. A student rolls ink on her block to demonstrate printmaking. The class had studied the prints of the Inuit people of Canada.

Fig. 11-4. First-grade students making embroidery. They were shown examples of stitchery made by Qolla Indian children in Peru, but use a simplified technique.

Fig. 11-6. In the art room, first-grade children help visitors make gyotaku, Japanese fish prints.

these sticks in order to make colorful canopies over the tables. At each booth a team of four students will demonstrate one of the projects —say, Peruvian embroidery—and some of the classwork can be hung behind the booth on the wall. A schedule should be worked out so that the teams change every half hour or so.

Invite people from the community to share their skills. For instance, there might be a booth where someone demonstrates Chinese calligraphy and, using a brush and ink, creates a few characters on colorful strips of paper to give the visitors. Or you might find a Polish artist who can demonstrate the art of wycinanki.

In the art room projects should be set up that everyone can do during the fair. These should involve inexpensive supplies. One suggestion from this book is Navajo sand paintings on small squares of cardboard. (The colored sand would need to be prepared beforehand.) Another suitable project is gyotaku— all you need is two or three fish, newsprint, and ink. Provide old shirts for people to use as smocks. A third suggestion is to make Japanese decorated papers. Instructions are given at the end of this chapter.

These projects should be taught by students who have mastered them—again, working in shifts, so that they can enjoy the rest of the fair.

There can be roving art: if the fair comes near the time of the Chinese New Year, students can create a papier-mâché dragon head, with sheets sewn together for the long body. With one student under the head and many students under the body, they can wend their way through the halls and into the gym among the visitors. Students who play the violin or guitar can be roving street musicians.

Fig. 11-7. Ikuko Mizukami and Masashi demonstrate origami folding at the Japanese booth. Next to them students make linoleum and woodcut prints inspired by Chinese woodcut prints.

Fig. 11-8. A student-made dragon emerges from a classroom, headed for the gymnasium. The dragon chases a pearl, part of the Chinese New Year tradition.

Fig. 11-9. The dragon makes its way through the crowds in the gym and welcomes a smaller dragon from another school.

Fig. 11-10. Dancing performed by the Bichinis Bia Congo (Dancers of the Congo) under the direction of Jean Claude Bahounguila-Biza. Students, taught by the dancers, also performed, and later the audience was invited to join in the dancing.

Performing arts can be in the auditorium. One school invited an African dance troupe to teach the students a dance. In the art room the students made beaded percussion instruments to accompany their dance, and then went on stage with the dance troupe. Students can sing the Puerto Rican song "¡Temporal!" found on page 211, accompanied by their handmade maracas. Your community may be rich in other dance or musical possibilities.

International and ethnic foods are very popular, and might be offered in the lunch room or cafeteria. Ask families to contribute food based on their own ethnic background, or to work from recipes found in cookbooks. Students who have made the Swedish cookie stamps described in this book may want to create decorated cookies for the fair. (You will need a permit to serve food to the public, and there may be rules—for example, that all food, except baked goods, must be prepared on the premises.)

One corner of the gymnasium might be set up as a sidewalk café with card tables and chairs—a place where people are able to sit and rest and have coffee, juice, and cookies. They can watch the passing crowds and be serenaded by the roving musicians.

A colorful program guide should be created and distributed, so that families and visitors will know what is happening throughout the school, will not miss the dance or music program, and know where to find the booths in the gym and the do-it-yourself projects in the art room.

The fair requires a lot of organization and preparation. Parents should be encouraged to help. It is useful to send a form home with the children to indicate where help will be needed,

Fig. 11-11. Topher plays his violin at the café in the gym.

Fig. 11-12. Japanese decorated papers made by the fold and dip-dye method. All the designs are based on dipping the corners, and sometimes the edges also, of paper folded into a triangle.

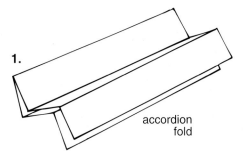

1.

accordion fold

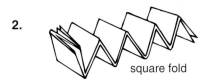

2.

square fold

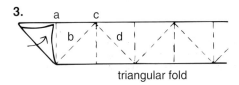

3.

triangular fold

asking for a time commitment: supervising children in the booths, donating food or staffing the food tables, putting up artwork, setting up tables in the gym, restoring order after the fair. It is well worth the effort, however, and is sure to be a fine time, bringing the community together to share art in its many forms.

JAPANESE DECORATED PAPERS

The Japanese make many very beautiful decorative papers using a wide variety of techniques. In some, leaves, blossoms, or other plant materials are incorporated into the handmade paper. Some designs are created using a resist technique that uses a paste and stencils. Others may be sprinkled with shiny or colored materials, or the design may be created by varying the thickness of the paper, letting the light shine through thin areas. One method is to create designs by folding the paper and dipping portions of it in different colored dyes.[1]

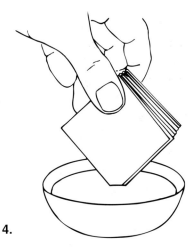

4.

Fig. 11-13. Making folded and dip-dyed decorative papers using the Japanese method. 1. Fold the paper in half and then accordion fold (in thirds). 2. Accordion fold again into squares or rectangles. Or, 3. make a triangular fold. First accordion fold the paper as in 1. Then fold the left corner up diagonally, fold to the back on *a*, forward on *b*, to the back on *c*, forward on *d*, etc., to the end. 4. Dip corners and/or edges into diluted tempera paint or food colors. Place the folded dyed paper between pieces of newspaper and step on it to spread the dye, unfold it, and dry on newspapers. Iron to smooth the paper.

[1] Hollander, Annette. "Fold-Dye Papers," *Woman's Day Studio,* September 1970, page 62. I am indebted to this article, the initial inspiration for the project on Japanese dip-dyed papers.

Fig. 11-14. Students demonstrate to a parent how to fold the paper before the dip-dye process.

Fig. 11-15. A young visitor to the fair takes a piece of paper from the roll to begin a decorated paper design. Participants leave their finished papers on the table to dry.

Making Japanese Folded and Dyed Papers

This is a fine project for families to learn at the fair because it is one they can continue to do later at home, using inexpensive materials, and creating their own beautiful wrapping paper for gifts. Copies of the diagram and instructions on these pages should be available for people to take home.

For the fair, industrial-strength paper towels that come on a roll work best. People work-

ing at home can use regular paper towels. For making extra-special papers at home, buy thin, white, absorbent (with no sizing) Japanese papers from an art supply store, or experiment with other available absorbent papers.

Cut a 12" piece of paper from a towel roll. Follow the diagram in Fig. 11-13. Dip just the tips and/or edges of the folded paper into diluted tempera paint (at school) or food coloring (at home). Use two or more colors. Place the dyed paper between clean cardboard or newspaper squares, put it on the floor, and step on it to spread the color and remove excess dye. Unfold the paper and examine it. If more color is desired it can be re-folded and re-dipped. Lay the decorated papers on newspaper to dry, or hang them on lines stretched across the room. It is a good idea at the fair, or in the classroom, for people to write their names on their paper in the beginning, before it gets wet with dye, so they can find their own piece to take home. After the paper dries it can be ironed to smooth out the folds.

Fig. 11-16. Folded and dip-dyed papers made at the fair. The bottom right piece was accordion folded into a rectangle and dipped on the ends, the other three designs are made with triangular folds.

Jade dips paper in the glue as she papier-mâchés the cover to her bowl. Kate's bowl is almost finished.

APPENDIX

SOME COMMON PROCESSES

Papier-mâché

The basic method for making objects of papier-mâché is simply to apply paste to torn pieces of paper and press them onto a base.

The base may be constructed of boxes, tubes, cardboard, or rolled or bunched newspaper. These items can be used separately or combined and taped together into a new shape. Or the base may be a blown up balloon (to create a spherical shape) or a plastic bowl or container. In the latter case, the bowl should be given a light coat of petroleum jelly so that it can be removed easily after the papier-mâché has dried.

Wheat paste, which is most commonly used for making papier-mâché, is available at wallpaper stores and craft supply stores. Sift the dry paste into a bowl of water while constantly stirring the mixture until it reaches a smooth, thick, creamy consistency. Mix only what is needed for the project at hand, as it does not keep well.

There are new products available in art supply stores that can be used instead of wheat paste, and have the advantage of keeping indefinitely. They are mixed in the same manner as wheat paste, but usually have to set fifteen minutes before being used. For strong papier-mâché, mix them using somewhat less water than is suggested on the package. They are used in the same manner as the wheat paste.

Apply the paste to both sides of *torn* pieces of newspaper. The edges of torn pieces tend to blend and make a smooth surface, whereas cut pieces of paper leave noticeable ridges. Overlap these pieces of newspaper on the object. Try to smooth out all the wrinkles. Large pieces of paper can be applied to large flat surfaces, but rounded or small sculptures should be made with small pieces of paper to avoid wrinkles. A strong piece will need four layers. After the first two layers are applied, let it dry a day or two before applying the third and fourth layers. It is easier to be sure each layer has completely covered the object if different papers are used. For instance, alternate layers of white and colored newspaper, or alternate newspaper with industrial strength paper toweling or Kraft paper.

If a very smooth finish is desired, the papier-mâché can be lightly sanded after it has completely dried. It is then ready to be painted or decorated. A final coat of varnish or polymer medium will strengthen the papier-mâché.

Glass Cutting

A glass cutter is an inexpensive tool. Buy one with a knob at the end of the handle. Place the glass to be cut on a pad of newspapers. The traditional way to hold the tool is to place it vertically, between the first and second fingers, where they join, gripping the handle just above the blade with your finger tips which are supported underneath with your thumb. (See Fig. 4-24.)

Press down firmly but not too hard and make one continuous pull toward yourself across the glass. You can feel the tool bite into the glass slightly if you are applying enough pressure. The tool will have scored a white line on the glass.

The easiest way to break the glass along the scored line is to use glass pliers (available at hardware stores). Place the line marked on the pliers on the edge of the glass, directly over the scored line, and press the handles together. The glass will break along the whole line. (If the pliers are upside down they won't work at all.)

To break along the line without glass pliers, place the knob of the cutter underneath the crack, and bear down with your hands on either side, using the tool as a fulcrum. The most common way to break glass is to place your hands, an inch or so in from the edge, on either side of the scored line, thumbs on top, fingers underneath, and rotate your wrists out so that you are simultaneously pulling out and down. If the glass has been well scored, it will break easily along the line. Roll the cutter blade through a drop of oil each time it is used to keep it running smoothly.

Safety goggles should always be worn when cutting glass, as sharp splinters may fly and cause injury.

To cut the glass to a particular size, measure the piece to be cut and make small guide marks with the glass cutter at the top and bottom edges. Place a ruler with a non-slip cork backing on these guide marks and run the glass cutter down along the ruler.

Small pieces may be created by cutting thin strips of glass and then cutting pieces from this strip. It is difficult to break off thin strips by hand, so for this you should use the glass pliers described above. After you have the strips, cut small pieces from the strip by using another tool, called a glass or tile cutting tool, that nips the edge of the glass. (See Fig. 3-32.) It will make a fracture straight across the narrow strip. This should always be done inside a clear plastic bag, because glass fragments may fly. With the glass and clippers inside the bag it is still possible to see clearly what you are doing.

Plaster of Paris

Although plaster of Paris has been used for many years, there is now concern that breathing the plaster particles that get into the air may be unhealthy. Therefore it is not recommended that students mix plaster themselves, and the teacher should mix it away from the workspace. The teacher may want to use a simple disposable mask, as well as eye protection, and also gloves to protect hands from possible allergic reaction.

Gather the containers into which the plaster is to be poured. Before mixing the plaster, set containers out on newspaper.

Put water into a plastic pail or bowl in an amount slightly less than the quantity of plaster needed. Sprinkle the dry plaster into the water *(without stirring it)* until it stops disappearing into the water and begins to form a large island of dry plaster. Then stir the plaster with your fingers, being sure it is smooth and there are no lumps. It should be a slightly thickened, creamy consistency. Immediately pour the mixture into the containers that have been set out. Tap the filled containers several times to level the plaster and make bubbles come to the surface. If the plaster hardens too quickly to pour, you have added too much plaster. Do not try to dilute it with more water. You will have to discard it and start over with a new mixture.

Do not rinse hands, tools, or containers in the sink, because the plaster will clog the pipes. Rinse your hands and tools in a bucket of water. When the plaster has settled, pour off the clear water. Then wipe out the container with newspaper or paper towels. If a flexible plastic pail is used, the plaster may be cracked out easily after it dries.

When students are carving plaster, dust in the air may be virtually eliminated by running the plaster very *quickly* under water, so that it is slightly damp (not wet). This will have to be repeated as it dries. However, if the plaster becomes too wet, it will be weak. Work on newspapers, and frequently dispose of plaster chips and scrapings before they dry out. In spite of all these precautions, children with asthma may have difficulty working with plaster.

Repairs may be made by mixing and adding small amounts of new plaster to a dampened piece.

To smooth a finished piece, use a damp cloth instead of sandpaper.

Wool Sources

This is a sample list and is not to be considered comprehensive.

Halcyon Yarns
12 School St.
Bath, ME 04530
800-341-0282
  Wool in batt and roving form

John D. Lindsay Co.
Box 218
Boston, MA 02124
617-288-1155
  Undyed wool of different types & colors—
  ask for samples and prices.
  White Merino top (very inexpensive).

Outback Fibres (From the Wool Shed)
Jill Gully
P.O. Box 153
Hewitt, TX 76643
800-757-2331 ext. 6164
  Beautiful, fine, clean Australian Merino top
  (roving) in 60 or more colors.

Peace Fleece
475 Porterfield Road
Porter, ME 04068
800-482-2841
  Felting supplies and kits

BIBLIOGRAPHY

Some books listed in the first edition that are now hard to find have been omitted. Those that remain in spite of being out of print are valuable references worth hunting for. Usually such books can be obtained through inter-library loan, and often secondhand copies can be purchased on the Internet. More recent references have been added that are relevant to both old and new projects.

CHAPTER 2
General African Arts

Blier, Suzanne Preston. *The Royal Arts of Africa: The Majesty of Form*. NY: Harry Abrams, 1998.
Arts of six West and Central African Kingdoms just before and after European contact. Includes long chapter on the arts of the ancient Benin Kingdom. Many color and black-and-white photos.

Duerden, Dennis. *African Art*. Feltham, England: Hamlyn Publishing Group Ltd., 1968.
An excellent introduction to African art, ancient and modern. Beautiful color plates of sculpture, architecture, adinkra cloth, and contemporary painting.

Hahner-Herzog, Iris; Maria Kecskesi, and Laslo Vajda. *African Masks from the Barbier-Mueller Collection, Geneva*. NY: Prestel Verlag, 2002.
Introduction concerning function and symbolism of the masks. 248 masks, 100 in color.

Jefferson, Louise E. *The Decorative Arts of Africa*. NY: Viking Press, 1973.
Excellent, comprehensive, and copiously illustrated book on a great variety of African arts, from metal work, carving, and fabric design (including adinkra cloth and symbols) to dress, hair styles, and many other decorative arts.

Newman, Thelma R. *Contemporary African Arts and Crafts*. NY: Crown Publishers, Inc., 1974.
Excellent book for use in the classroom. Covers all areas of contemporary crafts. Photo of aluminum panel by Olatunde, photos of contemporary fabrics: adire eleko, adire eleso (tie-dye), adinkra, and others. Description of processes involved in all these arts. Chapters end with brief suggestions to help the reader engage in similar art processes.

Parrinder, Geoffrey. *African Mythology*. Feltham, England: Hamlyn Publishing Group Ltd., 1967.
Fine photographs of bronze panels and a bronze leopard from Benin, Nigeria; brass from the Ashanti people of Ghana; carved wood Yoruba panels from Nigeria; beadwork; and carvings and masks from many other tribal groups. The book describes the myths and ways of life behind the artwork and also relates many delightful animal fables.

Sieber, Roy. *African Textiles and Decorative Arts*. NY: Museum of Modern Art, 1972.
Beadwork, jewelry, clothing, body decoration, and textiles. Includes many examples of weaving, appliqué, painted cloth, tied-and-dyed fabrics, and adire eleko.

Wahlman, Maude. *Contemporary African Arts*. Chicago: Field Museum of Natural History, 1974.
Wide range of contemporary arts, including a chapter on aluminum panels by Asiru Olatunde.

Willet, Frank. *African Art*. NY: Thames and Hudson, 1993.
Wide variety of African art including many shown in color: masks, Benin sculpture, jewelry, architecture, and contemporary art including a panel by Olatunde.

Williams, Geoffrey. *African Designs from Traditional Sources*. NY: Dover Publishers, Inc., 1971.
Black-and-white prints and drawings of traditional African designs used in many different media from all over the continent.

African Textiles

Ash, Beryl, and Anthony Dyson. *Introducing Dyeing and Printing.* NY: Watson Guptill, 1979.
> Methods of dyeing and printing with examples from Africa as well as other areas of the world.

Brooks, Lois. "Workshop: Adire Eleko". *Craft Horizons,* August 1971.
> An illustrated article on adere eleko techniques. See also general bibliography for books that include information about adire eleko.

Maile, Anne. *Tie and Dye Made Easy.* NY: Taplinger Publishing Co., 1971.
> See also the books in the general bibliography that have examples of African tie-dyed fabrics, and Nancy Belfer, *Batik and Tie Dye Techniques* under Indonesian Arts.

CHAPTER 3
Egyptian Arts

Davis, Peter. "Experiment in Harrania." *School Arts Magazine,* October 1963.

Forman, W. and B., and Ramses Wissa Wassef. *Tapestries from Egypt, Woven by the Children of Harrania.* London: Paul Hamlyn, 1961.
> This is a beautiful book with sixty-six full-color plates of Harrania weavings and of the young weavers themselves. In a short commentary, Professor Wassef describes his experiment at Harrania, which was not only to revive a craft, but to do so in a way that protected and nurtured the innate creativity of the children.

Freed, Rita E., Joyce L. Haynes, and Yvonne J. Markowitz. *Egypt in the Age of the Pyramids.* Boston: MFA Publications, 2002.
> A beautiful book published in conjunction with an exhibition at the Museum of Fine Arts, Boston. Many fine examples of hieroglyphs, jewelry, sculpture, and bas reliefs.

Malek, Jaromir. *Egyptian Art.* London: Phaidon Press Ltd., 1999.
> Whole range of Egyptian art—architecture, sculpture, wall reliefs, paintings, jewelry, pottery, including contemporary work. Color illustrations.

Rossini, Stephanie. *Egyptian Hieroglyphs: How to Read and Write Them.* NY: Dover Publications, 1989.
> A very useful resource for teachers—drawings of many hieroglyphs, descriptions of how they were used; arranged in categories such as consonants and phonetic signs.

Vilimkova, Milada. *Egyptian Jewelry.* London: Paul Hamlyn, 1969.
> Describes development of jewelry from prehistoric times through to the last dynasty and subsequent Greek and Roman influence. Ninety beautiful color illustrations.

Wilkinson, Richard H. *Reading Egyptian Art: A Hieroglyphic Guide to Ancient Egyptian Painting and Sculpture.* NY: Thames and Hudson, 1992.
> Beautifully illustrated guide to understanding hieroglyphs. Major signs and symbols, their meanings and applications in various art forms.

Israeli Arts

Katz, Karl, P. P. Kahane, and Magen Broshi. *From the Beginning: Archaeology and Art in the Israel Museum.* Jerusalem: Reynal & Co., 1968.
> Archaeological discoveries from prehistoric times up to the more recent past. Photographs of work in clay, bronze, stone, glass, gold, and silver from the museum's collection. Contemporary artwork also shown.

Roth, Cecil. *Jewish Art.* Jerusalem: Massada Press, 1971.
> A beautifully illustrated book with an anthology of articles by experts in their fields. The book covers over 3,000 years of Jewish art on five continents and includes many arts, from architecture and sculpture to painting, pottery, illuminated manuscripts, and ritual objects.

UNESCO. *Israel—Ancient Mosaics.* Norwalk, CT: New York Graphic Society, 1960.
> Thirty-two large color plates of mosaics in Israel with helpful preface and introduction by Meyer Schapiro and Michael Avi-Yonah.

Persian Miniature Painting

Bush, Sylvia T. "An Artist's Search for Colors." *Design Magazine,* Midwinter 1973.

> An article telling what is known about the materials used by Persian painters and their sources and preparation.

UNESCO. *Iran, Persian Miniatures, Imperial Library.* Norwalk, CT: New York Graphic Society, 1956.

> Beautiful color reproductions of Persian paintings in their original dimensions. The preface by Basil Gray and introduction by André Godard describe the art in general and the miniatures reproduced in the book.

Welch, Stuart Cary. *Persian Painting.* NY: George Braziller, 1976.

> Brilliant color reproductions of paintings from five Royal Safavid manuscripts of the sixteenth century. The introduction gives a history of Persian miniature painting, and each color plate is accompanied by very helpful comments that explain the story illustrated and point out delightful details that might otherwise be missed.

CHAPTER 4
Prehistoric Cave Paintings and Engravings of France and Spain

Denzel, Justin. *Boy of the Painted Cave.* NY: Philomel Books, 1988.

> A gripping novel for young people about a boy, Tao, who loves to draw and aspires to be a cave painter. Through many adventures he finally becomes one. The animals and ways of living in Paleolithic times come alive. Students from fourth to sixth grades will enjoy this story.

Gore, Rick. "People Like Us." *National Geographic.* Vol. 198, No. 1, page 90, July 2000.

> Beautifully illustrated with photographs, paintings, and diagrams. An excellent overview of the evolution of modern man during the final phase of the ice age.

Pfeiffer, John E. *The Creative Explosion: An Inquiry into the Origins of Art and Religion.* NY: Harper & Row, 1982.

> For the teacher who wants to dig deeper. A very carefully illustrated study that tries to answer the questions as to why art emerged. Detailed observations of the caves in France and Spain, including Lascaux and Altamira, and stories of their discovery.

Ruspoli, Mario. *The Cave of Lascaux: The Final Photographs.* NY: Harry N. Abrams, Inc., 1987.

> Excellent text and color photographs. Description of how people lived 17,000 years ago, the tools and materials used in making the paintings, and the animals that lived in those times.

Saura Ramos, Pedro A. *The Cave of Altamira.* NY: Harry Abrams, Inc., 1999.

> Photographs by Pedro A. Saura Ramos, with essays by others, edited by Antonio Beltran. Exceptionally beautiful photographs of the paintings, and essays on all aspects of the art: descriptions of the cave, analysis of materials and methods used, and theories as to why the paintings were created.

Thomas, Anne Wall. *Colors from the Earth: The Artist's Guide to Collecting, Preparing, and Using Them.* NY: Van Nostrand Reinhold Co., 1980.

> An excellent guide to using natural earth pigments to make one's own paints, chalks, pastels, and crayons. It is helpful both for beginners and for those who wish to explore the craft in more depth. Includes a history of how people have used earth pigments for art, going back to Paleolithic times.

Ancient Greek Sculpture

Boardman, John. *Greek Sculpture of the Classical Period.* NY: Thames and Hudson, 1995.

> The development of classical Greek sculpture. Black-and-white illustrations.

Hafner, German. *Art of Crete, Mycenae, and Greece.* NY: Harry N. Abrams, Inc., 1968.

> Superb photographs of Greek art from its earliest beginnings.

Ruskin, Ariane, and Michael Batterberry. *Greek and Roman Art.* NY: McGraw-Hill Book Co., 1968.

> Well written and illustrated.

Schoder, Raymond V., S.J. *Masterpieces of Greek Art*. Chicago: Ares Publishers, Inc., 1975.
    Exceptionally fine color photographs and descriptive text covering the entire range of Greek art.

English Stained Glass

Morris, Elizabeth. *Stained and Decorative Glass*. London: Quantum Books, Ltd., 2000.
    An excellent book covering stained glass methods and history from Gothic cathedrals to 21st-century art. Profusely illustrated in full color.

Morton, Jera May. *Glass: An Inspirational Portfolio*. NY: Watson-Guptill Pub., 1999.
    A well-illustrated book that includes the history of glass making until modern times, with full color illustrations. The emphasis is on the wide variety of techniques and artwork in contemporary glass.

Reyntiens, Patrick. *The Beauty of Stained Glass*. Boston: Little, Brown & Co., 1990.
    A beautiful book on the history of stained glass from the 12th through 20th centuries. Many full color plates of stained glass from this entire span of time.

Swedish Arts

Plath, Iona. *The Decorative Arts of Sweden*. NY: Dover Publications, Inc., 1966.
    A well-illustrated survey of Swedish arts, past and present: textiles, ceramics, wall paintings, and artwork in glass, metal, and wood.

Rycraft, Inc. A source for Scandinavian cookie stamps and recipes. 4205 S.W. 53rd St., Corvallis, Oregon 97333 or www.rycraft.com (800-479-2723).

Polish Wycinanki

Drwal, Frances. *Polish Wycinanki Designs*. Owings Mills, MD: Stemmer House Pub. Inc., 1976.
    A beautiful paperback with short introduction explaining history and purpose of the designs and techniques for making them. Fine black-and-white

wycinanki designs from all the different regions in Poland. Unfortunately the designs are not numbered and identification of styles is somewhat confusing.

Jablonski, Ramona. *The Paper Cut-Out Design Book*. Owings Mills, MD: Stemmer House Pub. Inc., 1976.
    A sourcebook for creating and adapting the heritage of American folk art, Polish wycinanki, Chinese Hua Yang, Japanese kirigami, German Scherenschnitte and others. An excellent introduction to paper cutting from many cultures.

Ukrainian Pysanky

Jordan, Robert Paul. "Easter Greetings from the Ukrainians." *National Geographic,* April 1972.
    Beautifully illustrated article on pysanky making among the Ukrainian-Americans of Minneapolis and St. Paul, Minnesota.

Luciow, Johanna, Ann Kmit, and Loretta Luciow. *Eggs Beautiful; How to Make Ukrainian Easter Eggs*. Minneapolis, MN: Ukrainian Gift Shop, 1975.
    A very comprehensive, beautifully illustrated book on making Ukrainian Easter eggs. All necessary supplies are available from this source.

Perchyshyn, Natalie. *A Kid's Guide to Decorating Ukrainian Easter Eggs*. St. Anthony, MN: Ukrainian Gift Shop, Inc., 2000.
    A fine guide to decorating pysanky for adults as well as children. Includes list of materials needed, how to make basic divisions of the egg for traditional pysanky, eight designs in full color, step by step, traditional colors and symbols and their meanings, how to empty the eggs and varnish them.

Books and supplies are available at:

Ukrainian Gift Shop, 2512 39th Ave. NE, Saint Anthony Village, MN 55421 or www.ukrainiangiftshop.com, 612-788-2545.

Ukrainian Book Store, 10215 97th St. NW, Edmonton, Alberta T5J 2N9, Canada, 866-422-4255.

German Flower-Related Arts

Bauzen, Peter and Susanne. *Flower Pressing.* NY: Sterling, 1982.

> Excellent small book with directions for pressing flowers and framing them under glass or plastic. Many other projects using pressed plants with cloth, wood, fiber, glass, and resin. The book also describes methods of preserving plants with lacquer, printing with plants, and using them as stencils.

Foster, Laura Louise. *Keeping the Plants You Pick.* NY: Thomas Y. Crowell Co., 1970.

> Illustrated with drawings by the author. Describes methods of pressing and preserving plants and many projects to make with them.

Kull, A. Stoddard. *Secrets of Flowers: The Message and Meaning of Every Flower.* Brattleboro, VT: The Stephen Greene Press, 1976.

> The folklore and symbolism of many flowers.

Russell, Francis. *The World of Dürer.* NY: Time-Life Books, 1967.

> A biography of Dürer, beautifully illustrated with many of his paintings, woodcuts, and engravings.

CHAPTER 5
Chinese Arts

Diehn, Gwen. *Simple Printmaking: A Beginner's Guide to Making Relief Prints with Linoleum Blocks, Wood Blocks, Rubber Stamps, Found Objects and More.* NY: Lark Books, Sterling Publishing Co., 2000.

> This is a beautiful, dynamic book, full of ideas and excellent, clear instructions. Illustrated with many fine color prints, ranging from ancient Chinese, through Japanese, Dürer, Edvard Munch, and Picasso, to contemporary artists.

Hwa, Khoo Seow and Nancy L. Penrose. *Behind the Brushstrokes: Appreciating Chinese Calligraphy.* Hong Kong: Asia 2000 Limited, 1993.

> Study of calligraphy, its philosophy, evolution of characters, and lives of great Chinese calligraphers. Well illustrated with a section on brushes, papers, inks, seals, and brush positions and movements.

Schachner, Erwin. *Step-by-Step Printmaking.* NY: Golden Press, 1970.

> Directions for making woodcuts, linoleum cuts, and other kinds of prints. Very fine illustrations from many sources, ancient and modern.

Smith, Bradley, and Wan-Go Weng. *China: A History in Art.* NY: Harper & Row, 1976.

> Beautifully illustrated with a great range of Chinese arts: early pottery and pictographs; sculptures in stone, bronze, jade, clay; calligraphy; woodcuts; and paintings.

Sze, Mai-Mai. *The Way of Chinese Painting: Its Ideas and Techniques with Selections from the Seventeenth Century Mustard Seed Garden Manual of Painting.* NY: Random House, 1959.

> The illustrations include many woodcuts from the Mustard Seed Garden Manual.

Wolff, Diane. *Chinese Writing: An Introduction.* NY: Holt, Rinehart & Winston, 1975.

> An excellent introduction to Chinese writing and calligraphy. Illustrated with photographs and with calligraphy by Jeanette Chien. For young students.

Japanese Arts

Basho, Matsuo. *The Narrow Road to the Deep North and Other Travel Sketches.* Translated from the Japanese with an introduction by Nobuyuki Yuasa. Baltimore, MD: Penguin Books, 1966.

> Five travel sketches by Basho, greatest of haiku poets. As he traveled through Japan by foot and horseback, he wrote of his adventures and the places that inspired his haiku.

Ekiguchi, Kunio, and Ruth S. McCreery. *Japanese Crafts and Customs: A Seasonal Approach.* Kodansha International, 1993.

> Beautifully illustrated book with essays on Japanese crafts, and diagrams and directions for making them. Many, including cloth fish banners, are appropriate for the classroom.

Henderson, Harold G. *An Introduction to Haiku: Translations and Commentary.* Garden City, NY: Doubleday, 1958.

> The best anthology for classroom use.

Lewis, Richard. *In a Spring Garden.* NY: The Dial Press, 1989.

> Beautifully illustrated by Ezra Jack Keats (Western style). A collection of twenty-three haiku selected for appeal to young children.

Terakazu, Akuyama. *Treasures of Asia: Japanese Painting.* Cleveland, OH: Skira, Distributed by The World Publishing Co., 1961.

Thompson, Kay Morrissey. *The Art and Technique of Sumi-e: Japanese Ink Painting as Taught by Ukai Uchiyama.* Boston: Charles E. Tuttle Co., 1994.

> A beautiful book. An excellent introduction to the art of sumi-e with fine illustrations by the artist. Chapters on the materials used and how the brush is held and different strokes made. How to make graded washes, and to paint particular plants, insects, birds, and landscapes.

Burmese Arts

Newman, Thelma R. *Contemporary Southeast Asian Arts and Crafts.* NY: Crown Publishers Inc., 1977.

> The first chapter discusses Southeast Asian arts in general and some similarities in these arts arising from shared influences. The book describes many arts and how they are done, including the lacquer ware process, with many photos.

Arts of India

Schulberg, Lucille. *Historic India.* NY: Time-Life Books, 1968.

> Well-written and beautifully illustrated with color photographs of the Taj Mahal, Moghul miniature paintings, and ancient sculpture.

Indonesian Arts

Anderson, Benedict R. O'G. *Mythology and the Tolerance of the Javanese.* Cornell, NY: Modern Indonesia Project Monograph Series, 1965.

> A rather technical essay but illustrated with pen drawings of sixty-five wayangs. These are very helpful in drawing the puppets.

Anderson, William M. *Teaching Asian Musics in Elementary and Secondary Schools.* Adrian, MI: The Leland Press (Box 301), 1975.

> Excellent introduction to playing Javanese gamelan music. Well illustrated.

Belfer, Nancy. *Batik and Tie Dye Techniques.* NY: Dover Publications, Inc., 1992.

> Includes a history of batik, with many fine illustrations of traditional Indonesian batiks and contemporary batiks as well. Step-by-step instructions for creating batiks and a list of sources for materials and tools. The book also has examples of tie-dyed fabrics and instructions for making many tie-dyed items.

Brandon, James R. *On Thrones of Gold.* Honolulu: University of Hawaii Press, 1993.

> A complete description of wayang kulit, its history and performance. Includes three plays, written as they are performed, with stage directions concerning the movement of the puppets, musical accompaniment, and the dhalang's songs and narrations. Illustrated.

Campbell, Joy. S*tart a Craft: Batik.* Edison, NJ: Chartwell Books, 1998.

> Brief history of batik and instructions for many projects, from simple to complex, using batik methods for decorating paper and fabric. Full color illustrations.

Newman, Thelma R. *Contemporary Southeast Asian Arts and Crafts.* NY: Crown Pub., 1977.

> Photographs and description of making shadow puppets and of a performance. Also contains a well-illustrated chapter on history and techniques of batik in Java.

Reiniger, Lotte. *Shadow Puppets, Shadow Theatres and Shadow Films.* Boston: Plays Inc., 1975.

> A brief description of wayang kulit and the history of shadow puppets from other countries. Directions for construction of many kinds of shadow puppets and theatres.

Wayang Kulit: The Shadow Puppet Theater of Java. Baylis Glascock Films. 22 mins., Color.

> A beautiful film, showing both puppets and gamelan in action. American Gamelan Institute, Box 1052, Lebanon, NH 03766. www.gamelan.org.

Kites of Southeast Asia and Taiwan

Hosking, Wayne. *Flights of Imagination: An Introduction to Aerodynamics.* Washington, DC: National Science Teachers Association, 1990.

> The principles of aerodynamics, and to illustrate them, instructions for making many simple kites that will fly, using easily available materials.

Hosking, Wayne. *Kites in the Classroom.* Rockville, MD: American Kitefliers Association, 1992.

> An excellent book for the classroom interested in making kites that will fly. The history of kites, explanation of what makes a kite fly, materials needed, instructions for making 15 different simple kites, and instructions for flying them.

Sheppard, Mubin. *Taman Indera: A Royal Pleasure Ground: Malay Decorative Arts and Pastimes.* Kuala Lumpur, Malaysia; Oxford University Press, 1972.

> This book has a well-illustrated and very informative chapter on kites and kite flying in Malaysia.

Sheppard, Tan Sri Dato Mubin. *Living Crafts of Malaysia.* Singapore: Times Books International, 1978.

> Ten traditional Malaysian crafts, featuring a particular artist for each. One short chapter on kite making with beautiful color photographs of Hashim bin Awang working on his prize-winning kites.

The Felt Rugs of Central and Northern Asia

Burkett, M. E. *The Art of the Felt Maker.* An exhibition catalog sponsored by Crafts Advisory Committee, Northern Art, Sotheby's, and Abbot Hall Art Gallery, Kendal, Cumbria, 1979.

> An indispensable guide to the history and techniques of felt making, and how felt is made and used in nine different countries. Abundantly illustrated.

Sjoberg, Gunilla Paetau. *Felt: New Directions for an Ancient Craft.* Loveland, CO: Interweave Press, Inc., 1996.

> An excellent, beautifully illustrated book on felting. History of felting and techniques in several cultures.

> Covers contemporary techniques and projects. One chapter on felting with children gives instructions for many items from the simplest to more demanding group rug making.

Vickrey, Anne Einset. *The Art of Feltmaking.* NY: Watson-Guptill, 1997.

> A fine colorful guide for beginners. Imaginative projects using flat felt and felt as sculpture and clothing. Easy projects for children, such as balls, beads, animal figures, and puppets.

CHAPTER 6
General Oceanic Arts

Buck, Peter. *Arts and Crafts of Hawaii.* Honolulu: Bishop Museum Press, 1964.

> A very comprehensive study of Hawaiian arts and crafts including chapters on canoes and tapa cloth.

D'Alleva, Anne. *Arts of the Pacific Islands.* NY: Harry N. Abrams, Inc., 1998.

> An overview of the art traditions of the Pacific Islands. Covers the rich variety of arts created in New Guinea, Melanesia, Polynesia, and Micronesia, including information on the arts of Belau and Yap. Concludes with a final chapter on contemporary Pacific art. Beautifully illustrated with color photographs.

Feldman, Jerome, and Donald H. Rubinstein. *The Art of Micronesia.* The University of Hawaii Art Gallery, 1986.

> Illustrated catalog for an exhibition of Micronesian Art with helpful essays. It describes the many fine arts from this area, including the gull bowls made on Puluwat.

Mitchell, Donald D. Kilolani. *Resource Units in Hawaiian Culture.* Honolulu: The Kamehameha Schools Press, 1992.

> In-depth studies of Hawaiian culture, including units on canoes and tapa cloth. Study guides and suggestions for student activities.

Thomas, Nicholas. *Oceanic Art.* London: Thames and Hudson Ltd., 1995.

> Arts of the Pacific islands, both historic and contemporary, and especially the context within which they are produced and their uses within the specific culture.

Hawaiian Canoes

Holmes, Tommy. *The Hawaiian Canoe.* Hanalei, Kauai, Hawaii: Editions Limited, 1981.

> A very comprehensive and well-illustrated book giving the history of the Hawaiian canoe, and how it was made, in meticulous detail.

Tapa Cloth

Kooijman, Simon. *Tapa in Polynesia.* Honolulu: Bishop Museum Press, 1972.

> Very detailed scholarly work that explores tapa making throughout Polynesia: the tools used, the dyes and their sources, the designs unique to each culture, and the methods of applying them.

Leonard, Anne, and John Terrell. *Patterns of Paradise.* Chicago: Field Museum of Natural History, 1980.

> A well-illustrated book on the making of bark cloth throughout the world, including the tapa cloth of the South Pacific.

Neich, Roger, and Mick Prendergast. *Traditional Tapa Textiles of the Pacific.* NY: Thames and Hudson, 1998.

> A beautifully illustrated book covering the techniques of tapa making and decorating in many South Pacific island communities, as well as how it is used within these differing cultures.

CHAPTER 7
Aboriginal Arts of Australia

Berndt, Ronald M., and Catherine Berndt, with John E. Stanton. *Aboriginal Australian Art.* Sydney: New Holland Pub., 1998.

> A beautiful and informative book. Covers work in all media by artists throughout Australia. Many illustrations of rock wall paintings, bark paintings, and work of contemporary artists.

Morphy, Howard. *Aboriginal Art.* London: Phaidon Press Ltd., 1998.

> A comprehensive book on art in Australia, with emphasis on its place in the society. Many fine illustrations.

National Gallery of Australia. *Marking Our Times.* NY: Thames and Hudson Inc., 1996.

> Selected works of art from the Aboriginal and Torres Strait Islander collection at the National Gallery of Australia. Beautiful photographs of contemporary Aboriginal art with accompanying text.

Sutton, Peter. *Dreamings: The Art of Aboriginal Australia.* NY: The Asia Society Galleries, 1998.

> Written to accompany an exhibition, this is a beautiful book with many fine photographs and explanatory text.

Sound Recordings

Australian Dreamings. An Audiovisual Cassette with Teacher's Guide. Tucson, AZ: Crizmac, 1996.

> Video with very informative teacher's guide and student booklet. Covers X-ray style painting and Desert acrylic dot paintings.

Didgeridoo—A Beginner's Guide. Black, Alastair, P.O. Box 384, Magill, S.A. 5072 Australia. Copyright 1995.

> A fine audiovisual cassette with demonstrations of how to play a didgeridoo, and of painting one. The didgeridoo player also accompanies an Aboriginal dancer as he portrays hunting and animals of the Australian bush.

Music of My People, Australian Aboriginal Music. Maza, Bob. Australian Music International, Inc. Twintrack Productions.

> This is a good tape to play while the students are working on their didgeridoo project. Beautifully narrated, it tells about the corroborees where music and dance tell of the Spirit Ancestors and their importance in Aboriginal society. Didgeridoo music, click sticks, and singing.

CHAPTER 8
Mexican Arts

Enciso, Jorge. *Design Motifs of Ancient Mexico.* NY: Dover Publications, Inc., 1953.

> Helpful black-and-white illustrations of ancient designs arranged by subject matter.

Harvey, Marian. *Crafts of Mexico.* NY: Macmillan, 1973.
> Chapters on weaving, reed work, metals, clay, wood, and paper, describing these arts, and giving directions for making some of the items described.

Lenz, Hans. "Paper and Superstitions." *Artes De Mexico—Myths, Rites and Witchery.* No. 124, Ano XVI, 1969, Page 93. Amores 262, Mexico 12, D.F.
> This article is primarily on amate paper cutouts, their historical beginnings, and contemporary use.

Sayer, Chloë, and David Lavender. *Arts and Crafts of Mexico.* NY: Chronicle Books, 1990.
> Brief description of each native group in Mexico and description of their crafts. Full-color illustrations including textiles, lacquer work, yarn painting, pottery, masks, and toys.

Toneyama, Kojin. *The Popular Arts of Mexico.* NY: Weatherhill Inc., 1974.
> Exceptionally beautiful color illustrations of many of the popular arts of Mexico: Huichol yarn paintings, amate paper cutouts and paintings, clay figures and pots of many kinds, tin sculpture, and many other arts.

Central and South American Arts

Anton, Ferdinand. *The Art of Ancient Peru.* NY: Putnam's Sons, 1972.
> Comprehensive well-illustrated history.

Anton, Ferdinand, and Frederick J. Dockstader. *Pre-Columbian Art and Later Indian Tribal Arts.* NY: Harry N. Abrams, Inc., 1968.
> Beautifully illustrated in black-and-white and color photos. Architecture and artwork in clay, metal, and textiles.

Brown, Pauline. *The Encyclopedia of Embroidery Techniques.* NY: Viking Studio, 1994.
> All major embroidery techniques—full color illustrations. Some traditional, but mostly contemporary examples.

Dockstader, Frederick J. *Indian Art in South America.* Norwalk, CT: New York Graphic Society, 1967.
> Well-illustrated history. Excellent photographs of artwork in gold and silver, clay, basketry, and textiles.

Jessen, Ellen. *Ancient Peruvian Textile Design in Modern Stitchery.* NY: Van Nostrand, Reinhold Company, 1972.
> The introductory chapter describes ancient Peruvian embroidered textiles in detail, with illustrations. The book has many diagrams of ancient Peruvian designs and directions for creating embroideries based on them using the cross-stitch and stem stitch.

Kapp, Captain Kit S. *Mola Art from the San Blas Islands.* Cincinnati, OH: K. S. Kapp Publications, 1972.
> Well-illustrated, comprehensive study of molas, their origin and development, how they are made, and an analysis of the many designs used.

Klotz, Roy. "The Mola: Artistry in Cloth," *Design* 73, No. 3, Mid-Winter 1972: 10.
> A short, illustrated article on molas.

Mattil, Edward L., "The Cuna Mola," *Everyday Art* 52, Spring 1974. Sandusky, Ohio. The American Crayon Company.
> Small paperback booklet with many full-color illustrations of molas.

Pasztory, Esther. *Pre-Columbian Art.* Cambridge, UK: Cambridge University Press, 1998.
> A range of arts, beautifully illustrated—stone sculpture, textiles, pottery, gold masks.

"Peruvian Children's Embroidery," *Woman's Day,* September 1967: 52.
> An article on the children of Chijnaya, their embroidery, and its origins, illustrated with photographs of the children and full color plates of several pieces of embroidery.

CHAPTER 9
Caribbean Arts

Christensen, Eleanor Ingalls. *The Art of Haiti.* Cranbury, NJ: A. S. Barnes and Co., Inc., 1975.
> Haitian history and culture from pre-Columbian times up to the flowering of the arts in the middle of the twentieth century. Illustrated with many black-and-white and color photographs.

Kurtis, Arlene Harris. *Puerto Ricans, From Island to Mainland.* NY: Julian Messner, 1969.
> A history of the island and its people, written for young children and illustrated with photographs.

Rodman, Selden. *The Miracle of Haitian Art.* NY: Doubleday, 1974.
> Information about the renaissance in Haiti that was fostered by the Centre d'art. Biographical sketches of prominent painters and sculptors, illustrated with many black-and-white and color photographs.

CHAPTER 10
General Native American Arts

American Indian Art: Form and Tradition. NY: E. P. Dutton & Co., 1972.
> An exhibition organized by Walker Art Center, Indian Art Association, and the Minneapolis Institute of Arts. A catalog of very fine examples of Indian art. Essays on art from each region, on the meaning of art in the daily life of the Indian.

Appleton, Leroy H. *American Indian Design and Decoration.* NY: Dover Pub., 1950.
> Black-and-white drawings of the design elements of North and South American Indian regional groups.

Billard, Jules B., ed. *The World of the American Indian.* National Geographic Society, 1974.
> Beautifully illustrated with color photographs. A comprehensive volume of Native American life from what we can guess of prehistoric times to the present. Gives a feeling for the many different Indian cultures, which were alike in their respect for and total use of environment.

Dockstader, Frederick J. *Indian Art of the Americas.* NY: Museum of the American Indian, Heye Foundation, 1973.
> Black-and-white and color photographs showing the full range of Indian art, with text.

Jones, Charles, ed. *Look to the Mountain Top.* San Jose, CA: H. M. Gousha Co., 1972.
> Contemporary views on all aspects of Indian heritage.

Whiteford, Andrew Hunter. *North American Indian Arts.* NY: Golden Books, 1990.
> This book provides a great deal of information despite its small size. The introduction gives an overview of the many different Native American arts, and then of the culture areas and tribal locations in North America. Chapters are arranged by type of work—pottery, weaving, etc., the relevant art methods are discussed, and there are color illustrations of items from each specific region. An excellent, informative guide.

Pueblo Indian Pottery

Bahti, Tom. *Southwestern Indian Arts and Crafts.* Las Vegas, NY: K. C. Publications, 1966.
> Along with other crafts, describes pottery-making process and has photographs showing differing styles from sixteen pueblos.

Baylor, Byrd. *When Clay Sings.* NY: Charles Scribner's Sons, 1972.
> A beautiful book about the pottery of prehistoric Southwest Indians. Brings to life the spirit of these ancient peoples, their respect for and delight in all forms of life, and their relation to Pueblo people of today.

Navajo Weaving and Sand Painting

Bennett, Noël, and Tiana Bighorse. *The Navajo Weaving Way: The Path from Fleece to Rug.* Loveland, CO: Interweave Press, 1997.
> A beautiful book that intertwines Navajo culture and weaving. It takes one through the whole process of creating a Navajo rug: shearing sheep, spinning wool, making natural dyes and looms, the weaving processes, and the deep meaning these rugs have in the lives of Navajo artists.

Rainey, Sarita R. *Weaving Without a Loom.* Englewood Cliffs, NJ: Prentice-Hall, Inc., 1977.
> Many techniques for weaving without a regular loom, using a wide variety of materials.

Tanner, Clara Lee. "Modern Navajo Weaving," *Arizona Highways,* September 1964, Arizona Highway Department.
> History of Navajo weaving and descriptions of all major regional styles with color photographs.

Villasenor, David. *Tapestries in Sand.* Healdsburg, CA: Naturegraph Co., 1963.
> Tells about the process of sand painting and, more

importantly, the spirit behind it—the myths and stories handed down for generations that hold, distilled, the Navajo beliefs about man and his place in the universe.

Plains Indians Arts

Catlin, George. *George Catlin Letters and Notes on the North American Indians,* Michael M. Mooney, ed. NY: Clarkson N. Potter, Inc., 1975.
> This book was originally published in 1841. It has been condensed and rearranged by the editor. Includes many engravings and paintings by Catlin.

Horse Capture, Joseph D., and George P. Horse Capture. *Beauty, Honor, and Tradition; The Legacy of Plains Indian Shirts.* Minneapolis, MN: Minneapolis Institute of Arts, and Washington, DC: The National Museum of the American Indian, Smithsonian Institution, 2001.
> This book was produced in conjunction with an exhibition of the same name. It is very informative and extremely beautiful in color and presentation. It includes a painted buffalo robe, and many shirts, all decorated with great skill and artistry in quill work, painted designs, beadwork, and fringing—a wonderful resource for teachers and students.

McHugh, Tom. *The Time of the Buffalo.* NY: Alfred A. Knopf, 1972.

Martin, Cy. *The Saga of the Buffalo.* NY: Hart Publishing Co., Inc. 1973.
> This book and the one above by McHugh both deal with the natural history of the buffalo and especially its changing relationships to man, from its role in the life of the Plains Indians to its near extinction by the westward movement of settlers to its present-day establishment in new herds through the efforts of the Canadian and U.S. governments.

Mason, Bernard S. *Dances and Stories of the American Indian.* NY: The Ronald Press Co., 1944.
> This collection includes directions for performing three buffalo dances from the Sioux, the Cheyenne, and the Jemez tribes.

Taylor, Colin F. *Buckskin and Buffalo: The Artistry of the Plains Indians.* NY: Rizzoli International Pub. Inc., 1998.
> A very beautifully illustrated book with color photographs of clothing, painted buffalo robes, and other objects. Enlarged details of decorative work in beads, shells, porcupine quills, feathers, and paint.

Woodland Indian Arts

The Art of the Great Lakes Indians. Flint Institute of Arts, 1973.
> An exhibition organized by the Flint Institute of Arts. Chapters on the history, art, and culture of Great Lakes Indians and careful description of porcupine quillwork and methods. Excellent diagrams and photographs. I have drawn heavily from this book in writing the chapter.

Hunt, W. Ben, and J. F. "Buck" Burshears. *American Indian Beadwork.* NY: Collier Books, 1996.
> A comprehensive paperback of Indian beadwork methods. Includes many color illustrations of Indian designs.

Ritzenthaler, Robert E. and Pat. *The Woodland Indians of the Western Great Lakes.* Prospect Heights, IL: Waveland Press, 1991.
> Fully illustrated, with much material on life and culture of Woodland Indians, especially the Wisconsin Chippewa.

Inuit Arts

Burland, Cottie. *Eskimo Art.* London: Hamlyn Publishing Group Ltd., 1973.
> Eskimo art and culture from prehistoric times to the present day. Beautifully illustrated with many color and black-and-white photographs.

Carpenter, Edmund. *Eskimo Realities.* NY: Holt, Rinehart & Winston, 1973.
> Aboriginal Eskimo art, especially prehistoric ivory carvings. An analysis of what art is to the Eskimo. A different point of view. Mr. Carpenter believes true Eskimo art is interchangeable with the Eskimo's life. He does not feel the sculpture and prints made for

sale are truly Eskimo art but are western in concept and execution.

Eskimo Art: Kenojuak, National Film Board of Canada, 1963. 20 min.

> A very beautiful film about the Inuit artist Kenojuak. She tells of her sources of inspiration, and we are shown the process of making a print from its conception in the mind of the artist to its being cut in stone and printed on paper. It would make a fine film to have in a school library. Contact the Film Board at www.NFB.CA or 866-267-7710, order #113C0164017. For rental call Transit Media at 800-542-2164.

Eskimo Graphic Art 1960. West Baffin Eskimo Cooperative, Canada.

> Exhibition catalogue.

Hessel, Ingo. *Inuit Art: An Introduction.* NY: Harry Abrams, 1998.

> A comprehensive study of Inuit art from prehistoric period to contemporary, with a wide range of art—sculpture, prints, drawings, and recent tapestries and wall hangings, but with a preponderance of stone carvings. Very fine color photographs.

Houston, James. *Eskimo Prints.* Barre, MA: Barre Publishing Co., Inc., 1971.

> How printmaking began in Cape Dorset in 1957. Mr. Houston introduced the concept but believes the images and ideas created are "based on centuries of ancient Eskimo traditions, myths, and skills."

Swinton, George. *Sculpture of the Eskimo.* Norwalk, CT: New York Graphic Society, Ltd., 1972.

> This book has 37 color photographs and 770 black-and-white photographs of sculpture. It covers the environment, history, and modern day culture of the Eskimo and traces the transition from making magical objects to making functional decorative objects for pleasure and market. Shows many styles and subject matters.

Early American Folk Arts

Bishop, Robert, and Patricia Coblentz. *A Gallery of American Weathervanes and Whirligigs.* Hong Kong: Bonanza Books, 1984.

> Beautifully illustrated and informative.

Burnell, Marica. *Heritage Above: A Tribute to Maine's Tradition of Weather Vanes.* Camden, ME: Down East Books, 1991.

> Beautiful color photographs by the author. Brief history of the development of weathervanes in Europe, and comprehensive information about the weathervanes of New England and especially those of Maine.

Flayderman, E. Norman. *Scrimshaw and Scrimshanders, Whale and Whalemen.* Ft. Lauderdale, FL: N. Flayderman and Co. Inc., 1972.

> A comprehensive and well-illustrated book on the history and art of scrimshaw.

Golden Book of Colonial Crafts. NY: Golden Press, 1975.

> Seventy craft projects from colonial times, with directions for making them with materials available today.

Jones, Iris Sanderson. *Early North American Dollmaking.* San Francisco: 101 Productions, 1976.

> Beautifully illustrated book showing a great variety of dolls with instructions for making many of them, including applehead dolls.

Jung, Pamela F. "Apple Dolls." *Design* 74, No. 1: 14.

> Illustrated article on the apple dolls of Mrs. E. E. Grannis of Lewiston, Idaho, and her methods of making them.

Klamkin, Charles. *Weather Vanes: The History, Design, and Manufacture of an American Folk Art.* NY: Hawthorn Books, Inc., 1973.

> A very comprehensive, well-illustrated book on weathervanes.

Linsley, Leslie. *Scrimshaw: A Traditional Folk Art, A Contemporary Craft.* NY: Hawthorn Books, Inc., 1976.

> How scrimshaw is done today—tools, materials, and methods of contemporary scrimshanders.

Miller, Steve. *The Art of the Weathervane.* Exton, PA: Schiffler Pub. Ltd., 1984.

> Beautifully illustrated with many examples of weathervanes, both those that were factory made, and also many wonderful unique ones made by individuals.

INDEX